Herbs for Health and Cookery

'While herbs have never lost their romantic appeal to the imagination we have tended to forget their practical uses . . . For those who would like to be more adventurous in their use and knowledge of herbs, however, there is no better encyclopaedia on the subject.' THE SCOTSMAN

'A wealth of information on herbs and how to use them.'
SHROPSHIRE STAR

'If you have a garden, then you should rope off a bit for herb growing and buy the book immediately.' NORTHERN ECHO

Claire Loewenfeld, originally a student of art, became a lecturer on food, health and diet after taking a diploma at Zurich. She founded Chiltern Herb Farms and has become an authority on the culinary and therapeutic use of herbs.

Philippa Back has studied herb cultivation and worked for Chiltern Herb Farms for some years. She has also had a cordon bleu training and therefore ample experience in trying out herb recipes.

Herbs for Health and Cookery

Claire Loewenfeld and
Philippa Back

Pan Original Pan Books London and Sydney

First published 1965 by Pan Books Ltd,
Cavaye Place, London SW10 9PG
8th printing 1982
© Claire Loewenfeld 1965
ISBN 0 330 25336 0
Printed and bound in England by
Cox & Wyman Ltd, Reading

CONTENTS

PREFACE

Our practical work with herbs over many years – Claire Loewenfeld as founder, and Philippa Back as lecturer, of Chiltern Herb Farms – has provided us with the experience on which this book is based.

Many requests have come to us for a book of herb recipes. We feel, however, health and cookery can and should go hand-in-hand. To many people, healthy eating conjures up tasteless lettuce leaves and expensive meats. We endeavour to explode this idea with tasty, inexpensive, and many easy to make dishes all using herbs.

The enjoyment we have had in compiling this book and trying out every recipe will, we hope, be apparent to our readers and will help to promote their interest. A fault of many cook books today is their vagueness in giving exact quantities. This cannot always be helped, but we have tried to be as precise as possible, thereby we hope to help and encourage the beginner.

A SHORT INTRODUCTION TO HERBS

WHAT IS IT that attracts people to herbs? There are many herb lovers and herb gardeners in this country, though relatively few herb cooks. Is it the graceful look of the growing herbs, their lovely scent, their quaint and sweet-sounding names and the charm of the herb garden? And yet, the actual purpose for which herbs are meant, and have been used since time immemorial, their flavouring, seasoning, and preserving properties and the magic they mean for good health and good eating has almost been forgotten.

We owe most of our culinary traditions to the Romans, who when they came to Britain, brought with them about 400 different herb plants for both culinary and medicinal use and without which they felt they could not live. The Romans, in turn, owed their knowledge of herbs to the Indians, Egyptians, and Greeks. Among the herbs which they brought with them were many we use today, such as Parsley, Onions, Lovage, Sage, Chervil, Thyme, and many more. They boasted that they had no need of doctors, as their knowledge of herbs for food and treatment was sufficient.

From then onwards, herbs have a long history of many 'ins' and 'outs'. Forgotten during the Dark Ages, reintroduced and cultivated by the Monks in the early Middle Ages, an important item in the still-rooms of the old manor house, and well known and much used by many generations until the nineteenth century, when the Industrial Revolution started the mass-production of synthetic substitutes for herbs and flavourings.

Now herbs are coming into their own again; a new trend can be felt, which started in the USA but is much in evidence in this country now. This reawakening of interest in the use of herbs does not appear to be a quaint revival, but seems to have its own historical necessity. Since the Industrial Revolution and the 'Chemical Age' so much has been done to food in the name of preserving, processing, 'beautifying', slashing prices, 'assuring a long shelf life', that the original flavours, natural colours, and tempting scents have vanished. We are meant to be tempted by the eye, the nose, and the palate and to use them as instruments for the judgement of the goodness of our food; but the eye, the nose, and the palate cannot in the long run be deceived by coal-tar dyes, sulphur-preserving agents, and sodium glutamate flavouring agents. A strong instinct for survival has recalled herbs to restore flavour where it has been lost.

However, once the palate regains the taste for herbs, it becomes necessary that they should be available all the year round. Ways and means had to be found to *retain* the herb's full flavour and colour when drying it. Freshly cut, they are mainly available for those with a garden and even for those only during certain periods of the year. If the flavour and colour of herbs are well looked after, most of the nutritional values can be retained; they are bound up together with volatile oils, minerals, trace elements, and the many important substances such as bitter principles, tannins, secretins, organic acids, etc., which give herbs their distinct flavour, and their digestive, disinfectant, antibiotic, or preserving qualities.

A similar development can be observed with herbs used for health and this is more fully discussed on pages 13–34. The experience of drugs having undesirable side-effects has increased interest in the safer but probably slower noticeable influence of herbs on minor ailments and improving health in general.

PART ONE

Herbs for Health and Beauty

Chapter 1

USES AND HEALTH PROPERTIES OF INDIVIDUAL HERBS

SINCE TIME began herbs have been used for maintaining health and as remedies. Many herbs were found to have digestive properties and from this some of the flavouring customs may have sprung, *eg* fennel with oily fish. As remedies, herbs were used up to the nineteenth century. During the Industrial Revolution, science began to invade the research into our remedies, many of the herbs and plants were chemically synthesized, but it was not endeavoured to find the individual reasons for the effect of herbs on health experienced by previous generations. In other countries some research on the substances which make herbs so useful for health has been carried out recently; some of this was used when compiling this book as in this country little research has been carried out on the qualities of herbs.

Modern drugs have sometimes unpleasant side-effects; this may be due to the synthetic nature of the drug, or to the fact that only certain substances of a plant may have been extracted and then concentrated; in this way the balanced effect of the plant may be lost. The known use of whole herbs – or infusions made of them – is safe and has no unexpected or even undesirable consequences. Unless they are used in increased or concentrated quantities – other than suggested in this book – they can be taken without fear. However, for those people who are used to strong stimulants, the effect may be delayed or even unnoticeable. In the following descriptions of the health properties of individual herbs, it is clearly stated which effects have been well known for generations and have often been experienced, and which uses have merely been reported and should be tried out.

Some herbs are mentioned in this book for their health qualities only, sometimes the health properties of those which are mainly used for cookery are given. The latter are described in more detail in Part Two, 'Twenty-four Herbs in a Chest', pages 127–68, and are printed in the following section in italics to distinguish them from the other herbs which are mentioned for their health qualities only. All these herbs are not meant to be used as a herbalist's treatment, but as wholesome, pleasant, and often health-restoring additions to the daily diet.

ANGELICA (Angelica archangelica)

This gigantic plant with large scented leaves and thick stems is mainly used for flavouring and confectionery, but it also has health properties. Angelica tea resembles China tea in flavour. Angelica is well known for its bright green candied or crystallized stems. The scented leaves are an excellent addition to potpourri.

BASIL (Ocimum basilicum)

The leaves of this most excellent flavouring herb have been used at one time as a snuff for nasal colds, and were said to clear the brain and deal with headaches. The leaves have been allowed to permeate in wine for a digestive tonic, and have also had the reputation of stimulating milk in nursing mothers. The herb stimulates perspiration and also digestion, because the leaves mixed with salad oil have been recommended for constipation. Like all strong tasting herbs it was considered to be antiseptic, which explains probably the tradition that it was mainly used with meat and fish. It has once been prescribed as a sedative, against gastric spasms, and has acted at times as an expectorant, a laxative, a carminative, and, by stimulating perspiration, it is supposed to reduce a temperature. Basil tea, page 37.

More details on Basil, page 128.

BAY LEAVES (Laurus nobilis)

The Sweet Bay from which the bay leaves come, is the true laurel and the only one of this genus which is used for human consumption. Apart from supplying leaves for wreaths for poets and heroes in ancient times, they were also used to decorate houses and churches at Christmas, and were once considered a cure for many illnesses. Apart from flavouring, bay leaves have been used for preserving and marinading, and their preserving qualities are useful for this purpose. Bay leaves also stimulate the appetite and were at one time used for rheumatic complaints externally, and as a protection against insects.

More details on Bay Leaves, page 130.

BERGAMOT, RED (Monarda didyma)

This old-fashioned perennial flowering plant is at the same time a useful tisane, well-known in Europe and in America, where it is called Oswego tea because it was used by the Indians. The American colonists used it instead of ordinary tea, when boycotting British tea at the time of the Boston Tea Party. Red bergamot provides a delightful tea; (page 38) when served hot it induces good sleep and has a soothing and relaxing effect. The leaves can also be added to China or Indian tea, to wine drinks, and lemonade. An excellent night-cap can be made of bergamot milk (page 38). From July to September bergamot has flowers of several colours, but scarlet flowers belong to the variety used for Bergamot tea.

BORAGE (Borago officinalis)

This plant of special beauty has had since the early days of the Greeks the reputation of 'making men merry'. In fact, its exhilarating effect accounts for the Greek proverb 'I Borage bring always courage', and for its name 'Herb of Gladness'. It is the juices in borage which give a cucumber-like coolness to wine or any alcoholic drink, nowadays used in Pimm's No. 1. Borage leaves are mainly added to claret cups and many other drinks, not only for the flavour but for the purpose of dispelling depressed moods and acting as a 'pep pill' without side-effects. The chopped leaves and the lovely blue, star-shaped flowers are also used in salads. Borage Tea, page 39.

CELERY AND CELERIAC LEAVES (Apium graveolens)

They contain a variety of vitamins, mineral salts, and many active principles which makes them into an important herb for health, quite apart from their much-liked flavouring qualities. They are also reported to have a hormone which has a similar effect to insulin. They are an excellent seasoning for certain types of invalids, such as diabetics, or for anyone on a salt-reduced diet.
More details on Celery, page 132.

CHAMOMILE (Matricaria chamomilla)

The flowers of the True Chamomile have been one of the most important medicinal herbs. It later lost some of its importance in England due to the fact that the two chamomiles, the true chamomile and the Roman chamomile (Anthemis nobilis) have been confused. The important healing blue oil is mainly found in the true chamomile, which can be recognized by the flower. This has a yellow receptacle which is hollow and markedly conical from the beginning. It also has a lovely scent which distinguishes it from the similar looking mayweed and other flowers of the same family. It flowers from May to October, and the flowers can be picked all the time whenever they arrive. They are dried for tea, but should be touched as little as possible. Chamomile tea (page 39) is drunk much on the Continent, mainly in France, as an aid to digestion after heavy meals, and has a soothing, cleansing, disinfecting, anti-spasmodic effect, particularly in the case of intestinal pain. It has also a soothing and healing effect on any part of the mucous membrane and on the skin, and that makes it not only a useful tisane but a most helpful herb for cosmetic purposes (page 63).

CHERVIL (Anthriscus cerefolium)

This most graceful, delicate-flavouring herb, which can be cut early in the year if sown in the autumn, is much liked in spring. The luscious green leaves are traditionally used in all spring soups and sauces because they have blood-cleansing and diuretic qualities, and are considered to have a specially stimulating effect on the glandular system. The juice of the leaves has been used as a cleansing treatment in spring and also been considered to be a good digestive. All this made it one of the Lenten herbs. As it also increases perspiration, chervil has been used for fever, jaundice, gout, skin troubles, and gall-stones. Lastly, finely chopped and warmed chervil has been known to be applied to bruises and painful joints.

More details on Chervil, page 134.

CHIVES (Allium schoenoprasum)

Chives, being the mildest type of onion, is also an antibiotic in a mild way. It is being added so often to clear broths and soups. It has the reputation of stimulating the appetite and strengthening the stomach, and it is also supposed to have a beneficial effect on the kidneys and to lower blood pressure. It is useful in an invalid diet, and in this case all salads, omelettes, egg dishes, and soups should be offered with plenty of chives during convalescence.

More details on Chives, page 136.

DANDELION (Taraxacum officinale)

A wild herb, though undesirable in the garden, it is of such high nutritious value that it should be used, particularly in spring. It is best taken as a fresh salad or chopped dandelion leaves with a salad, or as freshly pressed juice, or in combination with spinach. In this way dandelion can be used daily. Full of useful minerals and vitamins, it is considered helpful to the function of the gall-bladder. Dandelion salad in spring is also considered a blood-cleanser, owing to its diuretic and digestive qualities. All these qualities make it one of the most valuable herbs in spring and throughout the year, as long as young leaves can be found on any plant. Also a tea (page 40) is made of fresh or dried dandelion leaves, which is helpful to digestion, liver, and gall-bladder functions. The roots are used to make a coffee substitute.

DILL (Anethum graveolens)
Dill is a rather special herb for flavouring, and there are some countries in which dill is of such importance that their people, if away from home, go a long way to get dill. This may be due not only to its aromatic and pungent flavour, but also to the fact that dill is excellent for digestive purposes. Dill has always had the reputation of being helpful in the case of flatulence and tummy-ache, and for promoting good sleep. Therefore, it was used for the baby's gripewater. Though dill also sharpens the appetite, its seeds used to be chewed before a meal to avoid hunger pains, specially by early churchgoers, as it was done also with fennel seeds. Chewing dill seeds was also supposed to remove bad breath, an interesting suggestion which may be worth an experiment. Dill is rich in minerals and is thus an important addition to our food. It had the reputation of stimulating milk production in nursing mothers. The astringent quality of dill has been experienced by pressing out the juice of the plant, and this was used externally for piles. From a modern point of view, dill is a good flavouring for diabetics and for those on a low salt diet, because the salts contained in it are no burden to the system in general.

More details on Dill, page 137.

ELDER FLOWERS AND *ELDER-BERRIES* (Sambucus nigra)
The Elder Tree gives us in profusion the honey-scented elder flowers and its black berries useful in autumn and winter. The tree has been closely connected with legend and folklore, and it was believed to be unlucky to uproot elder trees. To this we owe many elder trees in the countryside and it is easy to collect the elder flowers which, apart from being used in cooking for elder flower fritters, have mainly medicinal and cosmetic properties.

They contain volatile oils, vitamins and many other substances, which are responsible for the main virtues of elder flowers. They increase perspiration, are diuretic and are supposed to purify the blood. Elder flower tea like lime flower tea, is useful in the case of colds and can also be taken as an alternative to aspirin, particularly if mixed with lime flowers and chamomile. The full value is obtained if taken hot in bed. Apart from this medicinal use, they make refreshing summer drinks, made with either water or milk, and their pleasant sweet distinctive flavour can be added to so many of our desserts, such as milk dishes, jellies, and jams. Elder flower water, an infusion, is safely used for eye and skin lotions and is a mildly astringent stimulant. Thus elder flowers are an excellent addition for washing and to the bath. Little bags made of elder flowers through which the hot tap runs can be very useful as a simple and quick bath addition. Also facial steam baths made of elder flowers or added to other herbs are useful, as elder flowers clear and soften the skin and are good against freckles and pigmentation. More about this is found on pages 68, 71.

The elder-berries can be cooked with jam or made into a juice and have medicinal properties of a different kind. They have the reputation of cleansing the blood-stream, and elder-berry juice is good for chills during winter and for people who suffer from pains originating from sciatica and neuralgia.

More details on the Elder, page 139.

FENNEL (Foeniculum vulgare)
Fennel is a relative to dill, both are fish herbs, and a number of their qualities serve the same purpose. Fennel also stimulates milk production in nursing mothers, it also has a similar kind of sedative effect, it also stimulates the appetite. In the same way as dill it acts as an anti-flatulent and is good for indigestion, which makes it in the same way as dill useful for the baby's gripewater. It has the reputation that it can be used as an expectorant and against catarrh. There is, however, one quality which is persistently mentioned, and that is that fennel is said to reduce overweight, and that therefore a tisane made with fennel could be useful and worth experimenting with for those who have to watch their weight. Amongst the many herbs expected to be helpful to the eye, fennel is one of the most useful. Compresses steeped in fennel tea, placed on the eyes, or bathing the eyes with fennel is good for inflamed eyelids, watering eyes, strengthening the

eyes altogether, and improving the sight. For cosmetic purposes a facial pack made of fennel tea and honey is recommended against wrinkles. (Cosmetic Uses, pages 66 and 72.)

More details on Fennel, page 141.

HIBISCUS FLOWERS
AFRICAN MALLOW
KARKADÉ

A delicious thirst-quenching ruby-coloured tisane, called Karkadé in its African homeland, is made of the flowers. They give it a beautiful burgundy colour and a slightly tart, lemony flavour. Two or three flowers can also be added to rose-hip tea (page 47) to improve the red colour and the flavour of this drink. This tea is drunk much on the Continent, particularly by students in University towns who do not like to prescribe to the alcoholic excesses of some of the University Societies, and is generally a useful summer drink without any stimulating substances. It is excellent either hot or iced, and can also be added to punch or a non-alcoholic punch can be made of hibiscus flowers (page 42). (Recipe, Chapter 12, page 328.)

HORSERADISH (Cochlearia amoracia)

The roots of the horseradish grow in most well-worked soils and are somehow more difficult to eradicate from a garden than to get them growing. The root has a delicious hot pungency and is at the same time cooling. This makes it not only an excellent flavouring but also a very healthy addition to many foods.

Horseradish belongs to the plants which have antibiotic qualities. It contains, in fact, substances which are hostile to bacteria, and is therefore not only most useful for preserving food to which it is added, but also for keeping the intestinal tract in a sound condition. It is stimulating to appetite and digestion, helps the liver to function, has a strong diuretic effect and is an excellent seasoning for diabetics.

For many different uses, see index.

HORSETAIL (Equisetum arvense)

This wild-growing herb looks like a minute version of the gigantic trees of prehistoric times. It contains a considerable quantity of silicic acid, which is useful medicinally, but at the same time has been used for cleaning and scrubbing all fine metals and the plants used to be sold in German-speaking countries for scouring. Owing to its content of silicic acid the herb has an astringent and strengthening effect on the tissue, and an infusion of it is excellent for curing brittle nails (Cosmetic Use, page 74). The green barren shoots, looking almost like minute Christmas trees, are the parts which can be collected during the summer months, in fact from May onwards until late summer, and are used for tea. They should not be bruised or broken and be dried carefully without losing their colour.

HYSSOP (Hyssopus officinalis)

The herb has a refreshing aromatic scent and its tea (page 43) is used as an expectorant for catarrh. The herb has a slightly bitter and minty taste and is, therefore, also a good flavouring when finely chopped in salads or as an addition to game, meats, soups and stews. The flowers and tops have also been used in some Continental sausages; hyssop is useful with the digestion of fat, meat, and fish, such as eel, or for rubbing into poultry or roast, before roasting. It has been suggested that hyssop 'cuts grease'. In America fruit cocktails, particularly those made with cranberries, are flavoured with a few leaves at the bottom of the dish, and it is also added to pies made with fruit, such as apricots or peaches. ¼ teasp. of hyssop sprinkled over the fruit before the top crust goes on is quite enough. Hyssop was mentioned in the Bible for cleansing purposes. It is also part of the famous Chartreuse, and there are probably more uses for hyssop in France than we are aware of in England.

JUNIPER BERRIES (Juniperus communis)

The shrub Juniper, regarded as a magic plant in the past, is connected with many legends concerned with evil spirits, devils, etc., but also with holy legends from the Bible. Its strong, aromatic scent emanates from all parts of the shrub and the berries are slightly bitter-sweet, fragrant, and spicy in flavour. They are used for gin and for all spirits which used to be thought good for the stomach. They are part of certain blends of kitchen spices, such as for beef and for game, especially venison. The Laplanders make a tea from juniper berries (page 43) which is used in all Continental countries and in Scandinavia, and a conserve is prepared and served with cold meat. The substances contained in the berries are stimulating for the appetite and the digestion and at the same time cleansing the blood. They stimulate all functions of the body and their diuretic effect make them useful for the functions of the kidneys. They also have disinfectant, antibiotic substances. During the nineteenth century school-rooms in Switzerland were not well aired as fuel was short; the air was then sweetened by putting juniper berries on red-hot burning coals. Meanwhile, research has found that while burning the sugar in the berries, a gas is produced which has a disinfectant effect and a germ-killing quality. This explains why it is also used to disinfect and clean the air in an invalid's room.

Smoked meat when smoked with juniper berries receives a special flavour.

The berries need three years to ripen. They are first green, then blueish and eventually black, and should not be used before they are ripe. In marinades for game and as a flavouring for sauer-kraut their preserving qualities come to the fore.

LADY'S MANTLE (Alchemilla vulgaris)
Lady's Mantle has an old reputation for healing. It was originally a wound herb used against bleeding, but its universal reputation has everywhere been connected with female ailments. Its active substances are not all fully understood, but the tea made of its leaves (page 43) has been considered to be of importance to all women. It has been said that lady's mantle clears inflammations of the female organs. Also cosmetic uses have been suggested against inflammation or other skin disturbances and against freckles. Although a very useful yet nowadays unknown herb, it obviously could be more useful for women of all ages.

LEMON BALM (Melissa officinalis)
Lemon Balm, which is growing profusely in many gardens and is often considered a weed, has many virtues, medicinal as well as flavouring, and very often the plant is not considered as valuable as it really is. The lemon-scented leaves have an anti-spasmodic effect, and as they at the same time stimulate the heart and have a calming effect on the nervous system, provide an excellent tea (Melissa Tea, page 46) to be used as a night-cap or as an early cup of tea. This experience is based not only on Continental uses of this tea, but on a particularly long and helpful experience of one of the authors.

There are a few people now in England who do not like to be without the tea for one day. Lemon Balm also has the reputation of securing a long life, and quite a few reports from the past confirm it. Lemon balm is also believed to induce perspiration in feverish patients, but for this purpose there is perhaps more help to be found with lime flower, elder flower, or chamomile tea. Lemon balm is considered effective for ear and toothache, and also reputed to be used against vomiting in pregnancy. This is very likely to be effective as vomiting is sometimes due to spasms against which this tea is particularly useful. There is also an unconfirmed reputation that it is good against bad breath. All the effects are mild and lemon balm can therefore be used for delicate people and over long periods and it is as such one of the most useful daily drinks.

Externally lemon balm has been used in an ointment for treatment of gout, and has been considered a wound herb for its cleansing and pain-killing effect; the same is also reported of external use for rheumatism. Cosmetically, washing with melissa tea or infusion is good for all kinds of skin conditions. Lemon balm leaves are useful in potpourri and herb cushions (pages 76–9.)

More details on Lemon Balm, page 143.

LIME FLOWERS (Tilia europaea, *or* cordata, *or* platyphyllos)
THE LIMES

The flowers of the limes can be collected mainly from three varieties of the Lime Tree, and are used to make a delicious and health-giving tisane from the dried flowers only. These are collected and used together with the large oblong leaf-like bracts. The flowers contain a number of properties which are mildly sleep-inducing and help to get rid of mucous. A tea made of Lime Flowers (page 44) soothes the nerves, aids digestion, and allays spasms, but it is also useful in cases of chills and colds, and can be used as a pleasant alternative to aspirin, as it also reduces temperature. Lime flower tea (tilleuil) is used in France as an after-dinner drink, and its calming and anti-spasmodic qualities help to provide a good night's sleep. Together with equal parts of chamomile and elder flowers, it is excellent against colds and 'flu – if taken in bed, because it increases perspiration. Lime flowers are also a cosmetic help against freckles, wrinkles, and impurities of the skin, and they are believed to stimulate the growth of hair. Lime trees take a long time until they bear flowers; they can often be found wild, in gardens, parks and avenues. The flowers should be collected from the lime tree during June and July, but should not be heaped up or pressed down, and be dried carefully on trays in a low temperature.

LOVAGE (Levisticum officinalis)

This is not only a herb with a very different kind of flavour – because it is reminiscent of yeast and similar to a yeast extract – but it has also an unusual health reputation. In many languages it has been considered a love-potion, though its name can be traced to its geographical origin and has really nothing to do with love; but it has also in several countries the reputation of being a deodorant, and therefore it is likely that having been used as such, it has been at the same time considered to be helpful in all things to do with love. The herb used in salads and cooking and as a tea (page 45) stimulates the digestive organs. It has a diuretic and general cleansing action. It is at the same time antiseptic, and it is very likely that its cleansing effect on the whole system acts as an external as well as an internal deodorant. From Czechoslovakia comes the report on a custom of country girls who used to carry lovage in small bags hanging from a ribbon round their necks when they went to meet their boy-friends. It has also been used as an addition to the bath-water, and been placed externally on wounds as an antiseptic and antibiotic. It has been used against flatulence, and is reported to stimulate the milk production in nursing mothers as other herbs do. Its general cleansing effect could probably be put to much better use. It may be worthwhile to experiment with its deodorant qualities internally as well as for a bath addition (pages 64, 70, 73.)

Lovage Cordial, page 45.

More details on Lovage, page 145.

MARIGOLD (Calendula officinalis)

The flowers of the Marigold have medicinal value, already mentioned in the twelfth century. Apart from their use with salads, rice, and as a substitute for saffron, all mentioned on page 146, marigold contains, apart from bitter principles, a colouring substance calendula, which is like carotine, and very small quantities of volatile oil.

The flowers soaked in oil and in ointments for the treatment of wounds, have an excellent effect on old or badly healed scars, *eg* for those which are left behind from chicken-pox in children. Marigold oil is also good for tired feet. It is used for any kind of skin eruption or small ulcers. Wounds also heal more quickly. An old herbal reports that only to look at marigold will 'drive evil humour out of the head'. It is the lovely sub-colour which probably does this trick.

Marigold Tea, page 46.
More details on Marigold, page 146.

SWEET MARJORAM (Origanum majorana)

Marjoram is a well-known flavouring herb and is discussed as such on page 148. Its disinfecting and preserving qualities have made it famous when added to sausages and other meat preserves. Marjoram, particularly the wild marjoram *or* origanum vulgare, contains thymol, which is a powerful antiseptic both internally and externally. Marjoram at the same time stimulates the appetite, and is probably for this reason added to all pulses and meat dishes. Marjoram also has the reputation for increasing white blood corpuscles, and this speeds healing of infections. Altogether it is supposed to improve the blood circulation. It has been noticed that it acts as an anti-flammatory agent in the mouth, and therefore an infusion of it is useful to be used as a mouth wash. It acts on mucous membrane, and therefore powdered marjoram has been used as a snuff to help with nasal congestion. Externally, bunches of warm marjoram herb can be placed on the affected parts to relieve rheumatic pains; marjoram oil has been painted on swellings of rheumatic joints.

More details on Marjoram, page 148.

THE MINTS

The various mints have certain health properties in common. Spearmint (Mentha viridis *or* Mentha spicata) can be used, for instance, as an infusion which is helpful in the case of skin troubles, for either washing or compresses for bathing the face, which gives to it a fresh and healthy complexion. Fresh leaves used as compresses in case of headaches have been found useful. Externally, mint rubbed on to places affected by gout or rheumatism will help to relieve the pain. Peppermint (Mentha piperita) has medicinal value, particularly as a tea. The tea is, in fact, a good pick-me-up when tired, and more details can be found on page 46. Peppermint tea relieves pain, cramps, nervous palpitation, and is a great help in settling the stomach after vomiting and all conditions caused by digestive troubles. It deals not only with a tummy-ache but also with a general upset and it has at the same time a pain-killing and anti-spasmodic effect. It stimulates production of bile, the functions of the liver and is altogether helpful with liver and gall-bladder trouble. In fact, it is a great help to the general digestion. Oil made of peppermint is antiseptic and used for flavouring toothpaste. It does not only ease headaches or neuralgic pains, but has an almost anaesthetic action.

Cosmetic Uses, pages 63, 70.

More details on the Mints, page 149.

MUGWORT (Artemisia vulgaris)
Mugwort has the reputation on the Continent of helping in the digestion of poultry such as goose or duck or fat meat and fish. It thus has become an indispensable seasoning for these foods, and it is difficult to find out now whether it was first known to improve the digestibility of fat food or whether its bitter substances and volatile oil created a flavour which goes particularly well with poultry and meat. Before hops were used, mugwort was also used for flavouring beer – this explains the name – and it can be found in digestive liqueurs, such as Vermouth and Absinth. It's a useful seasoning for diabetics, and a tea of mugwort was once used against rheumatism (page 47). It grows wild, but can be grown on any kind of soil. During July to September the high flower shoots – when in bud – are the parts to be collected before they fully open. The leaves can be discarded and only the buds are used for seasoning.

NASTURTIUM (Tropaeolum majus *or* minus)
Nasturtium is one of the popular garden flowers, the leaves of which can be eaten between bread and butter like watercress, but it is also one of the few herbs for which some modern health use has been discovered. It has antibiotic qualities and is therefore used in some countries on the Continent as a kind of herbal penicillin. This quality is probably due to its extraordinary content of Vitamin C. Modern research has discovered that the highest Vitamin C content was found in the leaves of the plants before they flower in July. As nasturtium grows in any garden, it is a valuable vitamin addition to the diet in any case, but in cases of an infection, a cold or a sore throat coming along, it is advisable to increase the intake of nasturtium. It can be dried for winter use, provided that the colour can be retained. As it is also a pleasant substitute for pepper, it is important for people with ulcers, who are not allowed to use pepper, and it adds to the appetizing value of a diet prescribed without salt and pepper. However, the quantity of nasturtium should be somehow restricted and should be used with a certain caution. In salads, on cream cheese, and on sandwiches altogether not more than a

third to two-thirds of an ounce should be eaten at one time, or one ounce per day at various meals during the day. Details can be found in Part Two, page 151.

NETTLE (Urtica dioica *or* Urtica urens)

Nettle is another tenacious weed, disliked by people for its sting, but the young leaves of the Stinging Nettle have especially curative values. They improve the quality of the blood because they contain iron and also a high content of the previously mentioned silicic acid. In fact, nettle is rich in many minerals and plant hormones. Because of its outstanding qualities, it could and should be used almost daily as a flavouring, added in small quantities to salads and vegetable dishes. A small quantity of dried nettles is hardly noticeable in food, but can on the other hand help with salt-reduced and diabetic diets, as nettles contain a salt which is not a burden to the system. Therefore, nettle is both a flavouring and a medicinal herb. Nettles must be picked with gloves and scissors, but all young shoots, even on older plants, are suitable for food. Nettles are best picked in spring, but it is possible to find young shoots at any time of the year. Boiling water takes the sting out of nettles, but they lose it also when dried. They are only valuable dried if they retain their green colour fully.

Nettle Tea *or* Broth can also be made (page 47).

PARSLEY (Carum petroselinum)

Parsley is such a generally used herb for flavouring that it is probably right to assume that practically every family gets some parsley each day, and this as a habit is more than justified from a health point of view. Parsley is one of the few herbs which is rich in Vitamins A and B and most of all in Vitamin C. As such, a small quantity every day is of help, as Vitamin C belongs to those vitamins which are not stored in the body but should be replenished every day. Though parsley's contribution is necessarily small, it is of importance as a regular source. It is considered to have an anti-flatulent, anti-spasmodic, and anti-fermentative effect. As it counteracts these three factors, it is useful daily for those who have a tendency towards these three conditions. It also stimulates the digestive glands and therefore improves the working of the whole digestive system. All this points to the frequent and daily need for parsley. Parsley tea (page 47) has an old reputation as a remedy for rheumatism in this country, obviously due to its diuretic qualities. Externally parsley water or infusion is believed to remove freckles or moles.

More details on Parsley, page 154.

ROSE GERANIUM (Pelargonium graveolens)

This is probably the most popular of the many sweet-scented Geraniums. The lovely scent of the leaves is reminiscent of roses, but has a slight suggestion of spice. The fresh or dried leaves can give a delicate flavour to many sweets, jams, and jellies and fruit cups. They are also used in baking at the bottom of a cake tin and their delicate flavour is added to custards, cooked fruit, puddings, and ice-cream. One of the smaller leaves in the bottom of a finger-bowl' will give a fragrance to the water. The leaves can also flavour other herb teas, and a tea can be made of them. For hot drinks use one crushed leaf in the bottom of a cup. Rose geranium leaves can also be used either at the bottom of jam-jars or used at the top for sealing. The dried leaves are a delightful scented addition to potpourri.

For Rose Geranium Tea, page 47.

ROSE HIPS
FRUITS OF THE WILD DOG ROSE (Rosa canina)
SHRUB ROSE (Rosa rugosa)
SWEET BRIAR (Rosa rubiginosa)

The fruit of the Wild and Shrub Roses are small red-orange mostly oblong berries which are left after the flowers have wilted. These colourful berries, an ornament for the hedgerows, are a nutritious and important fruit, a rich source of Vitamin C as well as Vitamins A, E, B, and P. Rose hips were reported to be twenty times richer in Vitamin C than oranges and sixty times richer than lemons, and were collected during the Second World War as an important Vitamin C source; but they are not only health-giving as a vitamin source, they also provide a tisane of long-standing reputation. Rose Hip Tea (page 47) made of pips and pods, is providing Vitamin C from the pods, and the pips have an age-old reputation of helping the work of gall-bladder and kidneys. Their diuretic quality, in fact all their qualities, make them useful as a daily tea, particularly for people who like to eat uncooked fruit and salads. When rose hip syrup is made commercially, the Vitamin C is extracted and mixed with syrup, thus providing babies with a readily taken Vitamin C food.

In many Continental countries a colourful orange-red rose

hip purée is made, which is served with desserts, for instance, the excellent rose hip sauce, which can be used instead of custard or chocolate sauce, providing all its health-giving qualities.

(Recipe, pages 290–1.)

ROSEMARY (Rosmarinus officinalis)

The popularity of Rosemary, which has increased recently, probably due to contact with Mediterranean cookery, should have an equally strong if not stronger appeal for its influence on health. When used as a flavouring it acts also on a weak digestion, and is helpful in the case of flatulence, but apart from its qualities as a digestive, it stimulates the circulation and various other functions. It widens the tissues and increases the supply of blood to those parts of the body to which it is externally applied. This has been found helpful in the case of nervous headaches. Greek students have been reported to have worn wreaths of rosemary round their heads when going to an examination. If a brain-worker feels tired and – through the external application of rosemary blood is rushed to his head – it is most likely that the brain cells will be freshly nourished and tiredness will be dispelled and the brain will start working anew. Experiments with this have supplied confirmative experience. Rosemary sprigs put into wine and allowed to permeate have been found to be a good stimulus for the heart, and this may also be due to the reasons given above.

Rosemary Tea, page 48.

More details on Rosemary, page 155.

Rosemary also has a wide reputation of stimulating the growth of hair when used as a hair-wash or a rinse. This general stimulation of functions is one of the important qualities of rosemary. Externally, it is also reputed to improve the skin when used for washing or as a bath addition, and for hair and skin alike rosemary has definite cosmetic functions. Rosemary kept in oil for some time produces an effective liniment in cases of gout and rheumatism.

SAGE (Salvia officinalis)

Sage has probably one of the oldest reputations for health amongst herbs, particularly in England, and this matches without doubt its popularity as a flavouring herb. The Arab proverb, well known in all countries, 'How can a man die if he has Sage in his garden', shows the importance which scholars of all civilizations applied to sage. Sage tea (page 48) which before tea was brought to this country was a popular and daily drink, was considered to be one of the reasons, if taken daily, why 'A man could not die'. It was considered a fine tonic, and was also used as a remedy for colds, rheumatism and fevers. It acts as a disinfectant, preventing colds, and as an expectorant in the case of lingering cough, and it is supposed to stimulate the circulation of the whole digestive system. Its healing powers – expressed in the Latin name 'Salvere' to save – illustrate its use as a universal remedy for all ills. The fact that it has been mainly used to flavour rich meats, such as pork and mutton, and fat fish, is probably due to the fact that it helped as a digestive. Its main health use, however, is as a gargle and mouth-wash in the case of a relaxed or sore throat. Red sage particularly has been considered to be an excellent disinfectant gargle in the case of a throat infection because of its astringent qualities; and as a mouth-wash; it also keeps the teeth white. Sage was believed to increase wisdom by strengthening the memory, and this is probably the explanation for the use of sage tea until old age. More details on sage tea for a gargle are given in the chapter on Teas, page 48. It has also excellent cosmetic properties when the herbs are added to a facial steam bath. As a steam bath it has an astringent effect on the skin and also therapeutic qualities in the case of a Severe Head Cold (page 53). If sage is steeped in oil, the same astringent qualities can be used on the skin.

More details on Sage, page 157.

SALAD BURNET (Sanguisorba minor)
Salad Burnet, the one herb which will be with us all winter, with luscious green leaves, can be used as a tonic. It has these qualities whether used with salads, or in drinks; a Tea (page 49) can be made of it as well. It is mildly diuretic. Salad burnet is also a useful ingredient as a bath addition or when added to a facial steam, it will strengthen and improve the skin.

More details on Salad Burnet, page 159.

SOLIDAGO
GOLDEN ROD (Solidago virgaurea)
Golden Rod has an old reputation of being an excellent wound herb and a more recent one of being helpful in the case of kidney and bladder troubles. Its old name was 'Heathen Wound Herb', and it was originally imported from the Middle East as being used by the Saracens. It was very expensive until it was found that

it grows in this country, and that it has not only the anti-flammatory effect speeding up the healing of wounds, but that as a
Tea (page 50) it is helpful with the functions of kidney and
bladder, it even has had the reputation of dissolving kidney and
bladder stones. It has also been used as a disinfectant and as an
ointment, probably all connected with its use as a wound herb.

SORREL, FRENCH SORREL (Rumex acetosa *and* Rumex scutatus)

The young green slightly acid flavoured leaves of Sorrel contain
Vitamin C, therefore they are a useful herb for salads and soups,
particularly in spring, and are considered to have blood cleansing
and blood improving qualities. They are also supposed to be
diuretic and helpful for kidney stones. They should, however,
not be used too regularly, because part of the plant contains
oxylic acid which can be damaging to health if taken in excess.
As a supplier of Vitamin C they are not therefore so generally
useful as nasturtium, which – if taken with the restriction
suggested on page 25 – can be taken over longer periods. Sorrel,
attractive as a flavour and useful for health, should be eaten in
moderation or at least not regularly over long periods.

More details on Sorrel, page 160.

SUMMER SAVORY (Satureia hortensis)

Summer Savory, in fact the savories – because there is a winter
savory which is coarser and stronger in flavour but remains in
the garden for the whole of winter – have a strong volatile oil as
a main constituent. Savory has above all a strong digestive effect,
and this may be the reason why it was originally used with beans
of all kinds, as on the Continent its flavour has been inseparable
from all kinds of beans from broad beans to runner beans. It not
only increases the flavour of beans (Part Two, page 162) but it
also helps with the digestion of beans which have a tendency to
cause flatulence with some people. Though the flavours are almost
inseparable, the origin of this combination was definitely a digestive one, and the volatile oil of savory has been infused as a
digestive medicine (Tea, page 50). Summer savory has also been
used for aromatic baths and its strong aromatic scent has a
strengthening effect. The leaves have been crushed and used on
bee stings to relieve pain and swelling. Summer savory has also
an old reputation of preserving sight and hearing, but it would
need research and experimenting with this to be certain.

More details on Summer Savory, page 162.

SWEET CICELY (Myrrhis odorata)

Sweet Cicely has the old reputation that it cures flatulence and that it is helpful with mild digestive troubles. It has also been recommended for coughs. But its main up-to-date contribution to health is that it is a definite sugar-saver. It is a sweet, slightly anise-flavoured herb which grows easily and is available throughout the greatest part of the year. It can easily be dried and obtained commercially green-dried; however, fresh as well as dried it helps to reduce the tart flavour of many fruits and even spinach. If cooked, particularly when dried, with fruit and fruit pies, or any sweet made of fruit, it reduces a fair amount of sugar, up to about half the sugar needed. White sugar is today disliked by many people for many reasons. For instance, by the figure-watchers, by mothers for their children's teeth, and because it is bad for health for people in general owing to the excessive way in which it is often used. Experiments made with, for instance, fruit tarts such as plum tart or pies, or in fact with stewed plums, have been so successful that it can be suggested to save sufficient sugar to make the still needed sugar for cooked fruit a minor disadvantage. In the case of those who are interested in a slim figure, it is certainly better to reduce the sugar by sweet cicely than by tablets. Here is a new function for a little-known herb which can be strongly recommended.

Tea, page 50.

More details on Sweet Cicely, page 163.

THYME (Thymus vulgaris)
LEMON THYME (Thymus citriodorus)

A valuable volatile oil thymol is contained in the leaves of Thyme, and is to a large extent responsible for its very old and often confirmed reputation. Though thyme is a very strong herb and can therefore only be used in small quantities, it has been considered to be good for indigestion and flatulence, and for minor intestinal affectations. Its main quality, however, is that thyme has, owing to its volatile oil and other constituents, strongly antiseptic and disinfectant qualities. For the same reason it can be found in the judge's posy or the Queen's herb posy for Maundy Thursday, both uses which were strongly connected with its antiseptic qualities. It has been considered a sedative and has been used in bronchitis, whooping cough, and other persistent coughs. Its strong scent made use of thyme for deodorants, gargles, perfumes, and soap, also as a pain-killer for toothache and in liquid dentifrices thyme or thyme oil was found. Thyme has always been an important part of a herb cushion which helps people to go to sleep and to sweeten the air in an invalid's room (page 78). It was also used for scented lotions and sachets, as a moth-preventative in cupboards and wardrobes. It has been used in potpourri where the strong scent of thyme and lemon thyme are most useful (page 76).

Thyme Tea, page 50.

More details on Thyme, page 166.

Lemon thyme has a still stronger scent and is more used for perfumes, but it also has an attractive flavour which – if used in small quantities – gives to fruit salad or any fruit sweet a soupçon reminiscent of brandy or Kirsch. It has been added to herbal tobacco; although its strong and perfumed qualities have, at the same time, an equally strong influence on health, the details of which still wait to be discovered.

VALERIAN (Valeriana officinalis)

The root of the Valerian is probably one of the best herb sedatives. Valerian Tea (page 50) made of the dried root, in fact from part of a plant without extraction or chemical interference, is not only the strongest herbal sleep-inducing remedy but has a general calming effect on the nervous system. It is really an excellent tranquillizer and particularly so in all nervous troubles which arise suddenly, when an infusion of valerian roots can be used with success. Though it is not 'everyone's cup of tea' and its smell can be upsetting, it has been used as a spice, and even as a perfume in the sixteenth century. Valerian can be found wild and cultivated; the roots are ready to be collected in the autumn of the second year. The tea is best made in the cold way, and instructions will be given on page 51. Valerian tea should not be taken uninterruptedly, after a while a break should be made, but it is most useful in times of strain and tiredness.

VERBASCUM

COMMON MULLEIN (Verbascum thapsiforme)

The Common Mullein, known to many people as a garden plant, is not only tall and beautiful in the garden, but it is also of great medicinal value. The bright yellow flowers, either freshly picked or carefully dried so that they retain their yellow colour, are an extremely health-giving tea in the case of chest troubles, particularly with a long-standing cough, or in fact for any surplus mucus in any part of the body (see page 51). This tea acts as an expectorant, and will at the same time help to counteract inflammation of mouth, throat, or any bronchial part. It is, however, necessary that the flowers should be brightly yellow as the healing qualities are connected with the colouring matter, and if the slightest discoloration takes place during picking, drying, or storing, the flowers are either less effective or become useless.

THE VERBENAS
VERVAIN (Verbena officinalis)
LEMON VERBENA (Lippia citriodora)
Both Verbenas are used to make health-giving teas: one is the native Vervain known by the Druids, called Verbena Tea (page 51); it has an old reputation as a slightly bitter tisane in France where it is used as a digestive, and is considered to be useful in nervous exhaustion and as a sedative tea as well as a digestive. Being slightly bitter and soothing, both these qualities offer the explanation for its effect.

Lemon Verbena is not a native plant, it came originally from Chile. The scent and taste of the leaves is that of lemon, and its fragrant tea, popular in Spain, is more attractive than the other verbena tea. Lemon verbena tea has also the reputation of having a sedative effect, particularly on the bronchial and nasal regions. It can be grown in poor dry soil and taken indoors as a houseplant when the bad weather starts. The delicious scented young leaves can be used in fruit drinks, salads, jellies, instead of lemon rind in sauces, and can be made into a tea blended with mint and drunk hot or iced.

WOODRUFF (Galium odoratum *or* Asperula odorata)
One of the sweetest herbs of the woods growing particularly amongst beeches, with its scent only noticeable after the leaves have slightly wilted and dried. Woodruff used to be put into drawers and wardrobes to keep the moth away, and to impart its perfume. It was also a strewing herb and was stuffed into beds amongst the linen. On the Continent woodruff has become famous as a flavouring for wine cups in May, which is the time it flowers, and before or during flowering it has the strongest flavour. Its fragrancy has the same reputation as borage, and its exhilarating effect, dispelling depression, was soon recognized

as a help for festive occasions. It increases the effect of good wine, and has the reputation of relaxing and at the same time uplifting. Suggestions for its use in drinks are found in Chapter 12, page 324, and its use as a tea as well as adding woodruff to China tea is found on page 52.

YARROW (Achillea millefolium)

Yarrow is mostly found wild and can be collected during its flowering period from June to August. The parts used are the leaves and the flowers, which, after the plant has been cut, can be pulled off the stem. The herb has a rather special, spicy scent, and while flowering, it has astringent qualities. Yarrow has, like chamomile, a great number of health properties. Owing to its bitter substances it belongs to those herbs which are good for the whole of the intestinal tract. It stimulates appetite, is anti-flatulent and helps with intestinal troubles, such as colitis, or gastric trouble. It is helpful in the case of fermentation and constipation, as well as for trouble with liver or gall-bladder. It stimulates both the functions of the kidney, and thus has a diuretic effect, and those of the circulation, and thus has an influence on the heart functions. Yarrow is also reported to have a regulating influence on the period and to have a wound-healing effect. It is supposed to help with gout and rheumatic pains, and is reported to have a favourable effect on a beginning diabetes. For all these purposes a tea made of yarrow (page 52) is the best way of taking it. Its most effective use, however, is a cosmetic one: yarrow is particularly good for greasy skins, and cleans and beautifies the skin. For this purpose it can be taken internally as a tea and as food, and externally for facial steams and face packs (Cosmetic Use, page 69). An infusion of yarrow can be used externally for a warm bath addition, or for washing when cooled. For food: freshly extracted yarrow juice is used, of which two teaspoons can be taken with cold water. Young leaves or flowers of yarrow can also be chopped finely and mixed with salads early in the season (Recipe for Yarrow Salad, page 89) and can be eaten between bread and butter; however, not too much of it should be taken during one day.

Chapter 2

DIRECTIONS FOR TEAS AND OTHER HERB MIXTURES

THE BEST WAY to extract the value of the herb as a whole – other than using herbs chopped or whole for food – are Herb Infusions or Teas. It is therefore advisable to make an infusion of a herb mostly with boiling or, in some cases, cold water. Such teas are wholesome and often health-restoring drinks, refreshing and cooling in summer, and warming in winter. Some of them are reputed to have specific therapeutic, others cosmetic, values for internal and external use, such as bath additions, etc. Some allow both uses.

Most of these tisanes can be used instead of ordinary tea, as a helpful addition to the daily diet. They are not necessarily meant to be treatment but used as first cups of early morning tea or as a helpful night-cap they can be of greatest value. Sometimes the herbs are used with water as a tea or tisane, sometimes with milk for a highly recommended bedtime drink. The word 'Tisane' applies to herb teas only. It is frequently used in England, though it originated in France, where herb teas were and still are being used daily.

There are many teas which can be made from different herbs and used for many useful purposes. These may appear overwhelming at first to the reader who has no experience with herbs; therefore a selection of the most useful teas and herb mixtures for day-to-day use follows at the end of this section. (Page 54).

Often herbs have been used as an additional flavour to either hot or cold China tea, or a sprig of mint or lemon thyme is used in iced tea. However, many refreshing and delicious drinks can be prepared by using herb leaves, flowers, or seeds without necessarily combining them with ordinary tea.

The flavours of these teas are usually most delicate and can be very easily impaired by using badly dried or badly packed herbs with their flavours mingled. Each herb should be packed strictly apart in airtight containers.

The herbs' delicate flavours are also easily affected by metal, therefore great care should be taken in using only earthenware, china, porcelain, glass, or unchipped enamel – but *never* metal. There are also other pitfalls. Too long steeping can ruin the flavour of any delicate herb, therefore it is best to steep the leaves a shorter time and rather use more of the herb if a stronger infusion is desired. One teasp. of leaves in either the strainer of a glass teapot or at the bottom of another non-metal teapot, gives a basic measurement per cup, the quantity of which can be added for each further cup. This results in a delicate and subtle flavour. There are, however, teas which require boiling for 10 minutes to bring out the full flavour and for each herb this is mentioned specially.

If dried leaves are used for the preparation of a herb tea, 1 teasp. of herbs for each cup and 1 teasp. for the teapot is generally considered adequate. Any deviation from this is specially mentioned in each recipe. Dried herbs for teas have a certain concentration, and, if well-dried, produce a definite flavour. Though for most cookery recipes the quantity given for a green-dried herb is often the same as for the fresh herb, for teas, however, the question of concentration is of special importance, and therefore it is really necessary to use three times as much of fresh herbs for making tea. If fresh leaves are used, the flavour is less concentrated as they still contain all their moisture; 3 teasp. of the herb for each cup is suggested. The fresh leaves should be bruised by crushing them in a clean cloth before infusing. The same applies to a tea made from aromatic seeds, where 1 tablesp. seeds per pint of water is suggested; the seeds should be crushed well before boiling.

METHODS OF PREPARING HERB TEAS are very simple and the results are subtle, soothing, and often very refreshing, all at the same time. Here follow three basic methods of preparing herb teas:

(a) *Teas Made from Dried or Fresh Leaves or Flowers*
1. Warm china or glass teapot.
2. Place green-dried or fresh, crushed herb leaves in teapot.
3. Pour boiling water over herb leaves.
4. Allow to steep 5–10 minutes only.
5. Strain.

Note: If a stronger infusion is desired, use more leaves at the beginning of the preparation.

Herb leaves can also be put into thin muslin – or paper bags. In some countries herb teas are available in bags similar to the tea bags used in this country for ordinary tea. It is difficult to judge the quality of the herbs if supplied in tea bags; if suitable strainers are used, it would be advisable to use whole or shredded leaves or whole flowers, the quality of which can be seen.

(b) *Iced Herb Teas*
1. Place crushed fresh herbs or dried herbs in an earthenware container.
2. Pour boiling hot water over the herbs.
3. Allow to steep for 5 minutes.
4. Strain and cover container.
5. Place container in a refrigerator to cool.

(c) *Herb Teas Made from Seeds*
1. Bruise seeds slightly, possibly with a pestle in a mortar, to bring out oil.
2. Pour boiling water into enamel saucepan placed over a strong heat.
3. Add bruised seed.
4. Simmer gently 5–10 minutes.
5. Strain quickly and serve hot.

Teas Made of Many Herbs

ANGELICA TEA. Angelica tea should be served hot as a digestive tonic. The leaves can be used fresh or dried if the colour of the leaf in drying remains light green as in its natural state. If the leaves are left whole it is difficult to measure them by teaspoon, therefore the equivalent of a teaspoon per cup has to be estimated.

ANISEED TEA belongs to the seed teas; 1 teasp. seeds should be used per pint of boiling water. (See above for method.) After straining, the tea should be served hot. Aniseed tea has a soothing influence and induces sleep; it is therefore suitable as a night-cap.

It has an anti-flatulent effect, and one cupful after meals is recommended unless seed tea is available, page 49. Aniseed can also be used with hot milk. Its aromatic flavour makes it a pleasant bedtime drink.

BASIL TEA was once famous for its sedative effect, particularly against gastric spasms and flatulence. It has been also used in the case of a cough and for stimulating perspiration to reduce temperature. For this purpose 1 teasp. of cold tea every hour was recommended. Its strong scent was used against head colds, and it can be used as a part of facial steam baths to clear the head. The tea is made of leaves in the same way as other leaf teas (page 36).

BERGAMOT TEA. Red bergamot is a pleasant tea which, served hot, induces good sleep and has a soothing and relaxing effect. It used to be called Oswego tea in America because of the Oswego Indians from whom American colonists took it over when boy-cotting British tea. Bergamot leaves also make an excellent addition to China or Indian tea, as well as to wine drinks and lemonade.

To make tea:
> To bring out the real flavour of bergamot tea, 1 teasp. bergamot per cup should be simmered for 10 minutes in an enamel or stainless steel saucepan. Bergamot tea can be sweetened with honey, if desired.

An excellent night-cap can be made with milk.

Bergamot milk:
> 1 tablesp. shredded dried bergamot leaves. ½ pint milk.
> Pour the boiling milk over the leaves. Allow to draw for at least 5 minutes. Strain and serve hot. This can be sweetened with honey and a little lemon added.

On the Continent the red flowers, after drying and retaining their strong red colour, are used as a sedative and relaxing tea, called 'Gold Melissa'.

BILBERRY TEA (Vaccinium myrtillus). Berries can be carefully dried and then chewed raw in cases of dysentery, or made into a tea for the same complaint.

To make tea:
> Soak 1 tablesp. of dried bilberries for some hours. Pour 2 pints of boiling water over the berries. Bring to the boil.
> Remove from the heat and allow to draw for 10 minutes. Strain and serve hot without sugar.

Bilberry Leaves Tea (see Wild Herbs in Spring, page 58).

BITTER TEA is made of a mixture of three herbs:

> Wormwood (Artemisia absinthium)

Centaury (Centaurium umbellatum)
Blessed thistle (Cnicus benedictus)

Equal parts of these three herbs will provide a tea which is most helpful for lack of appetite due to stomach disorder. It should be served hot as bitters.

BLACKBERRY LEAVES TEA. The leaves of the blackberry shrub are valuable if gathered in spring and an infusion or tea can be made for gargling and taking internally. They are an excellent addition to a mixture of other wild leaves. (See Spring Tea, page 56.)

BORAGE TEA. The excellent exhilarating qualities of borage used in drinks such as in Claret Cups and Pimm's No. 1 can also be experienced if borage leaves are used for a hot tisane or as an iced tea, made either with dried or fresh leaves. Those who do not like alcohol will feel the encouraging effect of borage when using it this way. Also borage flowers can be added to this tea, and are said to improve the functions of the heart. The leaves can be added to many other drinks shortly before serving.

CARAWAY TEA. Caraway seeds are part of seed tea; they have a carminative, ie anti-flatulent effect. In the case of flatulence, one cupful after meals of either caraway or seed tea is recommended. The boiling water should be poured over 1 teasp. bruised caraway seeds per cup and allowed to steep for 20 minutes and be strained.

CENTAURY HERB TEA (Centaurium umbellatum) is known to be a good tonic and a help in dyspepsia. (See Wild Herbs in Spring, page 55.)

CHAMOMILE TEA. The chamomile flowers – and a very little of the leaves of the True Chamomile (Matricaria chamomilla) – have a pleasant flavour, and a tisane is much drunk in France as an aid to digestion after heavy meals. It has a soothing action on the gastro-intestinal tract and all mucous membranes.

An infusion made of it is excellent for a mouth-wash after dental treatment, or for a sore mouth of any description, for a gargle, and for rinsing inflamed gums, or for a relaxed throat. It is excellent as part of the herbs used for a facial steam for a heavy cold, as well as an eye-bath in the case of inflamed eyelids.

To make tea:
For drinking as well as for infusions:

1 teasp. chamomile flowers per cup of boiling water. Do not steep
the flowers longer than 3–5 minutes. Strain quickly.
As a drink chamomile tea can be sweetened with honey, if desired.

Chamomile has excellent cosmetic qualities (page 63).

COLTSFOOT TEA (Tussilago Farfara). Rich in Vitamin C and
helpful for catarrh and cough. (See Wild Herbs in Spring, page
59) and Cosmetics (page 64).

COWSLIP TEA (Primula veris), made from flowers quickly
dried and also from roots if available, is a good bedtime tea as
a sedative effect has been observed. This tea can also be used as
an expectorant in the case of colds and as a Bath Addition, (page
71.)

CYSTITIS TEA. This is a mixture of the following herbs which
are helpful in cystitis:

> Equisetum (Horsetail)
> Sage leaves   in
> Uva Ursi (Bearberry leaves)   equal
> Mallow (Sylvestris)   parts.

1 tablesp. mixed herbs per cup of water. Bring to the boil and
boil for 5 minutes. Take one to three cups per day.

DANDELION TEA. As dandelion has diuretic and digestive
qualities and improves liver and gall-bladder functions as well
as rheumatic conditions, a tea is made from fresh or dried dandelion leaves, which is most helpful. The tea is made like other leafy
herb teas. The roots, when roasted, are used as a coffee substitute and have the same effect as the tea. (See Wild Herbs in
Spring, page 58.)

DILL SEED TEA. Dill has many helpful qualities and its richness
in minerals and volatile oil has provided many suggestions for
the use of dill seeds, in particular it has been used for insomnia,
and whether dill is used in the baby's gripewater or is suggested to be boiled in wine as a night-cap for adults it mostly
serves the same purpose.

The tea, made of 1 teasp. crushed dill seeds per cup of boiling
water and served unsweetened and hot as other seed teas (page
49), has been found effective for hiccoughs and vomiting.

ELDER FLOWER TEA is useful in the case of colds and as an

alternative to aspirin. Mixed with lime flowers and chamomile in equal parts it is very helpful in the case of 'flu and chills, if taken hot in bed, for it increases perspiration. A teaspoon per cup of tea and an extra teaspoon for the pot makes a very pleasant sleep-inducing tea.

Ordinary tea can be flavoured by adding one-third of elder flowers to the quantity of tea leaves used.

Elder flower drink:
    Refreshing summer drinks are made with cold water or milk. Half a jug filled with elder flowers to which boiling water is added should be strained when cold and slightly sweetened.

An infusion made of elder flowers and water can be used for an eye-bath or eye compresses and has also cosmetic qualities (page 63, 67,) etc.

Hot elder-berry juice:
    1 pint of juice, 8 oz. sugar. Wash and drain the berries, they need not be stalked. Heat them slowly in a stone or earthenware jar, covered by a lid in a slow oven. From time to time drain the juice which will develop.
    Put the remaining berries in a cloth (tied to the legs of a reversed kitchen stool). Place a bowl underneath and allow to drip overnight. Squeeze the cloth well. Boil 1 pint of juice with 8 oz. of sugar until ¼ of the liquid has evaporated (about ½ hour). Pour in dry hot bottles and seal well.

1–2 tablesp. of elder-berry syrup diluted with a glass of hot, not boiling, water is an old remedy for colds and coughs and is also recommended for people suffering from sciatica and neuralgic pains.

ELDER LEAVES TEA (see Wild Herbs in Spring, page 56).

EYEBRIGHT TEA. The small delicate flower grows in abundance in late summer and autumn. As a tea it improves digestion in general. (For its effect on eyes, see Cosmetics, pages 72–3.)

FENNEL TEA. Fennel seeds have the same quality as dill seeds and can be used for the same purpose. As fennel also has the reputation of being used as an expectorant and against catarrh, and as it is reported that fennel is said to reduce overweight, a tisane made of either fennel leaves or crushed fennel seeds may be useful for both purposes and worth experimenting with. Fennel tea can be most helpful for treatment of the eye; compresses steeped in fennel tea placed on the eye, or bathing the eyes with a fennel infusion for inflamed eyelids and watering eyes, have been found effective. The tea is also reputed to improve the sight. Fennel and fennel tea have also cosmetic qualities (page 63). (See also index.)

HIBISCUS TEA. The lovely red flowers of the African hibiscus, also called Karkadé, give a beautiful burgundy-coloured tea with a slightly tart lemony flavour. This tea is thirst-quenching in summer and warming in winter and is much drunk on the Continent, particularly by students. Though not exactly a medicinal tea, it is a delightful summer drink without stimulating substances, but is also very useful when used for punch, alcoholic, or non-alcoholic.

One heaped teasp. of hibiscus flowers are used per half-pint of water. If the flowers are placed in warmed and dried teacups or cup, the usual teaspoonful for the pot should be allowed. After pouring the boiling water over the flowers, the tea should be allowed to steep for 5–10 minutes and then be strained. This tea is most attractive in a glass teapot because of its lovely colour. It has the flavour of a tea to which lemon juice has been added and should be sweetened with honey for those who find this too tart. It is equally good hot or iced.

Karkadé punch:
  Without alcohol is made of hibiscus tea to which sugar, ½ stick of cinamon and 1–2 cloves are added.

2–3 hibiscus flowers, added to rose hip tea, will give this a beautiful burgundy colour and a lemony flavour.

HORSETAIL (Equisetum) a plant without flowers, with no special attractions, wilts soon after picking. It contains a great deal of silicic acid which makes the herb astringent and antiseptic; it has been used in folk-medicine for mending tissues, particularly for tears in the mucous membranes.

The tea, made of it, is a diuretic tea and is often found in mixtures for bladder and kidney teas. It has also cosmetic qualities such as strengthening and toning the skin and improving hair and nails (pages 73–74). This tea was much used on the Continent particularly by the famous Kneipp who had great success treating people with hydrotherapy and with herbs in the nineteenth century. (See Wild Herbs in Spring, pages 59, 70.)

Equisetum tea:
  For making the best use of the herb's properties, 1 teasp. of the herb per cup should be soaked for several hours, then be boiled in the soaking water for 10–15 minutes and be allowed to steep for another 10–15 minutes before straining it.

HYSSOP TEA is an expectorant and good in the case of a pernicious cough. In the case of intestinal catarrh, also catarrh of the bronchial tract and asthma it is a useful remedy. It has also been considered a vermifuge. It is made like any leafy herb tea (page 36) and is served as a hot tea; the herb is also used to flavour cocktails.

JUNIPER BERRIES. Juniper berries provide an excellent tea for liver and kidney conditions, though it is not advisable to take juniper berry tea during a chronic inflammation of the kidney.
  The berries, if chewed, have a cleansing effect on the whole system. They are antiseptic and also reduce excess fluid in the tissues. In fact, juniper berries stimulate all functions of the body.

Juniper berry tea:
  1 teasp. *or* 12–18 crushed berries are used per cup; pour over with boiling water and allow to draw for 10 minutes. Strain. To be taken in the case of stomach and intestinal trouble, also in the case of trouble with the respiratory tract, sweetened with 1 teasp. honey.

A similar infusion in larger quantity is suitable as a bath addition.

Juniper syrup:
  Boil 1 lb. of juniper berries with 6 pints water until tender. Crush and bring again to the boil and pass through a sieve. After it has cooled, add sufficient honey until a liquid syrup is obtained. Fill into containers with a wide opening and close well: 1 teasp. before meals stimulates the appetite and the circulation.

LADY'S MANTLE TEA, made of lady's mantle leaves, has been considered a protection for the female organs and at the same time improving the functions throughout the various periods of a woman's life, thus preventing female disorders. It has, in fact, been called 'a woman's best friend'. The tea has also been considered of importance during pregnancy, shortly before birth and immediately afterwards. It is supposed to have a regulating effect on the monthly cycle, and has been particularly recommended to be taken from the fortieth year onwards. It has been suggested that operations could be avoided if this tea was used in time and over long periods. The tea has been recommended also for the treatment of wounds, and an infusion of the herb is helpful against inflammations of the skin and acne (pages 63, 69, and 75).

LEMON BALM TEA, one of the most useful herb teas, probably in a range with chamomile and peppermint tea, the most widely used herb teas. The leaves have an anti-spasmodic effect and at the same time stimulate the heart, and as they also have a sedative effect on the nervous system, they provide an excellent tea to be used daily. Lemon balm does not actually induce sleep, but promotes it because it removes spasms and tension which can prevent sleeping. The tea is equally useful as an 'early cup of tea', when it helps to counteract over-tiredness left over from the evening before, even when it would otherwise develop into a headache or migraine. It is reputed to prolong life, and there are various reports of those who drank it every day and reached unbelievable years of age. It is supposed to help the brain-worker to overcome loss of memory, depression, and has the reputation of sharpening the wit and understanding.

It is made like all leaf herbs with a teaspoon per cup, but allowed to steep at least for 10 minutes if not longer. It is one of the teas which do not deteriorate from longer steeping.

LIME FLOWER TEA, similar to chamomile tea, is one of the most popular daily teas drunk for pleasure or for its medicinal value in France. It is a delicious tea (page 22) which also promotes perspiration and therefore belongs to those teas which, as a pleasant alternative to aspirin, are useful in cases of chills and colds. At the same time, the tea is mildly sleep-inducing. It soothes the nerves, aids the digestion and allays spasm. It is used as an after-dinner drink, is calming, and helps to provide a good night's sleep. In its quality to combat chills, it is one of the teas which, with equal parts of chamomile and elder flowers, should be taken in bed to increase perspiration; it is also part of the herbs to be used for a facial steam in the case of severe head colds (page 53). Its cosmetic qualities are mentioned on page 62.

LIME LEAVES TEA (see Wild Herbs in Spring, page 57).

LIVER TEA is a mixture of the following herbs, which are helpful to the functions of the liver.

$\frac{1}{2}$ oz. peppermint leaves (2 parts).
$\frac{1}{2}$ oz. dandelion leaves (2 parts).
$\frac{1}{4}$ oz. rosemary (1 part).
$\frac{1}{4}$ oz. blessed thistle (broken) (1 part).
$\frac{1}{8}$ oz. wormwood ($\frac{1}{2}$ part).

LOVAGE TEA. An infusion made of lovage has a distinctive celery flavour and is more similar to a broth than a tea. It can be served, therefore, as a relaxing savoury broth with a little herb or sea salt added, or it can be tried as a tisane sweetened with a little honey. This herb is also considered a deodorant and stimulates as a tisane the digestive organs, as well as having a diuretic and cleansing action. It is at the same time antiseptic and all this seems to point to the internal and external qualities of a deodorant. Lovage tea is also reported to stimulate the milk production in nursing mothers. It may be worth while to experiment with its deodorant qualities internally as a tea and externally as a bath addition. It has also cosmetic uses (page 64 and 72).

LOVAGE SEEDS have the same quality as the herb; they grow in pairs and look similar to caraway seed. Apart from being used for flavouring and cooking, they have been used in the past for a cordial.

Lovage cordial:
Freshly harvested seeds should be used for lovage cordial and a good quality of brandy.
1 oz. lovage seed.
1 pint brandy.
4 oz. sugar.

1. Crush the seeds slightly in a mortar with a pestle, or they can be tied in a clean muslin cloth and crushed with a wooden mallet.
2. Add the crushed seeds to the brandy.
3. Then add the sugar and stir well.
4. Put in a cool, dark place for 2 months, shaking the container occasionally.
5. Then pass the cordial through a paper filter.
6. Re-cork and serve at room temperature when desired.
   Note: It will yield 1 pint.

MARIGOLD TEA. A tea made of marigold petals (page 23) is soothing for intestinal conditions such as colitis, etc., and promotes perspiration. It helps the body to make better use of Vitamin A and has also cosmetic properties (page 63 and 73).

MARJORAM TEA. The fresh leaves of sweet marjoram can be infused and the tea made of it served hot or iced. The pleasure of taking it is increased by blending it with any of the mints, and its health-giving qualities are those mentioned in the description of this herb in Herbs for Health and Beauty (page 24).

MELISSA TEA (see Lemon Balm Tea, page 44).
The refreshing lemony flavour of melissa tea is more subtle when whole leaves are used, but shredded leaves are stronger in flavour.

THE MINTS. The various mints are all supplying refreshing teas made from either fresh or green-dried leaves. Spearmint, apple mint, or any garden or wild mint, gives a refreshing drink for cold summer evenings, if boiling water is poured over some freshly picked green leaves. In a glass teapot this tea shows its jade green colour; it can be sweetened with sugar and lemon juice, if desired.

Peppermint tea:
The most used and probably most attractive of the mint teas is peppermint tea. It is excellent as a daily tea, as it is not only most helpful when tired as a pick-me-up, but it will also deal with any discomfort after a meal, settle the liver, and is a perfect substitute for coffee, especially for those whose gall-bladder does not function satisfactorily. It is most helpful for an upset stomach, and with a few chamomile flowers added, it will settle cramps and relieve pain, particularly after vomiting. More details about its medicinal properties are given in 'Herbs for Health and Beauty' (page 24) and details about its cosmetic properties on page 63.
Peppermint tea made of whole leaves has a more subtle flavour, while a stronger flavour is found with shredded leaves. It can be used instead of ordinary tea, but after a period of taking peppermint tea regularly, a break should be made before using peppermint tea regularly again.

Peppermint milk:
It can be taken as a refreshing pick-me-up or as a helpful warm nightcap and is most useful against cramping pain in the abdomen, also soothing and refreshing.
1 tablesp. fresh or green-dried peppermint.
½ pint boiling milk.

Pour boiling milk over peppermint and allow it to draw for 5–10 minutes, then strain and serve hot.

MUGWORT TEA. Mugwort was originally used for flavouring beer and can still today be found as a part of bitter liqueurs. A tea made of mugwort leaves was once used against rheumatism. At the time of the Greeks and Romans it was used as a gynaecological medicine. Only the buds are used for making tea (see page 25) and it can be made like any leaf tea.

NETTLE TEA *or* BROTH. The medicinal qualities of nettle can be used also as a tea. As boiling water takes the sting out of nettles it can be made out of fresh or green-dried leaves. (See Wild Herbs in Spring, page 58.)

PARSLEY TEA. Parsley, which is such a useful herb to be used daily because of its content of Vitamin C, also provides parsley tea, a hot tonic of diuretic qualities, which helps to reduce excess fluid in the tissues. It has an age-old reputation for rheumatism, particularly in England.

Parsley is also used internally for cosmetic reasons (page 76).

RASPBERRY LEAF TEA (Rubus idaeus) is well known as a helpful herb before or during confinement, and for female disorders. It has an astringent and stimulant effect. For the skin, see page 57.

The leaves should be dried without stems.

Raspberry leaf tea:
  1 teasp. of leaves per teacup of boiling water. Allow to draw for 15 minutes.

ROSE GERANIUM TEA made of rose geranium provides a delicate rose-flavoured drink and can be served hot or iced. The tea can also be blended with various mints and rose geranium leaves can flavour other herb teas in the same way as they give their delicate flavour to sweets and fruit cups. For hot drinks, 1 crushed leaf should be used in the bottom of a cup.

ROSE HIP TEA is made from the complete fruit of roses, that means pods and pips after tops and tails have been removed. The hips can be picked in late autumn and dried carefully so that they retain their red colour. They can, however, be obtained commercially dried and with pods and pips in a balanced proportion.

Rose hip tea is an excellent tea for daily use and can be taken over unlimited periods. This drink is served twice daily at the famous Bircher-Benner Klinik in Zurich. The tea has the reputation of not only providing Vitamin C from the pods, but the pips are supposed to be helpful to the functions of kidneys and gallbladder. It has diuretic qualities and is important for all those who wish to slim on a diet containing plenty of salads and fruit.

Colour and flavour of rose hip tea can be much improved by adding a small quantity of hibiscus flowers, because it provides not only a beautiful burgundy colour but a lemon flavour, which makes it unnecessary to use lemon with the tea as often suggested.

To make tea:
   2 tablesp. rose hips (pods and pips in balanced proportion).
   Soak rose hips in water in a small container for 12 hours. Bring 3 pints of water to the boil in an enamel or other non-metal saucepan. Add the rose hips, and then simmer gently for 30–40 minutes. Strain.

The tea can be kept covered in a china or pottery jug for 1–2 days and re-heated when needed. If desired, a few more hips can be added for re-heating. Sweeten with brown sugar or honey (if desired).

ROSEMARY TEA. The fresh or green-dried leaves, young sprigs and flowering tops can be infused to make rosemary tea. This is a stimulant for the heart in the same way as Rosemary Wine (page 28). An infusion made of the same parts of rosemary is useful for the growth of hair and has many cosmetic functions (page 63). The tea can also be blended with lavender flowers, and can be served hot or iced.

RUE TEA (Rutae graveolens). This was once a well known tea in country districts and considered a remedy against dizziness and female disorders.

SAGE TEA was in general use in England before China and Indian tea became known. Many country people still believe that it ensures long life, and the proverb 'How can a man die with Sage in his garden' was one quoted at the Arabian universities. It is a wholesome drink in spring, served hot or iced. The tea can be blended with any of the mints. It has also been considered a valuable tonic, and was used for colds, rheumatism, and fevers. It is disinfectant and is supposed to stimulate the circulation of the digestive system. It was particularly used for a persistent cough; the reputation that it is the best gargle in the case of a throat infection came originally from the Continent, but this has been confirmed, though it is particularly the red sage that has been used for this purpose. Sage leaves are also an important part of the infusion made for a facial steam in the case of severe colds. The astringent qualities make sage tea useful all round, internally and externally The leaves also flavour drinks, wine cups, cocktails, or apple juice for the non-alcoholic. Its cosmetic properties can be found on page 63.

SALAD BURNET TEA (Sanguisorba minor) is a pleasant tea, which can be made from fresh or dried leaves. Served very hot it is helpful to the kidneys. It is useful as a tonic, and can also be served iced. The herb was originally used to flavour wine, especially claret, and has been reputed to have exhilarating qualities. It has the reputation of having a cleansing effect on liver, gallbladder, kidneys, and is supposed to stimulate the secretion of bile and altogether the glandular system. It has also been used as a bath addition and for cosmetic purposes (page 64).

SEED TEA is a carminative, an anti-flatulent tea. It is made of three seeds which were mentioned before:

Caraway seeds ⎫
Fennel seeds ⎬ in equal parts.
Anise seeds   ⎭

Crush the seeds with a pestle. Pour boiling water over the seeds. Allow to steep for 20 minutes. Then strain.

This is a very pleasant, warming drink. In the case of flatulence, drink one cupful after meals.

Another variation of the seed tea is used as a drink stimulating the milk production in nursing mothers. For this purpose either fennel tea, caraway tea or dill tea can be taken or the following mixture:

2 oz. Anise seeds.

2 oz. Dill seeds.

2 oz. Marjoram.

1 teasp. of this mixture is used per cup, otherwise the same

method as for seed tea should be used, 2–3 cups can be taken per day.

SOLIDAGO TEA (Golden Rod, Solidago virgaurea). This old wound herb, which was helpful because it has anti-inflammatory qualities, has also been found helpful with the functions of kidney and bladder. The upper part of the herb in flowering should be dried and broken apart.

Boil the herb for 1 minute. Allow to steep for 10 minutes. Then strain.

In cases of dropsy or inflammation of bladder and kidneys, 2–3 cups daily can be drunk and diuretic qualities will be experienced.

SUMMER SAVORY TEA. Summer savory has an old reputation of preserving sight and hearing, and it would be interesting to experiment with these qualities by making a tea of it. It has at one time been used as a digestive medicine by making an infusion of it. It also has been used as an aromatic bath addition. Proceed as with any other leaf herb tea, but steep a little longer.

SWEET CICELY TEA. Sweet cicely's reputation that it cures flatulence and is helpful with mild digestive troubles can be made use of by infusing the herb and making a tea out of it. Its main use is to flavour and to act as a sugar-saver, and the anise seed sweetness of it provides a tea that need not be sweetened.

THYME TEA (GARDEN *and* LEMON THYME). Fresh or dried leaves can be infused for making a tea. Served hot it has all the medicinal qualities of thyme (page 31) and in particular is useful for its antiseptic and disinfectant qualities. Thyme tea can be blended with sage and served hot; lemon thyme tea is more fragrant.

To make tea:
3–4 sprigs of fresh thyme, *or* 1 tablesp. of green-dried thyme (leaves and flowers). Pour 1 pint of boiling water over it. Draw for 10 minutes to make a tonic tea.

VALERIAN TEA. Valerian tea is made of the dried root of Valeriana officinalis, which is a slightly different plant from the decorative valerian, which can be found in so many gardens, particularly in Wales. It provides the best herbal sedative. The tea made of it has strong sleep-inducing qualities and a general calming effect on the nervous system. Its flavour and smell may not be liked by some people, but others get quickly used to it and can take it regularly without difficulties.

The tea can, like other infusions of roots, be made with boiling water using a teaspoon of root per cup, but it is infinitely more effective when made in the cold way.

Cold valerian tea:

Soak 1 level teasp. in one cup of cold water, cover and stand in cold place for 12–24 hours. Strain and drink approximately 1 hour before retiring.

If too strong, use half of this cup and dilute with water. Add water to the remaining half-cup and use this the next day.

It is advisable to soak this tea every evening or every second evening to have a regular supply for a period of 2–3 weeks, then a break is indicated; after this valerian tea can be taken again.

VERBASCUM TEA is made of the bright yellow flowers of the Common Mullein, which can be either grown in the garden or obtained dried. The flowers, however, must be bright yellow when dried because their medicinal value is bound up with their yellow colour. They provide a pleasant tea which gives dramatic relief to cases of a persistent cough, bronchial conditions and relieves the respiratory tract of mucus.

It is prepared in the same way as other leaf or flower teas, but should be allowed to steep until the tea becomes yellow. During an acute cold or in the case of chest troubles or cough, 2–3 cups per day can be taken.

VERBENA TEA. Vervain which is the Verbena officinalis, is a native plant of very old usage. It is a slightly bitter tisane used in France and in England as a digestive and is considered soothing in nervous exhaustion, and used as a sedative night-cap. It also is a good digestive, but is not as pleasant as lemon verbena.

LEMON VERBENA TEA. Lemon verbena is not a native plant; it produces a fragrant tea with a scent and taste of lemon, popular in Spain and often confused with the less attractive other verbena tea. Lemon verbena tea can be blended with mint and be taken hot or iced. Lemon verbena tea has a sedative effect and particularly so on the bronchial and nasal regions.

The delicious scent of its leaves – fresh or green-dried – can be used in fruit drinks.

WOODRUFF has always been a famous herb on the Continent because it provides the most delicious flavouring for wine cups in May. It is at its best when it flowers and is reputed to have the same exhilarating effect as borage and perhaps even more so. It therefore not only increases the effect and flavour of good wine, but as it is also reputed to be relaxing, and at the same time uplifting, it is not only useful at parties but has the same effect when used as a tea. Woodruff tea has additionally, also, the reputation of relieving headaches and migraines. As it is one of the herbs which have an anti-spasmodic effect, woodruff tea is also soothing and calming. In Scotland it was taken to increase perspiration in order to ward off colds. It is also considered diuretic and tonic and helpful to the functions of gall-bladder and liver. It has been credited with blood-cleansing qualities in spring and is also reputed to improve not only the quality of sleep but also the length of sleeping time. All these qualities make it a useful night-cap or even a morning cup of tea.

It is best picked during May when it flowers, but needs to wilt and dry to give off its particular fragrance. If the leaves can be picked and dried so carefully that they retain their green colour, they are excellent to use throughout the year for making tea or flavouring wine or fruit drinks. As the leaves are best dried whole when they 'stand like a ruff' round the stem, the equivalent of a teaspoon per cup or glass will have to be estimated. If used green-dried they should be soaked in a little wine before fixing the drink finally. For tea they should be infused in boiling water. Woodruff leaves can be added to China tea, which will give this subtle tea a special fragrance. (See also page 33).

Woodruff tea:
　1 teasp. per cup, but not more, should be used. The tea should never be boiled but can draw for a long time (up to 1 hour) in hot, but not boiling, water.

YARROW TEA has, like chamomile tea, many uses. It can be made of yarrow leaves and flowers and is good for the digestion. The milky juice of the plant is rich in minerals and vitamins.

The tea made of dry yarrow is also effective and can be taken during those seasons when fresh yarrow is not available. It is prepared as the leaf or flower tea. That is, a teaspoon per cup poured over with boiling water. A similar infusion can also be used for cosmetic purposes as a pack (page 67), for washing and as a bath addition (page 69, 70). Yarrow is particularly useful in spring and in combination with dandelion. (See Wild Herbs in Spring, and pages 75-6.)

Facial Steam for a Cold

An infusion made of the following mixture of herbs produces a steam which is most helpful for inhaling in the case of a persistent catarrh of the upper respiratory and the bronchial tract.

Ingredients:
   A handful of whole *or* shredded sage leaves.
   A handful of whole *or* shredded peppermint leaves.
   A handful of whole lime flower.
   A small handful of chamomile flowers.

Method:
   1. Place the herbs in an unchipped enamel bowl or heatproof glass or earthenware bowl (not metal).
   2. Have all equipment ready to make sure that the first steam is not lost.
   3. Expose neck and chest and then pour 2-4 pints of fast boiling water over the herbs.
   4. Immediately bend over the bowl and cover yourself with a large bath-towel in tent fashion.
   5. Inhale the steam – lift corner of bath-towel if the heat becomes uncomfortable.
   6. Carry on for 10-15 minutes, as long as there is sufficient steam and you feel comfortable.
   7. Wash face and all exposed parts with cold water immediately.
   8. Stay indoors for at least 1 hour, or do it in bed.
   Note: Only one facial steam per day should be taken for a cold, or every other day when strain is felt.

To this basic herb mixture for a steam, in the case of a cold, can be added smaller quantities of basil, elder flowers, lavender, verbascum flowers.

A similar steam with some further additions can be used for cosmetic purposes (page 64).

Herb Mixture for Abroad

When travelling abroad – particularly in more southern countries

– people have often experienced digestive upsets and one of the authors has been asked repeatedly, after lectures, whether herbs could be helpful in this connexion.

She then made up a mixture of hers – called 'Mixture for Abroad' – which she used herself with success and she also had satisfactory reports from other travellers. The mixture can be used sprinkled over food regularly and if carried in a small glass container in a pocket or handbag, the herbs can be added once, twice, or three times per day to food. They will add flavour and act as a disinfecting protective in the case of unfamiliar bacteria for which the body is not equipped to resist.

When mixing the herbs consult the Guide (page 127) for proportions and taste the flavour at the end so that there is not one overpowering herb and the mixture remains a pleasant over-all herb flavour.

*Fennel herb *or* fennel seeds (ground in electric blender).
*Basil
*Mugwort (if available).
Borage.
Nettle.
Salad burnet.
*Dill.
*Tarragon.
*Lovage.

*Marjoram.
Nasturtium.
*Rosemary.
*Sage.
Grated horseradish (if available without vinegar).
*Celery leaves.
*Thyme.
Hyssop.

Juniper berries can be added to this mixture or should be chewed during the same period.

Start eating 4 berries per day; they can be increased by 1 per day to 15 and then decreased by 1 per day down to 4.

A Selection of the Most Useful Day-to-Day Teas and Mixtures

PEPPERMINT TEA (page 46)   Settling after-dinner digestive; instead of coffee for liver and gall-bladder sufferers – Pick-me-up when tired.

CHAMOMILE TEA (page 39)   Digestive, after-dinner tea. Healing gargle and infusions.

* Essential herbs (can be obtained commercially).

LIME FLOWER TEA (page 44)	Pleasant after-dinner drink. Alternative to aspirin for colds.
ELDER FLOWER TEA (page 40)	Pleasant summer drink. Alternative to aspirin for colds.
HIBISCUS TEA (page 42)	Ruby-coloured thirst-quenching, stimulating summer drink.
ROSE HIP TEA (page 47)	Most wholesome daily tea, rich in Vitamin C and helpful to kidneys.
MELISSA TEA (Lemon Balm) (page 44)	Relaxing, anti-spasmodic and yet stimulating morning and evening drink.
SAGE TEA (page 48)	All-round wholesome tea; also for colds, coughs, and gargling.
VERBASCUM TEA (page 51)	Dramatic relief for coughs.
HERB MIXTURE FOR FACIAL STEAM (pages 53, 64)	For colds in the head and the bronchial tract and for beauty.
PARSLEY TEA (page 47)	Tonic, with diuretic qualities for rheumatism.
RED BERGAMOT TEA *and* RED BERGAMOT MILK (page 38)	Sleep-inducing night-cap. Pleasant – relaxing.
VALERIAN TEA (page 50)	Sedative and sleep-inducing tea before retiring (tranquilliser) (not pleasant flavour).
SEED TEA (page 49)	Anti-flatulent drink after meals.
MIXTURE FOR ABROAD (page 53)	For digestive upsets abroad.

Wild Herbs for Health in Spring

There are a number of wild herbs which have been used in many countries over centuries.

For those who are interested enough to collect some of these herbs and experiment with them, here are some suggestions. Quite a number of these herbs can also be found in one's own garden.

The wild herbs are grouped together according to the purposes for which they are used. There are, for instance, certain herbs which are useful to circulation and have, at the same time, a soothing influence on the nerves of exhausted or strained people.

Herbs Stimulating and Herbs Soothing

To this group belongs the leaves of the *Wild Strawberry*. They can be dried and the famous herbalist and hydrotherapist, Kneipp, reports on his experience that the leaves and roots stimulate the liver and have a general soothing effect. A tea made of them also acts favourably on intestinal catarrh.

Blackberry Leaves Tea (Rubus fructicosus). The leaves of the blackberry shrub are gathered in spring and as they contain a number of curative substances, they have been used in folk-medicine for gargling and particularly for skin troubles. (Cosmetic Suggestions, page 68). However, for a valuable spring drink, blackberry leaves should be mixed with equal parts of the leaves of *Wild Strawberries* and *Woodruff* with a pinch of *Thyme* added. This provides an aromatic tea equally good for an early cup in the morning or for a drink in the evening. This tea is thirst-quenching and diuretic.

Spring Tea:
   3 parts of:
      Blackberry leaves
      Wild strawberry leaves
      Woodruff leaves
      and a pinch of thyme

The leaves of the elder tree contain in spring a number of curative substances and when dried produce *Elder Leaves Tea* which is diuretic, improves the circulation, and has a cleansing effect; it is helpful after physical or mental strain and is also considered mildly sleep-inducing. The dried leaves and young tips can also be chopped up and added to soups and externally placed on inflammations.

An excellent means to stimulate the circulation is found in the herb *Centaury*. Tea made of this herb stimulates the glandular system, the liver, and improves the circulation. The tea should only be allowed to be steeped in water which is not boiling. Centaury tea made from 1 teasp. per cup should be allowed to draw for 10 minutes. It provides a drink for the early morning when it has a soothing effect on the nerves and a cleansing effect on the kidneys. It has been considered one of the best teas for cosmetic purposes because it improves the skin.

Wild Chicory growing near meadows provides leaves and roots which, when gathered in spring, can be taken either as a pressed fresh juice or they can be dried for tea. They improve the functions of liver and gall-bladder as well as the general circulation, if taken as freshly expressed juice, 1 teasp. four times a day or as a tea. Chicory, when complemented by the simultaneous use of woodruff, is most effective.

A soothing tea is made of the leaves of the lime tree. The young leaves of the tree, picked in spring, freshly chopped and allowed to steep in hot, but not boiling, water for about half an hour produce *Lime Leaves Tea*, a tea to relieve cramping pains and other nervous conditions.

The leaves of the *Wild Raspberry* and its flowering sprouts have a calming effect and are useful for skin rashes. A tea made from the fresh or dried plant and the chopped or pounded leaves can be used externally on the skin.

The *Hops* are one of the most famous nerve-soothing herbs which have been used for more than 1,000 years. The young sprouts of the wild hop in spring provide a pleasant tasting tea which is said to relieve restlessness, palpitations, insomnia. Should beer in which hops are used be liked for similar reasons?

The leaves of the *Walnut* and its male as well as female flowers can be prepared like the tea made of lime tree leaves and an infusion made with 2 teasp. of the chopped leaves in hot, but not boiling water is helpful in a similar way as lime tree leaves tea. The young freshly chopped walnut leaves have cosmetic properties against the loss of hair and skin troubles.

Spring Fatigue

Another group of herbs can help in spring to combat spring fatigue and to cleanse and renew the system. *Nettle, Dandelion,* also *Yarrow*, are useful for this purpose at this time of the year, as are the leaves of the lime tree. Young leaves of nettle are rich in minerals and Vitamin A. A few tablespoons of freshly pressed juice made of young leaves, or in a morning beverage, or leaves served freshly chopped on bread, or on cereals, are excellent and can be given to children if they can be made palatable by adding them to the right kind of food.

A cup of nettle tea in the morning and at night is excellent for liver, gall-bladder, and intestinal troubles. Only honey should be used to sweeten it.

Dandelion increases elimination and perspiration. It is activating and helps the body to get rid of winter deposits. The leaves and roots should be gathered before flowering in order to make a freshly pressed juice; 2–3 tablesp. daily can be taken early in the morning. Finely chopped leaves and roots can be added to salads, or soups, or on bread and butter. The effect of dandelion is often improved by the addition of yarrow as finely chopped raw plant, added to soups. Yarrow tea can be taken internally and used externally for healing wounds or as compresses for skin impurities. (See Cosmetics, page 69.)

Spring and the Figure

During springtime people become more figure-conscious than at any other time of the year. Some feel heavy and bulky and may be more aware of the weight they carry around; lean people may wish to add to a shape with which they are not happy.

Certain herbs have an effect on regulating the glandular system and are helpful in improving the functions and the shape of the body as well as that of the mind. To this group of regulating herbs specifically for people who are underweight belong in particular *Nettle, Dandelion, Centaury, Yarrow,* and *Blackberry Leaves.* The value of these herbs for spring has already been discussed. Furthermore, there is *Watercress* in salads and *Bilberry Leaves* which can be found in heath districts, *eg* in Surrey and parts of Scotland. These leaves collected in April and May before the fruit forms contain substances which have this regulating effect on the glandular system; they can be made into tea.

Amongst the herbs particularly useful for the figure-watchers concerned with overweight are *Wood Sorrel,* useful to elimination by the way of the kidneys. These leaves should be added to soups and salads. They have to be used in moderation as their flavour is very sour, but they can be used in combination with nettle and spinach by adding them in small quantities to spinach purée or a spring salad.

The fresh plant can also be expressed to make a juice which should be taken with three parts of water. A handful of fresh wood sorrel leaves should be steeped in 2 pints of boiling water and allowed to cool to be taken as a tea.

The leaves of the *Coltsfoot* can be used in a similar way. They are rich in Vitamin C and it is suggested not only to collect the flowers from March to May, but also the leaves from May to July. Both should be carefully dried without either losing their colour. The tea made of them has a spring-cleaning effect as it is diuretic and considered to be an expectorant, and clears the respiratory tract. Coltsfoot is also used for cosmetic purposes (page 69).

The leaves of *Ribwort Plantain* can be collected from the beginning of May to the end of August before the plant goes to seed. They should be dried well as they become easily dark and then are no longer useful for making tea. Some fresh juice can be expressed from the flowering plants and the root, straight after picking, and a few spoons of this as well as the tea made from the dried plant are useful in the case of obesity.

The leaves of *Fumitory* can be picked from May to July and can be found near fields and paths. When dried they make a tea useful for liver and gall-bladder trouble which are both sometimes connected with overweight. In ancient medicine they were recommended against depression, sometimes allied to the same condition.

The crushed leaves of *Wormwood*, together with the flowers, can be used to make a tea which helps all functions of the obese.

Horsetail Tea (Equisetum) mentioned before is most useful for obesity because of all its special substances and particularly its minerals. It is, however, necessary to find the equisetum in fields and waste grounds, rather than to pick the kind which grows near water or marshes.

Improving the Mood

The sluggishness which is often felt in spring, and for which these various herbs are suggested, produces often certain disturbances of mood. People are either exhilarated by the event of spring, but often the opposite can be found as any disturbance in the physical functions is more strongly felt during spring than at any other time of the year and may lead to contrasting moods.

For the consequent depressions and changes of mood certain herbs can be helpful. There are, for instance, the *Barberries* with their bright yellow flowers, often found in gardens and hedges. Later on in the year their berries can be made into an excellent juice or can be stewed and provide a sweet rich in vitamins; but it is not well known that the root of the barberries is a help against liver and gall-bladder troubles. The root can be boiled and the whole plant, added to a tea made of it, will help the flow of bile.

Also the roots of *Fennel* can be dug up as they contain volatile oils similar to the seeds. The tea helps cleansing the mucous membranes and the intestinal tract, has an anti-spasmodic effect, and improves the general feeling of well-being. Fennel is not only found in gardens where it is grown as a herb, but can be found wild particularly near the coast.

Fresh *Wood Sorrel* leaves, mentioned before, and made into a tea (page 59) provide a drink which is not only refreshing but thirst-quenching and of a stimulating and cleansing nature. It therefore is a suitable drink to improve spring moods. Also the juice serves the same purpose (page 59).

Chapter 3

THE NATURAL WAY TO BEAUTY

HERBS HAVE been used for cosmetic purposes almost since the beginning of time and, infused with water and mixed with oil, they have been the main constituents of cosmetics.

Until the chemical industry started substituting the properties of herbs, herbs were the only beauty aids, and after a century of chemicals there is a tendency nowadays to return once more to a natural way to beauty.

Fairly recently, Helena Rubinstein, who has probably had the greatest influence on beauty aids and who started as a chemical student at the beginning of the century, has returned to herbs and produced her new 'Herbessence' collection. She issued ten beauty preparations – after years of research – in all of which herbs play a major part. Thus from the Egyptian ladies who perfumed their hair with marjoram to the present day 'Herbessence', time has come full circle.

Herbs have many functions, both internally and externally, as the beauty of the skin is so much dependent upon the proper working of all body functions. Therefore the use of herbs in food is of equal importance to the external beauty of the skin as the herbs used *on* the skin. Amongst the many functions of herbs are those that improve circulation, have a tonic effect, can fade freckles and pigmentation, refine and whiten skin; some are cooling and astringent, others smooth out wrinkles, help blemishes. Others repair tissues, heal wounds, improve existing scars, and soothe pain.

Herbs can provide a natural approach to beauty if the appropriate individual herbs are carefully dried, and leaves, flowers, and seeds skilfully blended. Such mixtures are often based on centuries-old traditions of many countries. By infusing these fragrant herbs in hot water, the inherent qualities of the essential oils with their magic effects on beauty as well as their full aroma are made available.

Chemical extractions, which mostly only utilize part of the plant, can interfere with the effect of the whole plant as such.

Preservatives and colouring additives, often used in the cosmetic industry, can be damaging. If herbs are used in infusions, etc., the chemical aids become unnecessary and no changes in the essential qualities of the herbs take place.

The use of herbs have a psychological effect. The natural herb scents produce a feeling of relaxation and comfort and the volatile oils a stimulating influence on the nerves. Both of these qualities create an atmosphere which helps to make full use of the effects of 'herbal' cosmetics.

The beauty aids for which herbs are particularly useful are:

Facial steam
Face packs
Compresses
Bath additions
Herb pochettes (as a bath addition)
Eye compresses
Eye bath
Nail bath
Hair rinses

Herb preparations which rely on the scent for their effect:

Herb cushions
Herb potpourri

Herbs Used for Cosmetics

According to their effect, the herbs are divided into activating herbs and reducing herbs.

The activating herbs:

LIME FLOWERS
(page 22)

One of the best cosmetic herbs: slightly bleaching (good against freckles); improves circulation, helps to smooth wrinkles. Good for compresses; antiseptic and stimulating in facial steams. Demulcent and mucilaginous properties. Also stimulates growth of hair.

CHAMOMILE
(page 15)

Healing, soothing, disinfectant, anti-inflammatory effects, or astringent in cases of ageing skin, but not a tonic. If combined with yarrow — tonic; for blond hair.

PEPPERMINT
(page 24)

In facial steams, antiseptic, disinfectant, stimulating circulation. Also good for compresses.

FENNEL HERB AND
SEEDS
(pages 18, 41)

Antiseptic tonic, smoothes wrinkles, helpful for the eyes. Addition to packs with honey and for creams.

ROSEMARY
(page 28)

Stimulates growth of hair. Healing, warming, increasing blood supply to certain places.

ELDER FLOWERS
(page 17)

One of the best cosmetic herbs. For centuries used to cure sunburn, remove freckles, and wrinkles. As a lotion: to soften, whiten, and cleanse the skin. Helpful for the eyes.

YARROW
(page 34)

For greasy skins. Used for tisanes, facial steam, face packs; and as a hair tonic. For compresses on chapped hands.

NETTLES
(page 26)

Improving skin and hair. Used for packs, bath additions, hair rinse and oil.

The reducing herbs:

MARIGOLD PETALS
(page 23)

Excellent healing properties against acne; helps old and new scars, inflammation, and rough skins; in ointments and oil.

SAGE
(page 28)

Cooling and astringent for packs and facial steams. Good for hair rinse.

LADY'S MANTLE
(page 21)

Used by the Arabs as a cosmetic herb. Astringent and restoring beauty to the skin. Infusion against inflammation and acne. Taken as tea and used for compresses. Freshly expressed juice for freckles.

EYEBRIGHT
(page 41)

Infusion for eye-bath in case of tired eyes and for inflammation of the eyelids. Also for eye compresses.

VERBENA
(page 33)

Cleansing and strengthening effect on the eyes; helps with inflammation of the eyelids.

HORSETAIL
(page 19)

Owing to its high content of silicic acid has good astringent, antiseptic, and tonic properties. Strengthening tissues, hair, and nails.

COLTSFOOT
(page 40)

Infusion used as compresses for dilated facial veins (thread veins).

LOVAGE
(page 23)

Infusion to be used as a bath addition or shredded leaves in a muslin bag under the hot tap for a bath as a herbal deodorant and against impurities of the skin. Tea taken internally also acts as a deodorant and increases effect of the bath addition.

SALAD BURNET
(page 29)

A herb used for cookery which grows throughout the winter and can be used as an addition to the facial steam or to the bath; it beautifies the skin and strengthens the body.

Cosmetic Suggestions

Facial Steam for Beauty

This is the beauty aid with the most immediate effect. The skin of the face will always improve with the help of the humidity and the temperature of a facial steam. The effect can be much improved with the addition of either a mixture of herbs or some specific herbs for specific purposes. It is recommended particularly for any skin with large pores or impurities.

A general mixture of dried herbs for improving the skin of face and neck:

Sage (whole leaves if available)*
Peppermint (whole or shredded)*

Basil (small quantity)
Chamomile flowers*
Lime flowers*
Elder flowers
Marigold petals
Nasturtium flowers
Cornflowers
Lavender flowers
Verbascum flowers
Nettle leaves (if available)
Fennel
Yarrow (if available)
Salad burnet (if available)

Warning: Facial steams are not indicated and, in fact, should not be used at all on very dry skin because it is usually too thin and too sensitive to heat, particularly if there are any dilated red veins visible in the face. Also the steam is not good for people with heart trouble, difficulties in breathing, and for the asthmatic.

Method of Facial Steam. Cover the hair and clean the face as normally done in the evening. Place approximately 2 handfuls of the herbs in a bowl, bring 2 pints of water to the boil and pour over the herbs. Hold the head above the bowl at a distance of 8 to 12 in. Cover head and bowl with a big bath-towel and cover this possibly with a thin rug so that the steam cannot escape through the pores of the cloth, but remains to act on the face. After 8–10 minutes, provided you feel comfortable, you emerge red and steaming from underneath the cloth. The affected parts – face and neck – should be washed with a wet flannel, steeped in cold water, and the face allowed to cool down. Do not go out until one hour after the steam bath.

The steam can be taken once per week for cosmetic purposes. People suffering from acne will probably find that any black spots will come out easily after the steam, but one should be careful not to press or cause any inflammation. After the steam bath, some of the face packs are indicated (see pages 65–8).

Natural Face Packs

Method: A pack is usually made out of some material such as

* Essential herbs for a facial steam. The others are helpful as an addition and provide also good specific effects from each herb.

yoghourt, curd, Fuller's Earth,* a clay powder (Claydos)*, mixed with the help of an infusion or a herb tea into a thick paste. This paste should be applied thinly to the face with a broad brush. The surrounding of the eyes and lips should be left uncovered or be covered with wet cotton-wool pads. The pack has to be applied when lying down in an outstretched resting position, possibly with the legs higher than the face; after 10–15 minutes, remove paste and wash face with warm water. Finish with a cold compress on the face.

Eggs find several uses for face packs – egg yolk is particularly suited for dry skin on the face. For this purpose it is suggested to use:

The Mayonnaise Pack. Stir egg yolk well with drops of pure olive oil and add lemon juice. Add some fennel. Allow the pack to remain on the face for 10–20 minutes, then wash off with warm water, previously boiled.

A *White of Egg Pack* should not be used too often as it may be too astringent. Beat white of egg to a firm froth and add a few drops of lemon. This mixture can be painted with a soft brush on to face and neck. After 10 minutes, wash off the pack with boiled, but cold, water. The pack is tonic, refreshing, but not suitable for dry skin. With some finely chopped or green-dried *Yarrow* added the pack helps large pores and greasy skin.

Oil Pack – for the middle-aged skin (40–50 years). Warm pure olive oil in a small bowl standing in boiling water. Soak in it a layer of cotton-wool as large as the face and place on the face. Protect the eyes beforehand with pads of cotton-wool soaked in water. Remove when cold, and clean face with soft paper tissues. Finish with alternative compresses dipped in a warm infusion of *Chamomile Flowers* (and *Yarrow* combined), or *Peppermint*, or *Sage*, to be followed by a compress made of cold water. (See Compresses, page 68.)

Fennel Pack. For the ageing skin, a pack made of curd, yoghourt, or clay powder, with a strong infusion of fennel seeds or herb, plenty of honey and some additional fennel herb added helps to enliven the skin, to smooth wrinkles. Acting as a tonic, it is also antiseptic and allays irritation of the skin.

Linseed Herb Pack. Boiling linseed into a thick slimy consistency makes an excellent facial pack which contains oil and

* Available from chemists or health food shops.

Vitamins D and E; combined with chamomile it has an anti-inflammatory effect.

Yoghourt Herb Pack is valuable for bleaching and clearing the skin. Some clay powder mixed with yoghourt to which a strong infusion of *Fennel* (for the case of wrinkles) or *Yarrow* (for a greasy skin) and some honey is added can serve several purposes.

Curd Herb Pack. Add to curd a little milk and honey, a few drops of lemon and a small quantity of an infusion of *Sage* or *Horsetail* for a thick paste for large pores. It also refreshes the skin.

Wild Herb Packs. Dandelion, nettle, cowslip, and daisy are of great benefit to the skin, particularly in spring. Nettle and dandelion contain so many health properties including vitamins, minerals, and plant hormones, that they have a strong cleansing effect, improving the content of the blood, etc. For their effect on the functions of the body see pages 16 and 26.

The skin is much improved by the tonic and astringent qualities of the wild herbs. As *Nettle* and *Dandelion* supplement each other, they can be used together in equal parts. The young leaves of nettle and dandelion should be gathered if possible in the morning, finely chopped up, crushed and be simmered lightly for 10 minutes to provide a thick mash. The skin of the face should be prepared beforehand with warm compresses before the actual herb pack is put on. The herb mixture should be spread on to a piece of thin muslin and this can go as a pack or compress straight on to the face. The eyes must be protected by wet cotton-wool pads. After leaving the herb pack for 15 minutes, it should be washed off with lukewarm water to which some lemon juice has been added. This pack can be applied every second morning, and if this is done for two weeks in spring, the result will be surprising. The skin will become clear and fresh, small wrinkles will disappear and the pack has also a healing influence on spots which have a tendency to become inflamed.

Nettle Pack. The same method can be used for nettle leaves and sprouting tops alone.

Yarrow Pack can be made from fresh sprouts and buds in the same way.

Elder flower Packs are useful to improve the skin when mixed with yoghourt, buttermilk, whey, or any of the dairy produce which have undergone fermentation. The action of the elder flower is improved by the lactic bacteria. Elder flowers can be added to yoghourt or cream cheese for facial packs or other face packs such as clay powder, etc., and can be made with an elder flower infusion. These face packs are stimulating and tonic rather than soothing; they clear and soften the skin and are good against freckles and pigmentation.

Elder flowers should be mixed with yoghourt, etc., into a thick paste and be allowed to permeate; then either put straight on the face with a brush or packed in thin muslin and use like a compress. Elder flower tea should be drunk in combination with the use of Elder flower packs.

Blackberry Leaves Pack. Collect the leaves when young and tender; they should be dried without stalks for tea. Chop fresh leaves, boil with a little water into a pulp-like mash and wrap into muslin and apply warm on to the face or any parts which are affected by skin troubles. The packs should be left for 20 minutes before retiring. Blackberry leaves tea supports the effects of the face pack.

Valuable additions to Packs:

Lemon	Contains Vitamins C and P. Astringent, bleaching, also for hand creams.
Cucumber Juice	Bleaching, clearing, astringent.
Yeast	Excellent for a pack for greasy skin. Can be dissolved in milk or yoghourt or butter-milk; mixed with Fuller's Earth, *or* Clay Powder (Claydos).* After drying, pack will peel.
Honey	Tonic; honey and eggs.

Compresses

They have the advantage of producing a layer of humidity over the skin which acts like a moisturizer, particularly for dry skin which does not only need fat but also moisture. Compresses can be made with water, but very often are much improved by using herb teas for general or specific purposes. Before using compresses, the face should be cleaned thoroughly.

For people who do not suffer from too dry a skin or dilated

* Available from chemists or health food shops.

veins, alternative compresses with hot and cold water are most useful.

Prepare two bowls, one with warm and the other with cold water. Instead of the warm water, a herb tea can be used, and particularly for greasy skin, *Yarrow Tea* is recommended. Provide two soft pieces of lint which should be folded into a triangle and place each into one of the prepared bowls. First place the piece of lint from the warm herb tea bowl on to the face. It should be as warm as it is comfortable. Put the cloth around the nose so that the nose is free for breathing. This allows the face to relax, particularly when the body is stretched out in a comfortable position. Close the eyes. If the face has become warm under the compress, take it off and add immediately the compress from the cold water bowl. The first cold compress should only remain on the face for 10 seconds, approximately a third of the time of the warm compress. Then the warm compress is replaced and is followed by the cold again. This should be repeated according to the time available, but at least 3–4 times. The last compress should always be a cold one. This brings a great deal of fresh blood to the skin of the face and the functions of the skin become stimulated.

Cold Water Compress – this is suitable for many types of skin. Place soft pieces of lint big enough to cover the face, possibly two layers of lint, in boiled, but cold, water or in a cooled infusion of *Sage, Lady's Mantle*, or *Peppermint*. Leave for 10 minutes on the face. If the skin is dry, oil carefully beforehand, using little oil only. These compresses are a tonic for the skin and reduce large pores.

Coltsfoot Compress (for dilated veins). For those people for whom alternative or cold-water compresses are not possible because they suffer from dilated thread veins in the face, another type of compress made from an infusion of *Coltsfoot* is helpful. Use a teaspoon fresh chopped or green-dried coltsfoot leaves per cup, pour boiling water over and allow to steep for 10 minutes. When the infusion has become lukewarm, dip 1 or 2 cotton-wool pads into it, place it on the affected parts and allow the humidity in the cotton-wool to be soaked up by the pores. After removing, do not wash the part but use a little oil or cream on it.

This can be done twice a day. No lotions containing alcohol should be used. It is also possible to make compresses dipped into an infusion of *Chamomile* and *Yarrow* combined.

More about the treatment of dilated facial veins – (see page 75).

Dandelion Compress. The young shoots of *Dandelion Leaves* –
before they go into flower – provide an effective cosmetic compress improving the circulation of the face and with it removing
impurities of the skin. Chop young dandelion leaves finely, add
boiling water and allow to simmer for 5 minutes. Dip a clean cloth
(of linen, cotton or lint) into this infusion and put this compress
on to the carefully cleaned face. As soon as the compress starts
to become cool it should be renewed.

In the case of dilated veins, the procedure must be altered. The
finely chopped leaves are simmered with boiling water and
allowed to cool until the liquid is lukewarm. Dip the compress
into this lukewarm infusion and allow it to remain on the face
for 20 minutes.

Bath Additions

The effects of a full warm bath can often be much improved by
the addition of herbs, and particularly at the end of winter with
spring coming, people often get the urge to join in the renewal
of nature and add herbs to their bath. When people feel tired, the
skin looks grey and wilted. This is the best time to start refreshing
baths at home which cost little and make one feel younger. Water
belongs to the oldest and cheapest cosmetics and the addition of
cultivated or wild herbs, added over a period of perhaps six weeks,
may be as good as any spring cure in a distant place. An hour's
rest in bed after such a bath, will improve the effect.

A soothing effect on the nervous system can be expected with
the addition of *Chamomile, Valerian, Rosemary, Horsetail,* and
Pine Needles. Peppermint baths can be a great help to people
suffering from skin troubles (also with an addition of *Horsetail*).
It is best to try out which herbs in general are best for baths and
this may vary with different people, but mixtures may be used
and a mixture of *Lovage, Chamomile, Peppermint, Rosemary,
Fennel, Sage,* and *Yarrow* has an excellent effect.

For a full bath, about 10 oz. of dried herbs made into an infusion and allowed to stand for about 10 minutes would be an
excellent addition to the bath, particularly in spring. Some
people like to add Wheat-bran which contains fats, oil, and
vegetable hormones, and gives a velvety look to the skin in connexion with the effects of the herbs. In commercial cosmetics,
the Herbessence bath oil provides a kind of 'beauty bath' similar
to one for which the various herbs are used.

Elder flower Water is usually used for skin lotions because it is a mildly astringent stimulant and is therefore very good to be added to the wash-water or as a bath addition. Small additions of sea-salt are stimulating, strengthening, and increase the blood circulation.

FOOTBATHS. For a footbath the addition of an infusion of *Horsetail* and some sea-salt is helpful particularly to feet which have to stand a great deal of strain; finishing with cold water improves the effect. After such a bath, the feet should be rubbed with oil in which *Marigold Petals* have been soaked.

ALTERNATIVE BATHS FOR FEET AND LEGS. Two pails or tubs are necessary which allow the legs to be immersed in the water up to the knees. Fill one with warm water and add a strong infusion of *Lime flowers* or *Rosemary*. Fill the second with cold water of which the worst chill is taken off. Immerse the legs in the tub filled with the water which is as warm as it can be borne for 5–10 minutes. Then dip legs in the cold tub for 10 seconds (counting up to 20) then back into the warm tub for another 5–10 minutes, finishing with another 10-second dip in the cold water. Only two changes should be made. Allow to dry by rubbing the water into the skin and then go for a walk or into bed.

BATH ADDITIONS OF WILD HERBS. The wild herbs recommended for spring compresses, etc., are also suggested to be added to a bath, particularly during spring. They are *Dandelion* and *Nettle* with the addition of small quantities of *Cowslip* and *Daisy* if available. It is best to dry these herbs with care so that they retain their colour before use – only flowers and roots should be dried for cowslip. After drying, chop up the herbs, mix them well and infuse a large quantity of approximately 1 lb. in 6–8 pints of hot water for about 30 minutes. Drain and pour the infusion into the bath which should be filled up with warm water. The bath should have a temperature of 95–100° F. or 35–37° C., and should last not more than 10–15 minutes. This bath could be taken every second day in the evening for about two weeks not long before retiring, but not too soon after a meal. The effects should be felt from the third bath onwards.

For those who have difficulties in going to sleep, the addition of an infusion of *Valerian* will improve the night's sleep. A brushing massage of arms and legs under water into the direction of the heart, while cool water is being slowly added, will add to the effect. A further strengthening bath addition is a mixture of conifer sprouts from pine, fir trees, larch, juniper. The young sprouts should be poured over while fresh with boiling water and the resulting infusion added to the bath.

Blackberry Leaves. The leaves picked in spring without stalks, should be dried, then crumbled and about 10 oz. mixed with 6 pints of water at a temperature of 115° F. or 45° C. After allowing to draw for 3 minutes, strain and add to the warm bath-water.

Pochettes

Smaller additions to a daily bath can be achieved by packing the herb in question into a small bag of a porous material, hang this 'pochette' underneath the hot tap and allow the hot water to pass through this bag when filling the bath. The pochette can also be allowed to stay in the bath to increase the effect. This method, which is simpler than making a special infusion, is particularly suited to *Lovage* which can be used as a deodorant bath addition. Although the pochette can be hung up and dried and used for several baths, it is, however, advisable to fill a new pochette whenever one feels that the infusion becomes weaker.

Herb Mixtures for Improving:

Eyes

The following herbs are helpful to the eyes:

Eyebright cleans the eyes, improves the sight and, as a compress, improves inflammation of eyelids.

Elder flower Water – an infusion – is a mild astringent and stimulant and can be safely used for eye compresses or eye-baths.

Fennel Tea – compresses steeped in fennel tea placed on the eyes or bathing the eyes with fennel helps inflamed eyelids (conjunctivitis), watering eyes, strengthens the eyes altogether and helps to improve the sight.

Chamomile can be used for eye compresses for inflammation of the eyelids.

Verbena has a cleansing and strengthening effect on the eyes and is used for inflammation of the eyelids.

An infusion should be made of either of these herbs and used for compresses in cases of tired eyes or for inflammation of the eyelids or for an eye-bath.

A Herbal Eye-bath can be prepared from a larger number of herbs and an infusion of these herbs is useful for either eye-baths or eye compresses.

This mixture consists of larger parts of:

Eyebright
Chamomile
Fennel

and additions of carefully dried:

Cornflowers ⎫ They should not lose their bright
Marigold petals ⎰ colours in drying.

smaller parts of:

Lovage   Verbena
Horsetail   Lady's Mantle
Summer savory   Yarrow

and still smaller parts of:

Thyme
Rosemary
Mugwort (if available)

Method:

Use 1 heaped teasp. of this mixture per cup of boiling water. Allow to steep for 5 minutes; strain. Use either as an eye-bath or for eye compresses.

For compresses, cut 2–3 layers of white lint for each eye. Soak in the lukewarm infusion and place over each eyelid. Try to lie down and relax and repeat the freshly soaked compresses for 5–10 minutes. Finish with a cool, clear water compress. Even 3 minutes of compresses are better than none at all.

Hair

HERBAL HAIR RINSE. A special flower and leaf mixture has a stimulating effect on the glands and tissues of the scalp and stimulates growth and healthy development of the hair.

The hair rinse should consist of the following herbs, cultivated and wild mixed:

Cultivated	Wild
Lime flowers	Nettle
Chamomile	Horsetail
Fennel	Yarrow
Sage	
Rosemary	

The basis of the mixture should consist of equal parts of lime flowers, chamomile, and fennel, and smaller parts of all the other herbs. If the hair rinse is used for blond hair, the largest part should be chamomile, while for dark hair, less chamomile, but more rosemary is indicated.

Method:

Place 2 heaped tablesp. of the mixture into a china jug and pour over 2 pints of boiling water; cover and steep until the right temperature for rinsing; strain. Wash hair in the usual way. Rinse with clear water until all soap or shampoo is removed then rinse again and again with the infusion.

The scalp can be massaged with yolk of egg before washing or a whole egg beaten can be used for a dry scalp before or after washing. The same herbs mentioned for hair rinse can also be steeped in oil, allowed to stand in the sun (for a few weeks whenever there is sun) and can then be applied to the scalp and massaged with the fingers of both hands before washing. It stimulates growth and prevents dandruff and makes the hair strong and shiny. The scalp can also be massaged with oil in which *Nettles* have been steeped. The hair has to be well rinsed after washing to remove all oil.

Nails

Many people suffer from brittle or splitting nails. A warm oil bath should be taken twice per week for 10 minutes each, alternatively with baths of *Horsetail Infusion*. The high content of silicic acid helps to strengthen the nails. Both baths should be carried out over several weeks or months as nails cannot improve quickly. It is helpful to drink horsetail tea during the same period.

Herbs for Specific Conditions

Here follow cosmetic suggestions for certain conditions:

Dilated Veins [thread veins]

Those people who have a tendency to dilated veins which are often increased by the use of coffee and alcohol can be helped by drinking more herb teas instead of coffee; particularly *Chamomile Tea*, *Coltsfoot Tea*, or *Yarrow Tea*. People who have this tendency should never allow extreme temperatures to touch the face, but should protect the skin with the use of oil or creams from extreme weather conditions.

Facial steams, alternate compresses and cold compresses as well as alternatively splashing the face with warm and cold water which is normally so helpful to the skin, cannot be used. Instead, *Coltsfoot* compresses are suggested (page 69). Strong massage of the face is also not indicated, but to wash the face with milk and leave the milk to dry in for a few minutes before washing the face again, is useful.

Acne

Young people often suffer from acne and although they sometimes grow out of it, in some cases this appears to be difficult. The facial steam with herbs is a particularly good help for this condition. Apart from the herbs suggested as a general mixture for facial steam, special additions of *Chamomile*, *Lady's Mantle*, and *Yarrow* are advisable; 10 minutes after the steam is finished when the skin is soft and the pores are open it is possible to carefully move two fingers in small circles with a thin sterile paper tissue to get some of the blackheads or inflamed spots out. They should not be touched at any other time. It is also useful for this condition to make a pack with Fuller's Earth, or Claydos* (clay powder) mixed with *Yarrow Tea* or *Coltsfoot Tea* into a paste. At the same time, one cup per day at least of yarrow tea should be drunk and there are certain foods which are useful to be eaten in large quantities while suffering from any skin condition and in particular from acne.

* Available from chemists or health food stores.

Beauty from Within

During a period of using packs, compresses, steams, for the purpose of dealing with certain skin conditions, it is advisable to eat an uncooked salad daily in larger quantities than usual (page 80) to which as many herbs as possible are added for flavouring. Little salt and no spices should be taken. If salt is used at all, it should be sea-salt. It is further recommended to eat as much *Parsley* as possible which is good for the skin because of its content of Vitamin A Precursor. Apart from the daily use in salads and cooking, it can be eaten additionally, daily on bread and butter. All this applies also to all other skin conditions.

The external effect of *Dandelion*, for instance as face packs, can be supplemented if used internally as food at the same time. The freshly picked, tender, finely chopped leaves can be dressed with oil, lemon juice, and perhaps some milk or yoghourt and a small portion added to a salad. As these leaves have a tendency to be bitter, they should only be used finely chopped in combination with other herbs and possibly lettuce or other green salad leaves.

Yarrow Salad (page 89) and *Yarrow Tea* supplement the use of yarrow in packs for greasy skin; *Coltsfoot Tea* the use of coltsfoot in packs for dilated veins; *Blackberry Leaves Tea* and *Elder flower Tea* should be taken in conjunction with the packs made of the same leaves and flowers; and *Horsetail Tea* should be taken as a supplement while using nail baths.

Strawberries, bananas, and tomatoes are used sometimes for packs, but are better taken as food in as large quantities as available.

Sweet-scented Herbs

Herb Potpourri

Past generations liked large china bowls of potpourri in their drawing-rooms which were filled with dried flowers, mainly rose petals. Many detailed recipes distinguished between wet potpourri and dry potpourri, but all advised additions of fixatives, powders or salts and as time went on, the scent of the rose petals became musty and eventually was over-powered by the scent of the fixatives; sometimes even scented toilet waters or perfumes were added which gave the potpourri bowl an unnatural scent, different from the scents of nature.

Experiments with the scent of herbs and the new ways of drying flowers and retaining their bright natural colours allows a new kind of potpourri. The delightful, lasting, and natural scents of this potpourri come from the unspoilt and well-preserved, entirely natural scents of flowers, sweet-scented herbs and spices.

The colours are provided by the brilliant colours of well-dried flower petals, and the new way of keeping such potpourri in a contemporary living-room is in a clear glass or perspex bowl, with a clear lid firmly enclosing the scents while not in use but allowing the eye to enjoy the colours.

This new potpourri bowl should be kept in a dark cupboard of the living-room to be taken out when the room is occupied and the lid removed. The air is filled with the sweetest scent, cleansing the atmosphere, and the eye can enjoy the colours. When the room is emptied and the occupants retire for the night, the lid is replaced on the potpourri and the bowl can go back into the dark cupboard. In this way a potpourri can be enjoyed as scent and colour for a long time.

The following herbs, well mixed, provide the kind of scented leaf mixture which will give most of the scents needed:

Green-dried Peppermint leaves	Lemon Balm leaves
Sweet Cicely leaves	Red Bergamot leaves
Sage leaves	Lovage leaves
Basil leaves	Tarragon leaves
Rosemary leaves	Marjoram leaves
Angelica leaves	Rose Geranium leaves
Lemon Thyme leaves	Lemon Verbena leaves

The flower mixture consists of:

Lavender flowers	Nasturtium flowers
Elder flowers	Cornflowers
Verbascum flowers	Lime flowers
Chamomile flowers	Marigold petals

The following spices can be used for scent:

Cloves (whole).
Cinnamon sticks (broken).
Nutmeg (best freshly ground by an electric blender).
Coriander (best freshly ground by an electric blender).

Cardomom (best freshly ground by an electric blender).

Aniseed (half-ground).

Orange, grapefruit, and lemon peel (dried and crushed in a blender).

The bowl is best started with layers of brilliant flowers such as verbascum and cornflowers with the addition of marigold petals. Then a layer of herb mixture, a layer of flower mixture follows. In between the layers some of the spices and some dried and ground orange, grapefruit, and lemon peel can be placed. The top layer but one should be scented herbs such as tarragon, rosemary, rose geranium, lemon thyme, and lemon verbena with crushed bay leaves.

The very top layer should be arranged preferably using rose petals, chamomile flowers, lime flowers, lavender flowers, and whole dried flowers such as cornflowers, small roses, pansies, yarrow, and one or two angelica leaves to give an attractive and colourful pattern to the top.

Herb Cushions

Herb cushions have been used in the past to soothe and make people go to sleep more easily. In the course of years, herb cushions have been requested by all kinds of people – chronic invalids or old people. The cushions usually have two functions to perform – one is to soothe the nerves of those who have difficulty in getting to sleep, often through problems arising from the surroundings such as hospital wards, or people who, being invalid, have become over-sensitive to smells which surround them.

Originally, the lavender cushion probably fulfilled both these functions because it has a soothing effect on the nerves and also provides a clean and attractive scent; herb cushions can, however, be filled with a mixture which fulfils the functions of a refreshing, clean scent and has at the same time a soothing and sleep-inducing quality.

The herbs which should provide the basic needs of a herb cushion are:

Peppermint

Sage   } (Used in three equal main parts.)

Lemon Balm

Lavender   (About half of the above-mentioned herbs.)

and half again of:

Dill	Woodruff
Marjoram	Angelica
Thyme	Rosemary
Lemon Thyme	Lemon Verbena
Tarragon	Red Bergamot

A small addition of valerian, if available, should add to the sleep-inducing quality of the cushion, but it should not be enough to make it a predominant and unpleasant-smelling addition.

It is not necessary to use all the herbs mentioned above, but those which are underlined are most helpful.

It is best to use a porous material for the herb cushion; porous linen, for instance, is excellent. If the herb cushion is used regularly, it is better to enclose the herb mixture first in muslin or hessian and make another cover of coarse linen or another loosely woven material which can be changed and washed without disturbing the herb mixture.

However useful the gift of such a herb cushion may be for an invalid or for an old person, they are equally useful and attractive as a scented and soothing – even elegant – addition to any bedroom. Sachets or cushions of lavender have always been used in drawers – made of such a herb mixture they not only scent all drawers containing clothes or linen, but they also keep the moths away.

Chapter 4

EVERYDAY SUGGESTIONS AND RECIPES FOR HEALTHY EATING

THE DAILY SALAD

IT HAS THE highest health value of any dish in the daily diet. Some schools of thought on diet consider a 50 per cent intake of *uncooked* fruit and vegetables important. This is suggested not only to provide adequate vitamins and minerals from foods which are left as near as possible to their natural state, but also to balance the proportion of the important uncooked food to cooked food which should be about half each.

Nowadays it has been recognized that salads have become an essential dish of the first order and the 50 per cent intake can be easily achieved if an uncooked fruit porridge is taken, possibly twice a day, with the addition of an uncooked daily salad for lunch or the evening meal. This is important for the figure-watchers as they can be certain that half of their food will hardly add to the calories, and for everyone it becomes a daily vehicle for the intake of the important vitamins and minerals as well as an appetizer or *hors d'oeuvre*.

A small regular intake of these important nutrients is better than large quantities at greater intervals. If the salad is kept small and eaten before the cooked course as an *hors d'oeuvre*, or instead of soup, it not only increases the appetite and the enjoyment of the food, but decreases the quantity of the not so healthy food by providing part of the meal. Thus a small daily salad regularly is more helpful than large salads occasionally.

What the Salad Should Contain

The daily raw salad should consist of almost all parts of the plant and it is important that roots, leaves, and fruit are represented in it.

Root Vegetables such as:
  Raw grated carrots
  Raw grated beetroots
  Parsley roots
  Radishes, etc.
are important and indeed, available throughout the year.

The Leaves are represented by all kinds of green salad leaves such as:
  Lettuce
  Endive
  Watercress
  Mustard and cress
  Corn salad

The Fruit is usually:
  Tomato
  Cucumber *or can be*
    Avocado pear
    Courgettes
    Red pepper

The Flower is represented by:
  Raw grated cauliflower
  Raw grated broccoli
One of each of these three parts of the plant, leaves, root, and fruit, should be possibly represented in each salad. The flower part can be optional.

Serving the Salad
The uncooked salad, combined in the way suggested, is best arranged in a way that the vegetables are not all mixed up, but laid out separately like flower-beds or strips on an almost shallow dish, making use of the tempting colours and allowing people to choose more of some and less of others. This is helpful for those who are being gradually converted to eating more salad and, above all, for children.

The salad bowl should be preferably a wooden one, with salad servers to match. After use, each time rinse bowl with cold water. This method of cleaning keeps the faint flavours in the wood and in time the wood develops a fine patina. If any cleaning of the bowl is desirable other than cold water, some warm oil should be used, which is also the best cleaning for wooden salad plates which are excellent for salads, and if rinsed in water and then cleaned with warm oil they will remain beautiful and useful. Wooden forks and spoons do not bruise salad leaves as much as stainless steel or silver.

Mix the dressing in a small glass, or china bowl, or cup, particularly if some of the dressing or the basic oil and lemon mixture is to be kept for another day.

SALAD DRESSINGS

Mixing green leaves and raw vegetables in a large container with a dressing is a very old custom, originally an Arabian one. It has gone a long way through Greek, Roman, and European kitchens and many outstanding seasonings and dressings have been used.

Salad Dressing has two functions: One is to complement the flavours of a salad and the other is to add to its health value. It is still not sufficiently realized how important the salad dressing is, more important when the vegetable parts of the salad are not cooked. If 'What is healthy could just as well be enjoyable', and 'What is enjoyable will be eaten', it is well worth while taking trouble over the salad. Make it a daily habit, an essential addition to our menu, providing only a relatively small number of calories.

Vegetables have to be thoroughly cleaned for the purpose of an uncooked salad, and chopped, sliced, or grated.

Oil

The important health value of the salad dressing is found in the fact that the oil, cream, or other fatty substances which are used in every salad dressing, provide the necessary lubricant which helps to absorb the fat soluble vitamins, particularly Vitamin A in a salad. Without this the Vitamin A or its precursor contained in carrots, tomatoes, etc., can never be utilized by the body.

It is furthermore important that the oil in the dressing should be the cold pressed sunflower oil or corn oil. Although the controversy whether one kind of fat can be made responsible for certain conditions is by no means closed, there is no doubt that these oils can keep the balance of saturated and unsaturated fats in order and help to prevent troubles arising from disturbing this balance. The dressing, and in particular the oil in it, helps to cover the exposed surfaces, caused by grating, chopping, or cutting so that the vegetables do not go on losing important nutrients.

Many of the existing salad dressing recipes are suggested with olive oil and vinegar. Olive oil often has a special flavour and it is difficult to find a brand that is not too strong for some palates. People have frequently taken a dislike to salad dressings because of the predominant flavour of some olive oils. Apart from the health factor, the unflavoured sunflower oil or corn oil is often preferred. The lack of flavour in the oil helps to enjoy better the flavours of the salad and the herbs. It will not only have the advantages for heart and circulation, but it will furthermore not be a fattening 'fat', in fact, the unsaturated fatty acids will help to maintain a slim figure.

Lemon Juice and Vinegar
Lemon juice is preferable to vinegar, even to wine vinegar, and has an enhancing effect on the other ingredients; it will improve the flavour of the herbs rather than the vinegar which has an overpowering tendency. Lemon juice has not the habit-forming qualities of vinegar whereby more and more is needed or wanted for a dressing until the palate is blunted for the more delicate flavours. It also adds Vitamin C to the salad.

Dairy Additions
Useful additions to the salad are yoghourt, buttermilk, and skimmed milk, as they add some of the acid normally contained in vinegar and preferably contained in lemon juice and some milk protein at the same time; they are not only very tasty, but also a health-giving addition.

Seasonings
In the suggestions here, certain seasonings are omitted from the salad dressings, such as cayenne peppers, chilli powder, chopped capers, curry powder, freshly ground black peppercorns, mustard, Tabasco, or Worcester sauce; they all have a tendency to overpower the herbs and though they may be good at other times, they certainly should not be combined with the dressing of a health salad.

These dressings which are more complicated, and have many more ingredients, should not necessarily be used for raw daily health-giving salads; they are best for special salads offered for a party or as a summer luncheon dish. Recipes for these are given in Part Three, Chapter 2, page 186.

Herbs

The salad should be dressed and this is where the herbs play their important part. They make all the difference to the salad as a whole as they not only will improve its flavour and make it more wholesome, but with a wise use of herbs, changes can be rung and the appetite increased for the salad even if the herb mixture remains more or less the same. The herbs can be individually combined and varied with the various vegetables.

The housewife with a little time on her hands can try out endless variations of herbs in the dressing. The paragraph on Basic Dressings is followed by a Table (86) with suggestions for herbs and dressings to be used with a number of vegetables; also the Guide (page 127) should be consulted for proportions. Green-dried *bouquet for salads* consists of all the herbs suitable for salads combined in the right proportions; and an addition of this is always safe and will not spoil a salad.

Basic Dressings

The simplest and most wholesome salad dressing is the French dressing, and that is the basic one that can be used for all salads; the changes can be rung by using different kinds of herbs with different salad vegetables.

The French Dressing:

Ingredients per person:
1 tablesp. sunflower *or* corn oil   Some grated onion *or* garlic
1 teasp. lemon juice   (optional)
                                                            1 teasp. fresh *or* green-dried herbs

Mix all these ingredients well together, stirring vigorously to break up the oil.

Mayonnaise:

Ingredients:
1 egg yolk   Lemon juice according to taste
1 cup (10 oz.) oil

All ingredients must be of the same temperature. Whisk yolk; add oil drop by drop, whisking continually. The oil should not be too cold or too warm, or the mixture becomes too thick.

The above quantities are sufficient for 6–8 portions or even more if more oil is added. The mayonnaise will keep for days in a cool place and can be used for various dressings.

Mayonnaise Dressing:

Ingredients per person:

1 tablesp. mayonnaise   Some onion and garlic (if liked)
1 teasp. lemon juice   1 teasp. fresh *or* green-dried herbs
   Mix all these ingredients thoroughly but with a light hand.

Yoghourt Dressing (for those on a low fat diet):

Ingredients per person:

2–3 tablesp. yoghourt   Some onion and garlic if liked
A few drops of lemon juice   1 teasp. fresh *or* green-dried herbs
   Whisk all ingredients well together.

Yoghourt and Cream Dressing:

Ingredients per person:

2 tablesp. yoghourt   Few drops of lemon juice
2 tablesp. cream   1 teasp. fresh *or* green-dried herbs
   Whisk all ingredients well together.

Cream Dressing:

Ingredients per person:

2 tablesp. cream   Some onion and garlic if liked
1 teasp. cream cheese *or* yoghourt 1 teasp. fresh *or* green-dried herbs
1 teasp. lemon juice
   Whisk all ingredients well together.

Almond Purée Dressing (for those who should avoid animal fat and protein):

Ingredients per person:

1 tablesp. nut cream *or* almond purée Onion and garlic if liked
3 tablesp. water   1 teasp. fresh *or* green-dried herbs
1 teasp. lemon juice
   Add drops of water to nut cream until it becomes whitish and of a creamy consistency, add remaining water and mix all ingredients together slowly and thoroughly.

Further Simple Dressings:

1. Ingredients:

4 tablesp. cream   1 teasp. fresh *or* green-dried herbs
1 tablesp. lemon juice

Whisk cream well and add slowly, the lemon juice, constantly stirring.

2. Ingredients:

3 tablesp. oil	1 tablesp. lemon juice
(preferably sunflower oil)	1 teasp. fresh *or* green-dried herbs

Add drops of lemon juice to the oil, constantly stirring.

3. Ingredients:

4 tablesp. cream	2 tablesp. apple juice
1 tablesp. lemon juice	1 teasp. fresh *or* green-dried herbs

Add lemon juice slowly to the cream, constantly stirring.
Add apple juice.

Vinaigrette:

For a light diet, without egg, and using sunflower oil only:

Ingredients:

4 tablesp. (sunflower) oil	1 hard-boiled egg, chopped
2½ tablesp. lemon juice	1–2 chopped gherkins, parsley, *or*
2 tablesp. water *or* vegetable stock	chives
Salt	1 tablesp. diced tomatoes
½ chopped onion	

Whisk all the ingredients together.

Suggestions for Herbs Used in Salad Dressings

Quoted by kind permission of the author from Ruth Bircher's *Eating Your Way to Health*, Faber and Faber, translated and edited by Claire Loewenfeld.

Raw Vegetables	Method	Dressing	Herbs
Cabbage lettuce	Use whole leaves	French dressing	Chives, onion
Lettuce (thinnings)	Use whole leaves	French dressing	Chives, onion
French endive	Cut in ½-in. strips	French dressing *or* mayonnaise	Chives, onion parsley*
Cos lettuce	Use leaves whole *or* shredded	French dressing *or* mayonnaise	Sweet basil, marjoram†

* A small quantity of chives, parsley, and onion may be added to every raw salad.

† For proportions, see Guide, page 127.

Raw Vegetables	Method	Dressing	Herbs
Lamb's lettuce	Use whole leaves	French dressing or mayonnaise	Onion
Cresses	Use whole leaves	French dressing or mayonnaise	Onion
Spinach	Shred	French dressing or mayonnaise	Peppermint
Cabbage: white savoy, sprouts, sauerkraut	Shred finely	French dressing or mayonnaise	Lovage, savory, thyme
Tomatoes	Slice or dice	French dressing or mayonnaise	Basil, thyme, dill
Cucumbers	Slice finely	French dressing or mayonnaise	Dill
Fennel	Slice finely or chop	French dressing or mayonnaise	Onion, chives
Pepper	Shred finely	French dressing or mayonnaise	Chives
Large black or white radishes	Slice or grate	French or cream dressing	Chives
Small red radishes	Grate or slice	French or cream dressing	Chives
Celery	Shred finely	French or cream dressing	Onion, chives
Baby vegetable marrows or courgettes	Slice finely or grate roughly	French dressing or mayonnaise	Dill, basil
Carrots or young swedes, or other roots	Grate finely	French or cream dressing	Marjoram, lovage
Celeriac	Grate finely	Cream or French dressing	Basil, thyme
Beetroots, uncooked	Grate finely or roughly	Cream dressing or mayonnaise	Lovage, thyme, caraway seeds
Cauliflower	Separate florets, grate stalks	Cream dressing or mayonnaise	Basil, marjoram, walnuts
Chicory	Cut in ½-in. strips, shred	Cream or French dressing	Tarragon, marjoram
Jerusalem artichokes	Grate	Cream dressing	Thyme, lemon balm
Kohlrabi	Grate or chop finely	Cream or French dressing	Thyme, lovage

Raw Vegetables	Method	Dressing	Herbs
Red cabbage	Shred *or* grate finely	Cream *or* French dressing	Some grated apple, caraway seeds, lovage

SALAD RECIPES

Apart from the Daily Raw Salad – its combination and dressings are discussed on page 80 – there are some salads which are specially recommended for healthy eating, either because of the reasons mentioned before, or because they contain young wild herbs or vegetables with special significance for certain troubles.

Wild Herb Salads

Tender young dandelion, sorrel, and nettle leaves can be served as a salad in a dressing of sunflower oil, lemon juice, and, if liked, a little finely chopped onion; onion green, parsley, and chives can be added. The leaves are usually tender until the plant starts to flower. Later they become hard and have less value. The wild herbs should only be collected on ground which has not been chemically treated.

The dandelion leaves are most useful because of their bitter principles in the case of trouble with liver and gall-bladder.

Salad Made from Wild Herbs (*eg* Yarrow)

This salad is made of three wild herbs and is of cosmetic importance because it contains yarrow (page 34).

Ingredients:

Equal parts of yarrow, plantain, and watercress
A little garlic
½ oz. cucumber
Fresh chopped or green-dried chives and parsley

1 medium boiled cold potato
Salad dressing – consisting of lemon and cream, *or* No. 2 of lemon and oil, *or* No. 3 of lemon, cream, and a little apple juice (pages 85–6)

Method:

1. Select and clean herbs.
2. Wash them carefully and allow to drain.
3. Cut yarrow and plantain into fine strips, leave watercress whole and arrange in a bowl.
4. Grate cucumber and grate potato on to greens in the bowl.
5. Add herbs and salad dressing.
6. Mix well.

Italian Dandelion Salad (*serves 4*)

Ingredients:

½ clove of garlic
8 oz. young dandelion leaves
2 tablesp. sunflower oil
1 tablesp. lemon juice

A little salt
1 teasp. each fresh chopped or green-dried tarragon, chervil, and salad burnet

Method:

1. Rub the inside of a wooden salad bowl with a cut clove of garlic.
2. Tear the dandelion leaves into small pieces and place in salad bowl.

3. Gradually stir the oil with the lemon juice till blended, then add the herbs and stir well.
4. Pour over dandelion leaves.
5. Add the salt and toss the salad thoroughly with wooden salad servers.

Note: If liked, ripe black olives can be added to the salad. The salad can be served with herb bread (page 313) or garlic bread (hot).

Potato Salad with Dandelion (*serves 4–6*)

A main-dish salad, made more valuable by the addition of dandelion.

Ingredients:

1½ lb. boiled potatoes	4 tablesp. oil
1 large chopped onion	2–3 tablesp. lemon juice
1 clove garlic	2 tablesp. hot stock
1 teasp. each fresh chopped or green-dried chervil and parsley	Some grated celeriac *or* chopped celery
½ teasp. each fresh chopped or green-dried lovage and sage	*or* a large quantity of young dandelion leaves (approx. 5 oz.)
1 sour apple (peeled and diced)	cut into fine strips

Method:
1. Peel potatoes while hot and cut them into thin slices.
2. Keep them hot on a saucepan with boiling water.
3. Chop onions finely.
4. Grate or mince garlic.
5. Chop herbs or reconstitute green-dried herbs in lemon juice.
6. Make a dressing out of oil, lemon juice, and the hot stock.
7. Add the herbs and the apple to the dressing.
8. Mix all ingredients well with the warm potatoes and celery.
9. Add strips of dandelion leaves and mix well.
10. Allow to cool.

Potato Salad with Sorrel

Instead of dandelion leaves, add finely cut strips of sorrel and reduce lemon juice to 1–2 tablesp.

Three Chicory Salads with Three Different Types of Nut Mayonnaise

[a] Chicory Salad

Chicory is one of the best winter vegetables. It is always fresh, stimulates the appetite because of its slightly bitter flavour, can easily be digested, is rich in vitamins, and the bitter principles it contains are particularly valuable with liver and gall-bladder conditions. It is especially helpful to diabetics.

Ingredients:

8 oz. chicory, finely cut up
1 tablesp. sunflower oil
1 tablesp. sour cream
1 tablesp. tomato juice

1 teasp. each fresh chopped or green-dried chives and lemon balm
Lemon juice (according to taste)
½ teasp. each fresh chopped or green-dried tarragon and chervil

Method:

1. Wash chicory well and cut into small pieces.
2. Make a dressing out of all the other ingredients.
3. Mix with the chicory.

Note: The salad can be made without sour cream, just using sunflower oil and a little more lemon juice.

[b] Chicory Salad with Fruit and Herbs Dressed with Nut Mayonnaise

Ingredients:

8 oz. chicory
1 apple
1 banana
Nuts
Slices of orange
Sweet cicely and lemon balm

Nut Mayonnaise:

1 tablesp. sunflower oil
1 teasp. nut cream
2 tablesp. yoghourt
1 teasp. lemon juice
A little horseradish
Chives

Method:

1. Cut chicory and banana in slices.
2. Dice apple.
3. Chop nuts.
4. Mix with a dressing of nut mayonnaise and add herbs.
5. Decorate with orange slices.

Method for Nut Mayonnaise:
1. Add the sunflower oil drop by drop to the nut cream.
2. Add yoghourt and lemon juice.
3. Mix in a little finely grated horseradish and plenty of chives.

[c] Chicory and Grapefruit with Cream Cheese Nut Mayonnaise

Finely cut chicory and cut up grapefruit can be served in the following dressing:

Ingredients:

Juice of 1 lemon	Juice of 1 orange
½ teasp. nut cream	½ glass yoghourt
1 tablesp. curd *or* cream cheese	Grated horseradish

Method:
1. Add lemon juice drop by drop to nut cream and then add cream cheese, orange juice, and yoghourt.
2. Add horseradish according to taste.
3. Mix with chicory and grapefruit.

Fruit and Vegetable Salad with Nut Mayonnaise

Ingredients (Fruit Salad):

1 orange	1 piece of celery *or* celeriac
1 apple	1 tomato
2 slices of pineapple	3 walnuts

Ingredients (Nut Mayonnaise):

2 tablesp. nut cream	Dash of unsalted Marmite *or* yeast extract, diluted
2 tablesp. water	
1 tablesp. sunflower oil	½ teasp. fresh chopped or green-dried marjoram
1 teasp. lemon juice	
1 tablesp. yoghourt	A little grated horseradish
	1 clove garlic

Method:
1. Add water in drops to nut cream until it becomes whitish and emulsifies.
2. Add the oil, lemon juice, and yoghourt slowly and gradually with a few drops of diluted Marmite.
3. Mix in marjoram, horseradish according to taste, and the squeezed garlic.
4. Dice the fruit and vegetable and serve with nut mayonnaise decorated with nuts.

Fruit Salad with Nut Mayonnaise

Ingredients (Fruit Salad):
(Per Person)
1 apple
1 banana
1 orange
A few raisins
1 teasp. fresh chopped or green-
  dried sweet cicely
½ teasp. fresh chopped or green-
  dried lemon balm

Nut Mayonnaise:
(Per Person)
1 teasp. nut cream
1 teasp. sugar
Milk
Water

Method:
1. Cut the fruit, mix with herbs, and serve with nut mayonnaise.

Method for Nut Mayonnaise:
1. Stir nut cream with drops of water until it shows a creamy consistency.
2. Add more water and milk until the required consistency is reached.
3. Sugar according to taste.

Autumn Salad of Carrots, Radishes, and Kohlrabi, with Curd Mayonnaise (*serves 2–3*)

A nourishing yet healthy dressing, especially for those who should avoid animal fat.

Ingredients:
3 small carrots
1 small kohlrabi
1 small radish
1 tomato

Curd Mayonnaise:
1 tablesp. sunflower oil
1 teasp. nut cream
2 oz. curd (*ie* cream cheese with the cream taken off and no cream added)
3 tablesp. milk
1–2 tablesp. lemon juice
1 tablesp. grated apple
1 teasp. chopped onion (if liked)
1 teasp. chives
Pinch of paprika
3 tablesp. milk

Method:
1. Clean all vegetables thoroughly, wash.
2. Grate them separately on a two-way grater.
3. Serve the vegetables in individual small bowls and decorate with tomato slices.
4. Serve with curd mayonnaise served in a small separate bowl.

Note: Some parsley, lemon balm, or some coriander seeds, improve the flavour of the carrots. A little caraway or paprika improves the radish. A little chopped onion can be added if the raw salad is eaten at once and not left either for the evening or the next day.

Method for Curd Mayonnaise:
1. Add the oil drop by drop to the nut cream.
2. Add curd and milk and mix well.
3. Add lemon juice, grated apple, onion, and chives.
4. Add paprika according to taste.

Note: Curd Mayonnaise can be used with any other raw salad.

SAUERKRAUT is pickled cabbage – a valuable raw vegetable, particularly in winter, as it is rich in Vitamin C. It is easier to digest raw than when cooked. Therefore, Sauerkraut Salad is important, particularly in diabetic diets, and can be eaten daily in small quantities as *hors d'oeuvre* or with the Daily Raw Salad.

Sauerkraut can be bought in health food shops or in tins, but the best sauerkraut is made from home-grown cabbage in the autumn (see Recipe below).

Home-made Sauerkraut

Ingredients:

4 lb. cabbage (when shredded)
1 oz. coarse sea-salt
Sticks of horseradish (if available)

1 handful caraway and juniper berries *or* mixed sauerkraut herbs and spices containing caraway seeds and juniper berries dill, fennel, mustard seeds

1. Remove outer leaves and stalks.
2. Shred cabbage, preferably using a wooden shredder with two blades, or an electric shredder.
3. Using a large earthenware jar (preferably with straight sides),

put layers of cabbage alternately with sprinkled layers of salt, caraway, juniper, etc.
4. Add horseradish pieces from time to time.
5. Press down each layer with fists or a wooden masher until liquid rises and covers the cabbage.
6. Repeat this until the container is full.
7. Cover with a clean cloth, then with a wooden lid or a plate.
8. Put a heavy clean stone on top to press the lid firmly down.
9. Leave for 4 weeks; occasionally ladling out the rising liquid and washing the rim of the jar and the lid.

Note: After 4 weeks the sauerkraut is ready for use and can be eaten raw or cooked. At intervals of one week the cloth, lid, and stone must be washed. If the top layer of sauerkraut becomes soft and discoloured, it must be removed.

As long as these instructions are carried out with care, the sauerkraut can be kept until the warmer weather, usually about the beginning of April or longer, according to the season.

Sauerkraut and Apple Salad (*serves 3–4*)

Ingredients:

½ lb. sauerkraut
1 apple
½ cucumber

Chopped onion *or* leek
1 tablesp. sunflower oil
Some walnuts

Method:
1. Mix sauerkraut with diced apple and cucumber, or onions, or leek.
2. Mix all ingredients with the oil and with some nuts.

Note: All salad herbs can be added. If the sauerkraut is home-made, it is already pickled with sea-salt, juniper berries, dill, fennel.

Apple Horseradish Salad (*serves 2*)

Horseradish is often used for the preparation of raw salads because it is an excellent seasoning and it contains many plant ferments, which are important for health. For slimming, use yoghourt.

Ingredients:

1 eating apple
½ teasp. freshly grated horseradish

1 tablesp. sour cream *or* yoghourt
Lemon juice

Method:

1. Grate apple and horseradish quickly on the same grater and mix with the other ingredients immediately.
2. Serve at once.

Salad Made of Lettuce and Herbs (*serves 4*)

Ingredients:

1 head of lettuce
2 tablesp. sunflower *or* corn oil
1 tablesp. lemon juice

1 teasp. each fresh chopped or
  green-dried chives and dill
Some finely chopped onion and/or
  onion green
1 clove garlic

Method:

1. Wash lettuce well.
2. Allow to drain in a basket.
3. Make a dressing of oil, lemon juice, chopped herbs (and onion, if liked).
4. Rub salad bowl with garlic.
5. Prepare salad in a bowl and mix well with dressing.

Green Salad with Nasturtium Dressing (*serves 4*)

Supplies Vitamin C and acts as a vegetable antibiotic (see page 25).

Ingredients:

Lettuce, endive *or* corn salad
Nasturtium flowers
Juice of 2 lemons
3 tablesp. salad oil

1 dessertsp. finely chopped fresh or
  green-dried nasturtium leaves
1 teasp. finely chopped fresh or
  green-dried chervil
Salt

Method:

1. Arrange green salad leaves and nasturtium flowers in salad bowl.

2. Squeeze juice of the lemons into the salad oil in a small separate bowl and stir well.
3. Add nasturtium leaves, chervil, and a little salt, and mix again.
4. Pour this dressing over the salad and toss with wooden salad servers.
5. Serve immediately.

Radish Salad (*serves 4–6*)

This salad is most helpful for people suffering from gall-bladder and liver troubles, contains antibiotic qualities and has a nourishing dressing, softening its flavour.

Ingredients:
1 large radish (white or black)

Method:
1. Wash and peel radish.
2. Grate coarsely or pass through a Mouligrater on to a plate.
3. Sprinkle some salt on it.
4. Cover with second plate.
5. Allow to stand for half an hour.
6. Press out between hands and remove liquid.
7. Add special dressing.
   Note: Can be served immediately or kept in the refrigerator. It should be dressed before serving.

Salad Dressing for Radish Salad

Ingredients:
6 tablesp. yoghourt
3 tablesp. French dressing (sunflower oil and lemon)
3 tablesp. sour cream
1 tablesp. fresh chopped or green-dried chervil
1 tablesp. fresh chopped or green-dried tarragon

Method:
1. Mix all ingredients well.
2. Allow to permeate.
3. Keep in refrigerator until needed.

JUICES AS FOOD (*not as drink*)

A food of the highest quality for health as well as for the invalid and the baby

Freshly expressed uncooked and undiluted fruit and vegetable juices are one of the most concentrated and most health-giving foods which cause no disturbance to the intestinal work of the body as they are the most easily assimilated of all foods. There are now quick and easy ways of liquidizing all foods by mechanical means, such as electric liquidizers or, better still, electric juice extractors, and as these uncooked juices are rich in vitamins and minerals they are really an ideal nourishment, particularly for the invalid and the baby.

They are, of course, not meant to be the exclusive food of healthy human beings who must have some roughage to function properly. However, in all cases when roughage must be avoided, such as in gastro-intestinal conditions, for small babies who are not yet adjusted to digesting roughage, for old people whose teeth are no longer serviceable, or for all those who are rushed and strained – mothers, professional, and business people – juices are ideal. In the long run it is, of course, preferable that people should return to eating raw salads and fruit, as soon as circumstances permit.

Juices are food and not drink and therefore should not be gulped down, but should be taken by spoon and possibly chewed a little so that the saliva can do its pre-digesting work. They not only provide the extra vitamins and minerals so important for people after operations and during convalescence, but they also strengthen the resistance against disease and infection. The juices should be taken preferably before eating anything cooked, before breakfast, and certainly before a cooked breakfast, and before lunch, dinner, or supper.

All fresh juice must be drunk immediately after preparation because the oxidization from the air destroys valuable substances in a short time. Before any fruit or vegetables are either squeezed, as in the case of citrus fruit, or extracted, as in the case of stone fruit or berries, raw vegetables, leaf vegetables, and herbs, they should be finely chopped up before going into the fruit extractor.

It is not easy to make vegetable juices really attractive, and no food will be enjoyed in the long run if it cannot be made attractive to take. This is where herbs have to play their great part. A vegetable juice or cocktail which is really a pleasure needs experience. It is an art to make this kind of juice by using lemon, cream, or cereal cream, and, above all, the right kind of herbs in the right combination.

Fruit Juices should be served immediately after extracting because any delay will cause loss in value through oxidization. Fruit juices can be served either unmixed, such as in the case of oranges, tangerines, grapefruit, apples, pears, grapes, strawberries, raspberries, redcurrants, bilberries, peaches, apricots, and plums, or mixed as, for instance, orange and grapefruit, or juices made of soft fruit mixed with apple juice, or peach and apricot, or plum juice with apricot and mashed bananas, etc.

Apple Juice. As apples are fruit which fully ripen in most countries they are extremely suitable for juice. Quality has been improved and different varieties are available throughout the year. After the apples have been washed, only the stalk and the top have to be removed; the apple can then be cut into suitable pieces for the type of juice extractor available. It contains Vitamins A, B, and C as well as sodium and other minerals. Owing to the rich content of pectin the juice is agreeably mild. If we are the happy owners of good apple trees we can make our own apple juice throughout autumn and, often, winter. Lemon balm and sweet cicely combine with apple juice, also an occasional pinch of lemon thyme.

Orange, Lemon, and Grapefruit Juice are rich in Vitamin C. They should, however, be fully ripe and possibly not chemically treated. Orange and lemon peels contain volatile oils and therefore – if one can be sure that the skins have not been chemically treated – they can be squeezed with their cleaned peels because the volatile oils can then be utilized. If we only want the pure juice, the fruit should be halved and then pressed on an orange press. Grapefruit juice stimulates the functions of liver, kidney, and glands and is one of the best apéritifs; its tartness is reduced by the use of sweet cicely.

Soft fruit juices are rich in Vitamin A and contain many minerals. If sweetened with honey or brown sugar and if diluted with a little water they are good for quenching thirst, particularly for people running a temperature. When making a freshly expressed juice of soft fruit, the berries should be first put through a blender to make them into a purée and only then through a juice extractor.

Lemon juice should be immediately added to or, in fact, form the basis for each fruit juice to retain the colour; it also adds Vitamin C. Further additions of sugar, honey, cream, cereal cream, and the sweet herbs, such as sweet cicely and lemon balm are suggested for improving the flavour.

Herbs. Sweet cicely is an excellent addition to take away the tartness of any fruit, particularly if sugar is not liked or is not advisable, and a little lemon balm will also help to sweeten and to give the slight lemon flavour which is so pleasant with every fruit juice. The herbs can go straight into the blender or juice extractor with the fruit.

Nourishing Additions. Cream, yoghourt, nut cream, and almond purée add protein and make such juices a full meal. For those who find juices too tart or acid, they can be neutralized by using some cereal cream such as cream of rice, or barley, and add herbs such as sweet cicely and lemon balm.

Vegetable Juices. If served fresh, these have a high vitamin and mineral content. Each juice has in itself special value and provides special minerals and vitamins. Unmixed vegetable juices can be made of tomatoes, carrots, beetroots, white radishes, cabbage, celeriac – in fact of most leaf, root, and tuberous vegetables.

To prepare mixed vegetable juices, great care has to be taken to make the juices palatable. Too much of one ingredient can spoil the flavour of the juice. The best mixtures are carrots, tomatoes, and spinach in either equal parts or less spinach if spinach has been found too tart. Tomatoes and carrots, tomatoes and spinach, other mixtures and spinach, can be combined according to individual taste. It is, however, important to add less of the green leaf vegetables than one would in a salad because these are apt to spoil the flavour. It is preferable to have a good basis of either tomatoes or carrots before adding green leaves or any other vegetables.

A mixed vegetable juice is often called a vegetable cocktail and is equally good for the invalid and as an apéritif before a low calorie meal.

Various herbs will improve every vegetable juice, but should be used in small proportions; this has to be tried out for each individual taste. It is practically impossible to give hard-and-fast recipes as not only the individual appreciation varies but also the intensity in flavour of each vegetable and herb.

The herbs suggested for flavour and for health are:

Chives	Dandelion	⎫
Parsley	Young nettle	⎬ particularly in spring
Celery Leaves	Some sorrel	⎭

Herbs which will 'make' a vegetable cocktail are:

Lemon balm	Sweet cicely
Tarragon	Lemon thyme (pinch)
Chervil	Basil (pinch)

Carrot juice is one of the most popular because it is easy to take, not too tart and not too expensive. It contains Vitamins A, B, and C; minerals such as calcium, iron, and iodine. Its natural content of sugar has energy-giving qualities. Carrots have always been recommended to improve the sight and are important for those who must be aware of night blindness.

It is the first juice on which a baby can be started to add some uncooked vegetables and thus vitamins and minerals to its feeds; as it has not an acid flavour babies are happy to take a few teaspoons every day, when sweetened with honey. Pasteurized milk can be added.

Carrots should be well cleaned, scrubbed and scraped if young, or peeled. The juice can be made either by grating on a two-way grater on to a clean cloth and squeezing, or by putting into an electric blender and then passing through a muslin or by using a juice extractor. Parsley (pinch of marjoram and lovage), lemon balm, tarragon, and chervil are excellent herbs to add.

Celery and Celeriac Juice has a diuretic effect and is therefore useful for people with a tendency to rheumatism and for those who want to lose weight. Mixed with a little lemon juice and some cream, it is usually liked very much; it contains Vitamins A, B, C, and E, as well as minerals, such as calcium and potassium. Chives, parsley, and lovage, a pinch of basil and thyme, improve the juice.

Beetroot Juice is excellent for certain conditions of the liver and improves the haemoglobin of the blood. As beetroot made into a juice has not an attractive flavour by itself, it is advisable to mix it with some dairy cream or cereal cream and a little lemon juice. Chives, lemon balm, dill, lovage, a pinch of thyme, also add flavour.

Tomato Juice is an excellent apéritif if herbs are added such as basil, chervil, tarragon, parsley, celery leaves, or a dash of sweet cicely. The herbs can be mixed all together with the tomato juice or they can be tried out as separate additions. They give a superior flavour to tomato juice compared to any of the commercial sauce additions. Tomato juice contains Vitamins A and B and is an excellent basis for other vegetable juices, particularly for those which have tart flavours.

Cabbage Juice has been recently used as a therapy, particularly in America and Switzerland, as a help against duodenal ulcers. It is advisable to add a third of carrot juice without reducing the effect but making it more palatable. Cabbage juice provides calcium. Parsley, chives, lovage, caraway (pressed through a juice extractor) improves cabbage juice.

Radish Juice, expressed of either the large white or black radish, is helpful in the case of gall-bladder and liver troubles, but can only be taken in small quantities. Chives, lemon balm, and sweet cicely in not too small quantities, and chervil make radish juice milder and easier to take.

Spinach Juice is helpful for anaemic people as it improves the haemoglobin of the blood owing to its iron content, but it is tart in flavour and not easy to take. If wanted for therapeutic reasons, it should be either mixed with a cereal cream or small quantities be added to a vegetable soup. Small quantities can also be added to sweet vegetable juices such as carrot or to tomato. Chives are helpful, also chervil and peppermint.

Mixed Juices

These combine a variety of nutrients which supplement each other.

Carrot and Apple Juice. Carrots and unpeeled apple to be

passed through the juice extractor, to which chervil, sweet cicely, and lemon balm should be added.

> *Celery, Carrots, and Apple with Lemon Balm and pinch of Lovage.*
> *Beetroot and Apple with Lemon Balm and Sweet Cicely.*
> *Cucumber and Carrots with Dill and Chervil.*
> *Tomato and Carrots with pinch of Basil and Chervil.*
> *Carrots, Tomato, and Spinach with pinch of Basil, Chervil, Tarragon.*

When mixing these juices, nettle, dandelion, sorrel, and celery leaves can be added before extracting the juice. Also parsley, chives, onion green can be extracted with the juice for flavouring the juice. Chives or any other herbs such as parsley, chervil, a leaf of lovage, tarragon, very little marjoram or thyme can be added, unless specific herbs are suggested.

A little lemon juice and lemon balm are always a welcome addition and sweet cicely can be used in generous quantities for added flavour and as sweetener to any juices made from vegetables combined with fruit, such as apple.

Some milk or the top of the milk improves and softens the flavour of all vegetable juices and the added fat of the milk allows the better utilization of part of Vitamin A.

Freshly expressed juices are best supplemented by an addition of:

Cereal Cream.

Raw juices which contain acids such as citrus fruits, or have a tart flavour, are best supplemented with one-third of cereal cream which neutralizes tart fruit flavour and makes some of the juices easier to take, particularly for babies and advisable for people with gastro-intestinal conditions.

It is best to prepare such a cereal cream beforehand and keep it in the refrigerator to add to freshly expressed juices.

Cream of Rice or Barley:
1 heaped teasp. rice *or* rice flakes, *or* barley meal, *or* flakes
1 cup (10 oz.) water

> Mix cereal with cold water.
> Bring to the boil.
> Cook for 5 minutes, stirring constantly.
> Allow to cool.

Cream of Linseed:

1 tablesp. linseed   1 cup (8 oz.) water

Wash Linseed in a sieve under running water.
Boil in the water for 10 minutes.
Strain and allow to cool.

Examples:

Orange Juice with Cereal Cream:

Squeeze 1 orange, add some linseed cream, mix well, possibly in a blender.

Blackcurrant Juice with Cereal Cream:

2–3 oz. blackcurrant juice (expressed in a juice extractor)
1–2 oz. rice *or* barley cream
1 teasp. lemon juice
Sweet cicely (expressed with the juice)
Honey to sweeten
Top with dairy cream (if allowed)
2 oz. water (boiled and cooled if given to small children or invalids

Tomato Juice with Horseradish:

Peel and grate a small piece of fresh horseradish and add to a glass of freshly expressed tomato juice. Add 1 teasp. of rice *or* barley cream to soften the hot flavour of the horseradish.

Some fresh or reconstituted green-dried basil, *or* parsley and chives, can be extracted together with the tomatoes.

Horseradish contains some antibiotic substances which are of importance to the diet in cases of inflammation of the intestinal tract.

Juices with Protein – *A Complete Meal*

Some excellent fruit drinks can be made with or without a blender if fresh berries or freshly expressed fruit juices are used, or a clean concentrated juice such as blackcurrant juice.

Strawberry Milk:

5 oz. T.T. milk   A little honey for sweetening
Some fresh strawberries

The same fruit-milk can be made with all other berries. If the berries are tart, the milk can be sweetened by the addition of sweet cicely and honey.

Bilberries, owing to their pectin, tannins, and volatile oils are extremely wholesome and should be used in cases of all intestinal disorders. They are, however, difficult to get in this country, with the exception of a few heathland districts, *eg* near Guildford and in the north in Scotland. If a good strong undiluted bilberry juice could be imported, this would greatly add to such a health drink.

Savoury Curd Drink:

A nourishing liquid food, rich in protein, easy to digest:

5 oz. butter milk	½ teasp. grated horseradish
1 tablesp. curd	½ teasp. each freshly chopped *or*
½ teasp. nut cream	green-dried tarragon and chervil
1 tablesp. concentrated fruit juice	

All these ingredients should be mixed in a blender.

Other variations of such liquid food are health-giving, particularly in cases of chronic conditions of liver or in a post-operational diet.

5 oz. butter milk	1 teasp. tomato purée
1 tablesp. curd	Some fresh chopped or green-dried
½ teasp. nut cream	basil
5 oz. Jersey milk	Some malt
1 tablesp. curd	Some fresh chopped or green-dried
	sweet cicely
3 oz. Jersey milk	1 teasp. nut cream
1½ oz. orange juice	1 teasp. fresh chopped or green-dried sweet cicely
1 tablesp. curd	

Juices with Non-animal Protein and Fat

Fruit Nut Milk:

An excellent and valuable substitute for dairy milk and cream; according to analysis, similar to mother's milk.

Ingredients:

3 oz. water	1 teasp. nut cream
2 oz. orange juice	1 teasp. honey

Well mix equal quantities of nut milk and honey.

Add water drop by drop, stirring well.

This produces a creamy consistency which, through the addition of water and orange juice, eventually provides a fruit nut milk.

A general quantity of either fresh chopped or green-dried sweet cicely, *or* lemon balm, *or* chervil, will add to the flavour and value of these protein foods.

Freshly extracted juices of fresh blackcurrants, raspberries, bilberries, can be added to the nut cream.

Also vegetable juices flavoured with herbs can be combined with Nut Cream.

For those who should avoid animal fat:

The nut fat becomes such a fine emulsion in the fruit nut milk that it can be well tolerated even in the case of liver and gall-bladder trouble, provided that these are not in an acute state.

Nut cream made of hazel nuts contains 68 per cent fat.

Nut cream made of almond nuts contains 59 per cent fat.

Nut cream made of cashew nuts contains 49 per cent fat.

The cashew purée contains somewhat less fat than the almond or hazel nut cream and is therefore suggested for fruit nut milk, if there is a particular sensitiveness to fat.

MEATLESS AND HEALTH DISHES

The following dishes are grouped on their own because they provide – together with Salads and Juices given elsewhere in this chapter – further alternative menus for those interested in healthy eating.

Tomato Soup with Soya Dumplings

Ingredients:

Soup:
1 lb. tomatoes, diced
1 tablesp. sunflower oil
½ onion, finely chopped
1 tablesp. wholemeal flour
1 pt. vegetable stock
A little yeast extract
1 teasp. each fresh chopped or green-dried basil and parsley

Dumplings:
⅓ oz. butter *or* special margarine
1 triangle of processed cheese
1 tablesp. wholemeal flour
1 tablesp. semolina
1 tablesp. soya flour
1 teasp. bouquet for omelettes *or* 1 teasp. mixed fresh chopped or green-dried parsley and chives

Method (Soup):

1. Sauté onion in the heated oil until transparent.
2. Add basil and parsley.
3. Add the diced tomatoes and cook until tender.
4. Sprinkle with flour.
5. Smooth with vegetable stock.
6. Pass through a sieve and season with some yeast extract and a trace of sugar.

Method (Dumplings):

1. Work fat with the processed cheese, flour, semolina, soya flour, and herbs into a paste.
2. Form small dumplings, wetting the teaspoons or the hands with hot water.
3. Allow to simmer for 3 minutes in the hot tomato soup.

Health Vegetable Soup

Ingredients:
2 tablesp. sunflower oil
3 small carrots, finely diced
1 small kohlrabi *or* other root, diced
1 stick of celery, diced
or 1 small celeriac, diced
1 leek, chopped
3 small potatoes, diced
2–2½ pints vegetable broth *or* any stock

A small quantity of yeast extract
1 tablesp. fresh chopped or green-dried parsley
1 tablesp. mixed fresh chopped or green-dried celery leaves and lovage
A pinch of fresh chopped or green-dried summer savory and marjoram
If available, the finely diced root of Hamburg parsley

Method:

1. Sauté all vegetables in heated oil.
2. Add the herbs and sauté.
3. Add the diced potatoes and add vegetable stock.
4. Simmer until tender.
5. Before serving, the soup should be tasted and more herbs added if necessary.

Note: If necessary, the whole of this soup, when finished, can be placed into the blender and served as a purée which makes it easier to digest.

Nettle Soup

A health-giving soup, especially in spring. After nettles are cooked, they lose their sting.

Ingredients:

3 oz. young nettle leaves
1 tablesp. butter *or* oil
1 small onion, chopped
¾ lb. potatoes, peeled and diced
2–2½ pints stock

1 teasp. mixed fresh chopped or green-dried marjoram, basil, sage
1 dessertsp. fresh chopped or green-dried lovage
½ tablesp. butter
2 tablesp. cream

Method:

1. Wearing rubber gloves, pick only young nettle leaves.
2. Select nettles and free from stalks; wash and allow to drip.
3. Cook in saucepan without additional liquid over low heat until tender.
4. Allow to cool, then chop.
5. Sauté onion in fat until golden.
6. Add potatoes and sauté again; add boiling stock.
7. When potatoes are cooked, add nettle and all herbs.
8. Allow to simmer for 15 minutes.
9. Allow to stand in warm place for 15 minutes.
10. Before serving, add butter and cream.

Tomato Cottage Cheese Spread

Ingredients:

3 oz. curd *or* cottage cheese
3 tablesp. milk
1 tablesp. sunflower oil
1 teasp. tomato purée

½ teasp. nut cream
Lemon juice
1 teasp. each fresh chopped or green-dried chives and basil
A little chopped onion, if liked

Method:
1. Add the oil drop by drop to nut cream.
2. Add lemon juice and all other ingredients.
3. Use as a spread on Ryvita *or* Pumpernickel.

Red Radish Spread

Ingredients:

1½ oz. curd *or* cottage cheese
1 tablesp. sunflower oil
1 tablesp. milk
1 bunch small red radishes

Some lemon juice
1 teasp. each fresh chopped or green-dried celery leaves and tarragon
A little salt (if permitted)

Method:
1. Grate radishes.
2. Mix with all other ingredients.
3. Use on rye bread, Pumpernickel *or* Ryvita.

Carrot Cheese Spread

Ingredients:

2 oz. curd (without cream) *or* cottage cheese
1–2 oz. grated carrot
Some milk
1 teasp. sunflower oil
1 dessertsp. fresh chopped or green-dried parsley
1 teasp. each fresh chopped or green-dried lemon balm and sweet cicely
A pinch of fresh chopped or green-dried marjoram
Lemon juice according to taste

Method:
1. Grate carrots finely on two-way grater.
2. Mix with curd, milk, and oil.
3. Season with the herbs and lemon juice.
   Note: Best prepared in a blender. Used as a spread on Ryvita *or* Pumpernickel.

Spinach Sauté

Ingredients:

½ lb. spinach
1 small onion
1 teasp. fresh chopped or green-dried onion green
1 tablesp. sunflower oil
Lemon juice

A little vegetable stock
Yeast extract
1 teasp. fresh chopped or green-dried lovage
1 teasp. mixed of chopped nettle, dandelion, and sorrel (optional)

Method:
1. Sauté finely chopped onion and onion green in heated oil until transparent.
2. Add two-thirds of the washed spinach and allow to cook for 5 minutes in covered saucepan.
3. Put this spinach, together with the remaining uncooked spinach, into the blender and make into a purée for some seconds on No. 2.
4. If the spinach has not provided enough liquid for the blender, add some vegetable stock.
5. Before serving, season with some lovage and wild herbs, according to taste.

Chicory au Gratin

Ingredients:

½ lb. chicory
1 tablesp. sunflower oil
1 oz. cheddar *or* Gruyère cheese
Yeast extract

1 teasp. each fresh chopped or green-dried parsley, and onion green *or* chives
1 teasp. each fresh chopped or green-dried chervil and fennel

Method:
1. Cut chicory fairly coarse.
2. Heat oil in a flameproof dish and add parsley and onion green.
3. Sauté chicory in this for 5 minutes.
4. Add other herbs and season with yeast extract.
5. Cover with the grated cheese and place under grill for 20 minutes.

Vegetarian Stew

Ingredients:

1 cooked beetroot, diced
1 large apple, diced
1 cucumber pickled in brine, diced
1 tablesp. sunflower oil
¼ pint vegetable stock
1 tablesp. bouquet for soups and stews
    or 1 tablesp. mixed fresh chopped or green-dried parsley and lovage
¼ teasp. each fresh chopped or green-dried marjoram, thyme, and chervil

Caraway seeds
Lemon juice
Yeast extract (diluted with a little water)
1 tablesp. sour cream

Method:
1. Sauté cooked beetroot, apple, and cucumber in the vegetable oil.
2. Add vegetable stock.
3. Allow to cook for 5 minutes on low heat.
4. Add herbs, caraway, lemon juice, and yeast extract.
5. Add sour cream.

Strawberry Cream (milk protein food)

Ingredients:
3 oz. curd *or* cottage cheese
6 oz. fresh strawberries
  (reserve a few for decorating)
2 tablesp. milk

1 tablesp. brown sugar (or according to taste)
1 teasp. each fresh chopped or green-dried lemon balm and sweet cicely

Method:
1. Wash and hull strawberries.
2. Pass the berries through a sieve together with the herbs, curd, or cottage cheese and milk, or mix it all in a blender.
3. Add sugar according to taste.
4. Leave some of the best fruit to decorate the mixture.
  Note: This is an especially good sweet for everyone; even children find it delicious and it does provide vital substances for their growth and well-being.

Banana Cheese Cream

Ingredients:
3 oz. curd *or* cottage cheese
2 small bananas
1 tablesp. fruit juice *or* syrup

4 tablesp. milk
Linomel*

  * Available at health food stores. Linomel is made of linseed, crusted with pure bees' honey. It is a valuable addition to fruit and cream cheese and tastes very good.

Method:
1. Mash the bananas with a fork.
2. Beat until frothy.
3. Add the curd and all other ingredients to the banana froth.
4. Stir until smooth.
5. Decorate with Linomel and banana slices.

Chapter 5

HERBS IN INVALID COOKING

DURING ILLNESS and convalescence food can play a decisive part in fighting a condition and speeding up recovery. In spite of the special study made of invalid food, the very great help provided by herbs is barely understood. Where we have to restrict certain foods such as salt in feeding a patient with heart trouble, or are trying to tempt a convalescent after an operation, far too little use is made of this important aid. The first-class catering trade – the livelihood of which depends upon the flavour of its dishes – may have shelves full of drums or glass jars of green-dried herbs; yet the hospital and nursing home diet kitchens are not so much concerned with the help which first-class fresh or green-dried herbs can give to the diet when nursing a patient back to health. With some 'culinary cunning' to which herbs are of such significant help, so much could be done for the invalid.

However, when the invalid is at home, the housewife or mother can tempt the patient with herbs to encourage eating. This requires skill in presenting food which not only tastes good but is wholesome and helps recovery. Herbs should make invalid food far from dull, even when salt-restricted diets have to be followed. These are only some of the qualities which herbs bring to invalid feeding, apart from the important minerals, trace-elements and essential oils they provide.

The following recipes will show in which way herbs can be used as an instrument for restoring the patient to full health.

Breakfast Frumenty (*serves 2*)

Ingredients:

3–4 heaped tablesp. whole wheat flakes

4 tablesp. milk *or* yoghourt

2 apples

Lemon juice and 1 teasp. honey *or* orange juice

1 teasp. each fresh chopped or green-dried lemon balm and sweet cicely

1 teasp. milled nuts (optional)

Method:
1. Mix wheat flakes with milk or yoghourt.
2. Grate the apples into this.
3. Flavour with lemon juice and honey (according to taste) or with orange juice if used without sweetening.

Note: Apple is always an ideal supplement to whole cereals, and this is also the idea on which the famous Bircher muesli is based. Apples are available almost the whole year. When grating apples on a stainless two-way grater it is necessary to avoid them becoming brown because the apples oxidate so quickly in contact with the air. Mix them quickly with the prepared wheat flakes and then serve *as quickly as possible*.

This breakfast dish can also be made with strawberries, peaches, apricots, plums, oranges, or pears, cut up finely. Any berries should be mashed with a fork beforehand.

Wheat Breakfast (*serves 2*)

1½ oz. freshly crushed wheat *or* cracked wheat*
Lemon juice
Water for soaking

4–6 prunes
1½ apples
1 teasp. each fresh chopped or green-dried sweet cicely and lemon balm
1 pinch fresh chopped or green-dried lemon thyme

Method:
1. Wheat and prunes should be soaked overnight in separate bowls.
2. In the morning, cut the prunes finely and, together with lemon juice, add to the soaked wheat.
3. Then grate apples into it and mix all quickly.

Note: Any freshly crushed wheat will become more digestible when warmed for 15 minutes over steam. Instead of prunes, dried apricots, raisins, or mixed dried fruits can be used. A little top of the milk (shortly before serving) will improve the flavour.

Whole Cereal Apple Breakfast (*serves 2*)

A valuable breakfast.

Ingredients:
1½–2 oz. cracked whole wheat* *or* freshly crushed whole wheat
¼ pint water
¼ pint milk *or* some yoghourt
1 teasp. honey
1 teasp. fresh chopped or green-dried sweet cicely

Method:
1. Soak the wheat overnight in water.
2. Add a little water in the morning and cook over low heat, constantly stirring.
3. Allow to cook for 3–5 minutes.

* Available at health food shops.

4. Sweeten with honey and sweet cicely.
5. Grate an apple into the porridge.
6. Add some fresh milk or yoghourt before eating.

Mixed Vegetable Drinks with Milk

The following drinks are a liquid milk protein food and are important for post-operational cases and for providing nourishing food to an invalid without being a burden to the digestion. The drinks are best mixed in a blender; the vegetable juices can be varied and to all of them some freshly chopped or green-dried herbs should be added according to taste or by using the herbs suggested with individual vegetable juices (see page 100). If yoghourt or buttermilk is preferred, some of this can be added instead of some of the milk. More details about making vegetable juices are given on page 100.

(*a*) 2 oz. milk   ⅓ oz. celery juice
       1 oz. spinach juice   A few drops of lemon juice
       ¾ oz. tomato juice   Herbs

(*b*) 2 oz. milk   A few drops of lemon juice
       1 oz. carrot juice   Herbs
       1 oz. celery juice

(*c*) 2 oz. yoghourt *or* butter   A little grated horseradish
       milk   A few drops of lemon juice
       1 oz. carrot juice   Herbs

(*d*) *Enriched Milk Protein Food*
3 oz. milk   1 teasp. tomato purée
1 tablesp. curd   Herbs
½ teasp. nut cream

(*e*) *Beetroot Milk*
   An excellent milk food for the anaemic made palatable by milk.
2 oz. milk   ½ teasp. honey
½ oz. freshly expressed beetroot   ½ teasp. lemon juice
   juice   Herbs
¾ oz. apple juice

Spreads

(a) *Cheese Spread (oil protein food)*

Ingredients:

1½ oz. curd *or* cottage cheese
½ portion processed cheese
2 tablesp. milk
1 teasp. sunflower oil

1 pinch paprika
1 teasp. finely chopped onion
1 teasp. fresh chopped or green-dried chives

Method:

1. Mix curd, cheese, milk, and oil in blender until creamy.
2. Add paprika, according to taste.
3. Add onion and chives last.

(b) *Horseradish Cheese Spread*

Ingredients:

1 pkt. soft cheese (gervais, etc.)
2 teasp. grated horseradish (approx.)
1 tablesp. single cream *or* top of the milk
1 teasp. fresh chopped or green-dried lovage

A pinch of each fresh chopped or green-dried thyme and summer savory
Slices of tomato for decoration
Fresh chopped or green-dried basil for decoration

Method:

1. Mix all ingredients well together.
2. Spread on Ryvita or similar biscuit.
3. Decorate with tomato slices and sprinkle with basil.

Diet Cereal Soup (oatmeal reinforced with nut cream)

Ingredients:

2 tablesp. whole oat flakes *or* whole oatmeal
1 teasp. nut cream
1 teasp. each fresh chopped or green-dried parsley and lovage
2 teasp. bouquet for soups and stews
or 2 teasp. mixed fresh chopped or green-dried chives, celery leaves, basil and chervil (see GUIDE, page 127, for proportions).
Yeast extract

Method:

1. Start cooking oatmeal in cold water, add parsley and lovage and allow to boil for 10 minutes.

2. Pass through a sieve.
3. Add drops of water to nut cream until it is of a creamy consistency, then add to the soup.
4. Add some unsalted yeast extract and bouquet for soups and stews *or* 2 teasp. mixed herbs.

Note: If used for salt-restricted diet, use more yeast extract, otherwise season with salt.

Invalid Chervil Soup

For special diets or invalid food because it contains no flour.

Ingredients:

1 small onion
1–2 tablesp. oil
A good handful of fresh chopped chervil
or 1–2–3 tablesp. green-dried chervil
1 potato
Hot vegetable *or* yeast stock up to 1 pint

1 teasp. fresh chopped or green-dried parsley
½ teasp. fresh chopped or green-dried celery leaves
Lemon juice
1 clove garlic, minced

Method:

1. Heat oil carefully, add finely chopped onion and sauté.
2. Add fresh or green-dried chervil and sauté.
3. Grate raw potato into this mixture.
4. Add hot stock.
5. Allow to simmer on low heat for 5–10 minutes.
6. Add finely chopped parsley and celery leaves.
7. Flavour with drops of lemon juice and the minced garlic.

Note: This soup avoids flour as it uses potatoes for thickening and is therefore more valuable for certain diets or for the invalid.

Cooked Carrots

Ingredients:

¾ lb. carrots
1 tablesp. sunflower oil
1 tablesp. fresh chopped or green-dried parsley
1 teasp. mixed fresh chopped or green-dried lovage and lemon balm

A pinch of fresh chopped or green-dried marjoram
1 teasp. lemon juice
A little yeast extract
Water or vegetable stock
Fresh parsley (if liked)

Method:

1. Clean the carrots carefully, wash and cut into small sticks or cubes.
2. Heat oil in a saucepan.
3. Add parsley.
4. Add carrots and sauté
5. Add all other herbs, lemon juice, and yeast extract.
6. If necessary, add a little vegetable stock and cook until tender.
7. Add freshly chopped parsley before serving (if liked).

Sweet Fennel (Finocchio)

Ingredients:

2 sweet florence fennel
1 tablesp. sunflower oil
¼ pint vegetable stock
1 tablesp. sour cream
1 teasp. fresh chopped or green-dried fennel leaves

1 teasp. fresh chopped or green-dried parsley
½ teasp. each fresh chopped or green-dried chervil, tarragon, and borage (optional)
Yeast extract

Method:

1. Clean fennel and take away the outer parts.
2. Heat sunflower oil carefully and add the cut-up fennel and parsley.
3. Sauté.
4. Add some vegetable stock.
5. Allow to simmer on low heat.
6. Add sour cream, fennel, and other herbs.
7. Add a little yeast extract.

Baked Rosemary Potatoes

Method:

(*a*) 1. Brush potatoes well under running water to clean.
    2. Halve lengthwise.
    3. Dip surfaces on to rosemary leaves.
    4. Place cut surfaces downwards on a tin which has not been buttered.
    5. Allow to bake in the oven or under the grill until ready.
(*b*) 3. Dip cut surfaces on to rosemary leaves and salt.
    4. Place cut surfaces downwards on an oiled flat tin.
    5. Brush with vegetable oil and bake in the oven.

Risotto with Tomato Sauce

Ingredients:

Risotto:
1 teasp. oil
1 cup whole rice
½ teasp. fresh chopped or green-dried rosemary
1 pinch of curry
3 cups of water
½ teasp. marigold petals, if available
1 pinch yeast extract, preferably salt-free

Tomato Sauce:
¾ lb. tomatoes
Lemon juice
Garlic, minced
Paprika
½ teasp. fresh chopped or green-dried basil

Method (Risotto):
1. Heat the oil.
2. Sauté rice with rosemary and curry for a few minutes.
3. Add the water and marigold petals.
4. Allow to come to the boil.
5. Then put into a cool oven for 25 minutes.
6. Before serving, add yeast extract according to taste.

Method (Tomato Sauce):
1. Cut tomatoes into quarters and then put through a sieve.
2. Season with lemon juice, paprika, garlic, and basil.
3. Put into fireproof container and warm over a saucepan of boiling water.

Asparagus with Scrambled Egg

Ingredients:

Asparagus:
½–¾ lb. asparagus, fresh or tinned
Paprika
½ oz. fresh melted butter
1 teasp. fresh chopped or green-dried tarragon

Scrambled Egg:
2 eggs
1 tablesp. milk
1 pinch of sea-salt
Fresh chopped or green-dried chives
Chives and parsley for garnishing

Method (Asparagus):
1. Clean asparagus.
2. Cook in boiling water until tender (approximately 25 minutes).
3. Drain.

4. Serve on a flat dish.
5. Sprinkle paprika and tarragon in two strips each over the flatly arranged asparagus.
6. Serve with the butter.

Method (Scrambled Egg):
1. Beat eggs with the milk.
2. Add salt and chives and beat well again.
3. Butter a small shallow container, fill with the eggs and allow to set in a pan with boiling water.
4. Garnish with chives and parsley.

Calves' Liver from the Grill

Ingredients:

1 slice of calves' liver	Sea-salt
1 slice of apple	Horseradish
1 teasp. sunflower oil	1 tablesp. thick double cream

Method:
1. Brush the slice of liver with sunflower oil on both sides.
2. Add the slice of apple.
3. Put under hot grill and grill for 6–8 minutes.
4. When grilling is finished season with a little sea-salt.
5. Serve with grated horseradish mixed with the cream.

Apricot Dumplings with Soya Flour

Ingredients:

3 peeled boiled potatoes	4 fresh apricots
2 tablesp. wholemeal flour	4 lumps of sugar
1 tablesp. whole semolina	1 teasp. fresh chopped or green-dried sweet cicely
1 tablesp. soya flour	
1 egg	

Method:
1. Grate the peeled potatoes and mix with flour, semolina, and soya flour.
2. Mix with the egg and knead well.
3. Divide the pastry into four parts.

4. Take the stone out of the apricots and put a lump of sugar and ¼ teasp. sweet cicely in each.
5. Roll out the pastry and wrap the apricots with pastry.
6. Drop the dumplings into boiling water.
7. Allow to simmer for 10 minutes on low heat.
8. Serve with stewed apricots.
   Note: Dessert plums can be used instead of apricots.

Rice Pudding

Ingredients:

½ cup whole rice
½ oz. butter *or* vegetable fat
1 tablesp. sugar
2 eggs
3 oz. curd *or* cottage cheese
3 tablesp. milk
1 tablesp. raisins

Grated peel of lemon
Sugar in which vanilla pods have been stored
1 teasp. each of mixed fresh chopped or green-dried sweet cicely and lemon balm

Method:

1. Put rice into boiling water in a saucepan and allow to simmer for 20 minutes or until cooked.
2. Pour into a sieve and rinse with cold water.
3. Allow to drain well.
4. Beat butter, sugar, and egg yolks until creamy.
5. Add curd and milk and, lastly, rice and raisins.
6. Add lemon peel, vanilla sugar, and herbs according to taste.
7. Add white of egg beaten to a stiff froth.
8. Butter fireproof dish and bake quickly in the oven.

Orange Cheese Cream

Ingredients

3 oz. curd *or* cottage cheese
1 orange
1 teasp. nut cream
1 teasp. honey
2 tablesp. milk

½ teasp. fresh chopped or green-dried sweet cicely
½ teasp. fresh chopped or green-dried lemon balm

Method:

1. Squeeze the orange.
2. Add all other ingredients.
3. Mix well, possibly in a blender.

Cherry Cream

The cherries in this recipe, particularly if made in a blender, are so finely dissolved that they can be tolerated by sensitive people who suffer from liver or gall-bladder conditions. If, technically speaking, the cherries are totally mashed into a purée, all the old restrictions on stone fruit do not apply.

Ingredients:

3 oz. curd
6 oz. cherries
3 tablesp. milk
1 tablesp. brown sugar

1 teasp. fresh chopped or green-dried sweet cicely
½ teasp. fresh chopped or green-dried lemon balm
Retain a few cherries for decoration

Method:
1. Stone the cherries.
2. Pass through a sieve, or mash in a blender.
3. Mix cherries well with other ingredients.
4. Decorate with the remaining cherries.

Note: The curd for this sort of sweet must always be very fresh and should not taste bitter.

Fresh Fruit Mould (*serves 2*)

Ingredients:
¼ pint freshly expressed juice of raspberries, blackberries, red or black-currants, grapes
or ¼ pint juice of orange and grapefruit, *or* lemon – half each – (strained)
¼ pint water
Sugar according to taste
1 teasp. fresh chopped or green-dried sweet cicely
½ teasp. fresh chopped or green-dried lemon thyme
2 tablesp. cornflour

Method:
1. Mix fruit juice with the water.
2. Bring two-thirds of the mixture to the boil.
3. Add sugar and herbs.
4. Smooth cornflour with remaining cold liquid.
5. Add to the boiling juice and boil until clear, stirring all the time.
6. Pour into mould rinsed with cold water.
7. Leave to set.
8. Turn out and serve with thin or whipped cream, if desired.

PART TWO

Herbs for Cookery

TWENTY-FOUR HERBS IN A CHEST

A Guide to the Strength of Individual Herbs

HERBS HAVE individual flavours, varying immensely in kind and strength. Some have to be used in large quantities, others in very small ones. It is practically impossible to give exact quantities for the use of herbs. In no other field do tastes differ quite so much. The palate changes when using herbs and, as it becomes more discriminating, wants either more or less of certain herbs.

The following Table is intended to be a basic guide to avoid errors caused by unknown pungencies and is meant to be a warning and encouragement at the same time. It is often suggested by herb books and recipes that it is always better to use less rather than more herbs. This is not correct as erring on the other side may not make the best use of the flavouring qualities of a herb. Even more caution is advised when dealing with dried herbs. Though this warning may be justified when using powdered herbs, it is certainly not a precaution to be used with green-dried herbs which reconstitute to the size of fresh chopped herbs, and are similar in strength of aroma to the fresh herb.

Therefore, once the nature of a herb has been fully understood the actual quantity has to be determined by its individual strength and one's own taste and this has to be discovered by one's own experience; this Table is merely to guide one's first steps. This same approach should be applied when using herb mixtures, unless one feels one can trust a reliable bouquet of a specialist firm, mixed by an expert.

BASIL	Sparingly.
BAY LEAVES	Cautiously, until familiar with flavour.
CELERY LEAVES	As much as desired to give a celery flavour.
CHERVIL	Generously.
CHIVES	According to taste.
DILL	Wisely sometimes generously.
ELDER FLOWER	Lavishly.
FENNEL	Wisely.
LEMON BALM	Lavishly.
LOVAGE	Economically, until familiar with flavour.

MARIGOLD	..	..	..	**Lavishly.**
MARJORAM		..	..	**Judiciously** at first – easily overpowers other flavours.
MINT ..	..	..	..	**Generously.**
NASTURTIUM LEAVES			..	**With caution.**
ONION GREEN		..	..	**According to taste.**
PARSLEY	..	..	..	**Generously.**
ROSEMARY		..	..	**Economically.**
SAGE ..	..	..	..	**With discretion.**
SALAD BURNET		..	..	**Generously.**
SORREL	..	..	..	**Carefully.**
SUMMER SAVORY	..		..	**Carefully,** until familiar with its strength.
SWEET CICELY		..	..	**Lavishly.**
TARRAGON ..		..	..	**Judiciously** – beware of hidden tang.
THYME	..	..	..	**With care.**

GENERAL INFORMATION

Basil (Ocimum basilicum)

Basil, strong and powerful, is king amongst herbs. It is invaluable in the kitchen, because it can make an impact on so many dishes and gives a sweet, delicate, pungency to food. Growing abundantly in India where it is used a great deal in curries, it also grows wild in the hot Mediterranean sun; there it enhances tomato dishes of every kind and rarely is one served without it. Newcomers to this herb should, however, use it carefully as otherwise it can dominate other flavours.

Common or sweet basil is an annual, growing to about 3 ft high with quadrangular stems and light green leaves of a fair size (3 in. by 1½ in.) grey/green beneath and spotted with dark oil cells when held against the light. The flowers are whitish and appear in whorls in the axils of the leaves. It is a difficult plant to grow because of its great need for warmth and nourishment. It needs a well-drained light soil and a very sheltered place, possibly sloping to the south. It can only be started after all the frost has disappeared and in many ways it is less risky and does better in pots in a fairly rich soil. Its excellence and the small quantity needed more than compensates for the trouble needed to grow it.

Although basil is comparatively little known in this country, those who have visited Italy and tasted there the delicious tomato spaghetti dishes will realize how much it imparts a special flavour, very difficult to compare with the flavours created by any other herb. It can be added to egg, cheese, and fish dishes and to any sausage mixture; basil was an ingredient of the famous Fetter Lane sausages.

Years ago farmers' wives grew pots of basil to give to their visitors, a gift which was gladly accepted because, apart from the basil's use as a flavouring, the pots were known to keep flies away; for this quality the French still put pots of basil on the tables of their pavement restaurants. If basil leaves are allowed to permeate wine this makes an excellent digestive tonic and the crushed leaves used as a snuff clear the head in cases of headaches and nasal cold.

Basil is one of the few herbs which increases its flavour when it is cooked. While it can be added liberally on tomatoes for use in sandwiches, in cooking it should be used SPARINGLY.

Pizza Napolitana with Basil
   (page 316)
Spaghetti with Tomato Meat
   Sauce
   (page 276)

Stuffed Tomato with Basil
   (page 184)
Genoese Pesto to be used with
   Spaghetti
   (page 289)

Day-to-day dishes for which Basil is traditionally used:

APPETIZERS	Tomato juice; shrimp and prawn cocktails.
SALAD AND SALAD DRESSINGS	On tomato or cucumber salads; in French dressing. Freshly chopped fresh or green-dried basil, possibly reconstituted, added to fresh tomato or mixed green salad or to their dressing.
EGG AND CHEESE	With creamed eggs, cheese soufflés, and fondue.
SOUPS, STEWS, AND CASSEROLES	Tomato soup, minestroné, pea, and in turtle soup.
FISH	Sole, shellfish and mackerel. With melted butter as a sauce or a seasoning for fish and shellfish. Basil, parsley, onion green, and summer savory to be added to the

	water in which fish is to be boiled, poached.
MEAT	With all meats – sausages and stuffings. Finely chopped or shredded green-dried basil sprinkled on to fried tomato slices while they are still very hot as a garnish for pork chops.
POULTRY AND GAME	Rubbed on poultry before cooking – in chicken and rabbit stews and with game.
VEGETABLES, POTATOES, RICE, AND PASTA	In all tomato dishes, with mushrooms and fungi. Flavours insipid vegetables, also spaghetti and rice.
SAUCES, DIPS, AND ACCOMPANIMENTS	Basil sauce, basil butter.
SANDWICHES AND SNACKS	On tomato sandwiches. Finely chopped fresh or green-dried basil and parsley added to any herb butter.

Bay Leaves (Laurus nobilis)

Bay leaves come from the handsome laurel, which, in ancient times, was a symbol of glory for poets and heroes – hence the Poet Laureate. Nowadays it glorifies the flavour of many dishes from the kitchen. It is the only one of its genus which was and is used in cookery. The volatile oil of the sweet bay provides an aromatic, slightly bitter, but important, flavour and stimulates the appetite.

The shiny leathery leaves are typical of this evergreen aromatic shrub-like tree, which can reach a height of about 30 ft and is usually pyramid-shaped. The dark green leaves are a pale yellowish green on the underside and the flowers are greenish yellow growing in small umbels.

The bay tree is a hardy perennial in the south of England, but it needs some protection and for this reason grows well in the shade of other trees. It cannot withstand long periods of severe frost. However, if the leaves go brown because of frost it is wise to keep the tree or shrub until well into the following summer as it may grow green leaves again. Small trees can be successfully grown in tubs in moderately rich soil and in a sunny position and taken indoors during winter, or into a sunny greenhouse. The leaves can in any case be picked all the year round, though it is quite easy and better to dry them; then the flavour becomes stronger.

They should be dried in the dark, not in the sun, in thin layers and must retain the exact colour and not become brown. They should be pressed under a board and packed into hard, dark, uncrushable containers, not bags, as otherwise volatile oil exhudes all the time.

Bay leaves are an important part of a bouquet garni necessary for roasting fowls and in stuffings; shredded, they are an important part of the green-dried bouquet for poultry and game, and bouquet for fish; in marinades for poultry and game, especially venison which has the reputation of being tough, the marinade should consist of oil, wine, and herbs to which shredded bay leaves or half a bay leaf has been added. They should always be added to court bouillon or to stock in which fish has been boiled. A bay leaf alone gives a new taste to the old-fashioned vegetable soup. It gives a subtle flavour when boiled with vegetables, such as artichokes, aubergines, etc., even potatoes, and it improves tomato juice and tomato soup. Two leaves can be added to the water for boiling ham and tongues.

The bouquet garni, however, is most often used and for so many dishes. This should contain 2 sprigs of parsley, 2 of chervil, 1 of marjoram, 1 of thyme, and $\frac{1}{2}$ a bay leaf. Whilst the proportion of bay leaf to other herbs seems small it should be remembered that it is a strong herb, that it becomes stronger when shredded and for all purposes it should be used CAUTIOUSLY and experience allowed to be the guide.

Chilled Salmon
(page 225)
Chicken in Vegetable Soup
(page 220)

Sauerkraut Spareribs
(page 243)

Day-to-day dishes for which Bay Leaves are traditionally used:

APPETIZERS — Dried and shredded in aspics (also sea-food) and tomato juice.

SALADS AND SALAD DRESSINGS — In French dressing for green or vegetable salads.

SOUPS AND STEWS | Dried and shredded in beef, lamb, mutton stock; chicken soup; 1 whole leaf or shredded equivalent added to bouquet garni.

FISH | In fish and shellfish; in court bouillon for poaching; with almost any fish if used with discretion.

MEAT | With beef, steaks, pot roast, lamb, or veal stews. Corned beef, tripe stews, with all smoked meat such as ham and tongue for boiling; in pickled meat; in marinades for meat. As part of bouquets for beef, lamb, or mutton stock in court bouillon for poaching; 1 or 2 leaves in bottom of roasting pan.

POULTRY AND GAME | In chicken fricassee and stews for roast chicken and duck and for all roasted birds, 1–2 leaves into the roasting pan. In chicken pies. Dried and shredded for all poultry stuffings. With almost any game. In all marinades for game, particularly for venison, stew, and steak.

VEGETABLES, POTATOES, RICE, AND PASTA | Dried in spaghetti dishes and almost all their sauces. Into the water for boiling potatoes and carrots. With artichokes, beetroot, aubergines; for pilafs.

SAUCES, DIPS, AND ACCOMPANIMENTS | For meat sauce, tomato, and wine sauces.

SWEETS AND DESSERTS | In custards and creams.

Celery Leaves (Apium graveolens)

Celery leaves are a seasoning of such world-wide reputation that they are a necessary addition to the herb and spice shelf. They are actually a bi-product when growing celery or celeriac as a vegetable, but the season during which celery leaves are available is very short. Only when the plants are ready to be harvested can the leaves be used and it is therefore a great help that celery leaves are also available green-dried. They are wanted in all recipes where celery flavour is called for and most soups, sauces, and stews are much better for a liberal addition of celery leaves.

The celery plant was originally a medicinal plant and is rich in various vitamins, mineral salts, and also has many active principles. Celery also has an effect on the whole glandular system, stimulates the digestion and is good for gout and rheumatism. All parts of the plant are edible – the leaves, stalks and roots, either raw or cooked. The leaves are as tasty and aromatic as the stalks and even the seeds have the same nutty flavour. Their sharp pungency has, at the same time, an almost sweet flavour. They are an excellent seasoning for diabetics and for anyone on a salt-reduced diet.

If celery leaves are dried it is most important to retain the colour and the specific flavour. To soups, sauces, stews, clear broth, and stuffings, celery leaves can be added at the last moment. They should not cook for more than 3 minutes with any of these dishes. The stalks of celery and the roots of the celeriac are also used chopped and grated raw in many salads, and when cooked give a basic flavour to any good strong soup. Enough celery leaves should be used to provide a celery flavour.

Cold Cucumber Soup
   (page 214)
Celery Sticks with Cream
   Cheese
   (page 177)

Macaroni and Shrimp Salad
   (page 187)

Day-to-day dishes for which Celery Leaves are traditionally used:

APPETIZERS	With cheese, fish, meats, shellfish and all canapés. Add 1 teasp. chopped celery leaves to ingredients. Use leaves and stalks as garnish.
SALADS AND SALAD DRESSINGS	Blend chopped celery leaves with all fruit and vegetable salads before adding dressing. As a garnish.
EGG AND CHEESE DISHES SAVOURIES AND SNACKS	Add chopped or green-dried celery leaves to creamed, devilled, stuffed eggs, and omelettes. Blend chopped celery leaves with soft cheeses.

SOUPS, STEWS, AND CASSEROLES	With cream, fish and shellfish chowders, meat and vegetable. In stews of fish, meats, shellfish, especially clam oyster. Add ¼ cup chopped celery leaves to milk when preparing fish and shellfish stews; also in game stews.
FISH	In court bouillon. With stuffed fish. As a garnish.
MEAT	Season all meat dishes: beef, lamb, mutton, veal, pot roasts. Place celery leaves in pot with ingredients; may be removed before serving. In stuffings.
POULTRY AND GAME	Use leaves as a flavouring in all game ragouts. In stuffings.
VEGETABLES	Mix with carrots, onions, peas, tomatoes, green peppers, and other sweet vegetables as a flavouring.
SAUCES	With brown and cream sauce for meat and vegetables.
SANDWICHES AND HERBS	With canned and chopped meats, fish, shellfish, and tomato.

Chervil (Anthriscus cerefolium)

The aroma of chervil is as fragrant and as delicate as the appearance of this lovely feathery bi-annual. It is a most useful herb for the cook because of its very special subtle flavour, which needs experience to be appreciated. It is slightly sweetish and has a pleasantly aromatic scent and taste, difficult to describe. As it is not dominant, it can be used in large quantities; at the same time it improves the flavour of any other herb with which it is combined. It has therefore always been an important part of 'fines herbes', a mixture of herbs called for in so many dishes.

The Romans brought us this herb, but it is more cultivated and used throughout Europe than in this country. It is more widely used in France where it often takes the place of parsley, even for garnishing, and is almost as common. On the Continent the delicious chervil soup is extensively made and many famous sauces are based on this herb.

Chervil, similar also in appearance to parsley, is more delicate and fern-like and the leaves are a lighter shade of green. It grows to the height of 1–1½ ft with small white flowers growing in umbels; in many cases it will remain smaller and become bushy. A hardy biennial, it grows best when sown in late summer, in well-drained light soil, for harvesting in the spring, and it is one of the first herbs to be used after the winter has gone. A weed-free sunny spot is liked by chervil during winter, but it prefers half shade in the summer. It is a mild-flavoured herb and is used rather in the quantity of a vegetable, for instance, for soup; it should, therefore, be grown in greater quantities than other herbs. Sown in flat boxes it will grow inside or on the window-sill, and the contents of half a box to a box can be used for a soup.

It has always been known that chervil has blood-cleansing qualities and in years gone by was used in particular for lent dishes to help the spring cleaning of the body. With its refreshing flavour it has been greatly welcomed after the winter as the first fresh, green, yet spicy addition to whet the appetite. It was also taken to increase perspiration and the leaves finely chopped and warmed were applied to bruises and painful joints.

Chervil improves every dish to which it is added and can flavour all foods for which parsley is used; Béarnaise sauce requires chervil and it should be put in vinaigrette and wine sauces. It plays an important part in the Frankfurter Maundy Thursday soup. It will benefit all salads, particularly in spring, and while its flavour is most noticeable when added to food which need not be cooked, it is at its best in chervil soup; for this and the equally good chervil sauce it must be used GENEROUSLY.

Chervil Soup
  (page 215)
Baked Potatoes with
  Chervil
  (page 272)

Chervil Sauce
  (page 279)
Chervil Soufflé
  (page 202)

Day-to-day dishes for which Chervil is traditionally used:

FRUIT AND VEGETABLE
  COCKTAILS,
  APPETIZERS AND
  HORS D'ŒUVRES

Vegetable cocktails; with crab; on canapés.

SALADS AND SALAD DRESSINGS	Raw vegetable salads, on green salads, potato, and cucumber salads.
EGG AND CHEESE	Added to cream cheese; in chervil omelette and any egg dish.
SOUPS, STEWS, AND CASSEROLES	Chervil soup, spinach soup, sorrel soup, and green or spring soup.
VEGETABLES	Sprinkled on boiled or buttered vegetables, also spinach, tomatoes and peas before serving.
SAUCES	Melted chervil butter on steaks and fish. Béarnaise sauce, green sauce, and all sauces for poultry.

Chives (Allium schoenoprasum)

The smallest of the onion family, chives, the 'Infant Onion', has the mildest flavour of them all. Widely known today it has been used for centuries in many parts of the world, its history going back to the days of the ancient Chinese in 3000 B.C. It is an excellent herb for flavouring, even for those who dislike onion taste, and it avoids the slight digestive disturbances which are sometimes caused by onions. Chives also have a stimulating effect on the appetite and are important in invalid cookery.

A hardy perennial, chives have slender grass-like leaves growing from small white flat bulbs which are close together in clusters. The small, round mauve flowerhead grows from the main stem, but this is usually nipped off because the plants are grown only for their 'grass'. They are easy to grow if the soil is not too poor and require little attention. They are important for the gardener because chives will be available for use early in the year before other onions are ready. Indoors they will flourish in pots in good rich soil.

Chives is really one of the most indispensable herbs for our daily use. Its delicate savour is a great improvement to salads, raw vegetables, cheese, and omelettes. Soups, thick or clear, potatoes, pancakes, and sauces would never be the same without chives. It is also the main ingredient of the famous Frankfurter Green Sauce, excellent with new potatoes, boiled beef, or cold meat. Chives butter – chopped chives mixed with butter – makes an excellent accompaniment for grilled meat or fish. Finally, the little flat bulbs can be pickled like small onions. Only with delicate vegetables must chives be used with care; in most dishes it can be used GENEROUSLY.

Frankfurter Green Sauce   Vichyssoise
    (page 285)   (page 213)
Chive Potato Cakes   Sausage Salad
    (page 271)   (page 188)

Day-to-day dishes for which Chives are traditionally used:

APPETIZERS, HORS D'ŒUVRES	Can be mixed with nearly any *hors d'œuvres*.
SALADS AND SALAD DRESSINGS	In green salads, mixed vegetables, potato, or cucumber salad; shell-fish salad.
EGG AND CHEESE DISHES	In cottage and cream cheese, omelettes; pancakes; stuffed eggs.
SOUPS, STEWS, AND CASSEROLES	In asparagus, bean or potato soup; in clear consommé; vichyssoise; in stews and casseroles where mild onion flavour is required.
VEGETABLES, POTATOES, RICE, AND PASTA	As a garnish over potatoes, carrots, and other vegetables; add to plain rice just before serving.
SAUCES, DIPS, AND ACCOMPANIMENTS	In white and tomato sauce add before serving; in herb butters.

Dill (Anethum graveolens)

Dill cannot be compared with or substituted by any other herb; it stands alone. Such is the nature of this herb that once tasted its fascinating flavour is demanded again and again. It is sharply aromatic and yet slightly sweetish with a fragrance peculiarly its own. Its popularity stretches from America to Russia.

In Scandinavia dill is as popular as parsley and is used not only for most of the fish dishes and vegetables but also for decoration. Poland, Czechoslavakia, Austria, Germany, in fact, the whole of Central Europe are also passionately interested in the traditional dill flavour. It is most used for pickling cucumbers, probably with the intention to make them and fish more easily digestible. At the same time, bland vegetables are greatly improved by dill flavour.

Apart from its flavour it has digestive and sedative qualities. Its name arises from the Norse word 'dilla', to lull, and its digestive power is illustrated by its traditional use in the babies' gripe-water in this country. It may be that as a solution to digestive uneasiness, in the baby as well as in the adult, it leads to quietening the baby and makes it sleep. At the same time, dill seeds, called 'Meeting House' seeds, were taken at church in the early morning to prevent people from feeling hungry.

Dill is an annual which can grow to about 3 ft high with a hollow stem and finely-cut thread-like leaves. These are similar to fennel but are set more widely apart and are bluish-green in colour. At the top of the main stem grows the flower umbel, consisting of tiny yellow flowers, which appears from June to August. These flowerheads, when already starting to develop seeds, are used for pickling cucumbers. The root structure is weak so transplanting is not usually successful. It should not be grown near fennel as cross-pollination takes place and the resulting plants are neither dill nor fennel.

Dill is grown from seed. While it needs no special requirements as to soil it will be found that it is, however, a tender fragile plant which has difficulties in withstanding adverse conditions. With favourable soil and good weather conditions dill grows like a weed, but if dill becomes dry in light soil during a drought or has to stand stagnant humidity, it may not grow at all. A well-drained soil and a sunny spot gives dill the best chance, and if kept well watered it will produce a mass of foliage.

Dill can be planted in pots or boxes indoors as it is a quick-growing plant, but it will never reach the height of outdoor dill. Leaves can be picked from the indoor plant when needed.

The difference between dill herb and dill seed lies in the degree of pungency and there are occasions where the seed is better because of its sharper flavour. Where a salt-free diet must be followed the seed, whole or ground, is a valuable replacement. In the kitchen, dill seed is used as a flavouring for soups, lamb stew, and in grilled or boiled fish. It can also add spiciness to rice dishes.

The most frequent use for the dill herb is with fish, salads, and delicate vegetables, and in particular for pickling cucumbers. Fresh leaves, finely chopped or green-dried mixed with cream cheese, make an unusual spread. For many dishes dill can be used generously but it is a herb which improves rather than dominates the flavour of food. For this reason it should be used WISELY, sometimes GENEROUSLY.

Dill Potatoes   Avocado Dill Dressing
   (page 271)   (page 194)
Dill Meat Cakes
   (page 238)

Day-to-day dishes for which Dill is traditionally used:

APPETIZERS   With fish spreads; for canapés.

SALADS AND SALAD   With green salads, cucumber, potato
   DRESSINGS   and tomato salads; with sour
                                cream on cucumbers; pickled
                                cucumbers; seeds in dressings;
                                for avocado pears, potatoes and
                                cucumber.

EGGS AND CHEESE DISHES   Egg sandwiches; with cottage or
SAVOURIES AND SNACKS   cream cheese; pancakes; ome-
                                lettes.

SOUPS, STEWS, AND   A little with bean, pea, tomato,
   CASSEROLES   chicken soups, fish soups.

FISH   With halibut, mackerel, salmon, sea
                                trout, in fact with most fish
                                recipes.

MEAT   On grilled steaks, on chops and with
                                boiled meats; seeds in meat pies,
                                lamb stews.

POULTRY   With roast chicken, turkey, or duck;
                                seeds in fricassees.

VEGETABLES AND   Use with string beans, peas and
   POTATOES   tomatoes; on mashed potatoes
                                and parsnips; seeds with cabbage,
                                beets, and cauliflower; dill pota-
                                toes.

SAUCES   In all fish sauces; on its own as
                                dill sauce.

SANDWICHES   In cucumber sandwiches in place of
                                salt and pepper.

The Elder (Sambucus nigra)

The elder tree is the most useful plant. All parts were used in
former times; the hollow stem, the leaves, the flowers, and the

fruit. Due to the fact that at one time it was supposed to be a protection against witches, people are even now afraid to cut down elder. The elder tree can, therefore, be found practically everywhere. We are mainly concerned here with the flowers which have versatile uses; they are usually white and can be detected through their sweet heavy scent in June and July. The dried flowers contain a volatile oil and a number of other important constituents which explain their manifold uses for culinary, medicinal, and cosmetic purposes.

The elder grows to a considerable height. It has large dark green leaves; the flowers hang in umbel-like clusters and have to be picked carefully. The outer flowers open first and there is difficulty in harvesting as all the flowers must be out, but not over. The flowerheads must be carefully handled, not bruised, and should be spread out, without touching each other and their heads down, on fine nylon net over a frame for drying. If all this care is taken they will retain their colour. The little fruits which ripen in September or October when they become shiny/violet are excellent for sauces, juices, and have a reputation of being very helpful against autumn and winter colds.

The fresh flowers can be used for one of the best summer desserts – elder flower fritters – made from fresh elder flowers picked from the hedgerows (Recipe, page 304). The flowers also make an excellent refreshing summer drink, very popular with children. They add a pleasant distinctive sweet flavour to milk dishes, jellies, jams, to gooseberry, and apple tart. They can be tied in a muslin bag, boiled or baked with milk, cooked with jam, and be removed before serving. The dried flowers make a delightfully flavoured tisane, strongly reminiscent of muscatel. It promotes perspiration in the case of colds and is a pleasant alternative to aspirin, particularly if mixed with equal parts of lime flowers and chamomile, most effective if taken hot in bed. This tisane is also sleep-inducing. It has the effect of stimulating the glandular system.

Indian or China tea can be flavoured by adding 1 part dried elder flower to 2 parts of tea.

Elder flower water or tea has been used for eye or skin lotions and it is good for washing and as a bath addition. For cosmetic suggestions, see page 63.

The elder-berries can be added to jam or made into a juice. They have the reputation of cleansing the blood-stream. Juice made of elder-berries is good for chills and people who suffer from sciatica and neuralgia. Wherever they grow, both flowers and berries are found in large quantities and can be used LAVISHLY.

Elder Flower Fritters   Elder Flower Drinks
   (page 304)   (page 40)
Elder Flower Milk   Elder-berry Sauces
   (page 329)   (page 291)

Day-to-day dishes for which the Elder is traditionally used:

SAUCES	Elder-berry sauce.
SWEETS AND DESSERTS	Elder flower fritters; with apple dishes; in milk dishes; jams and jellies.
DRINKS	Elder flower milk; on its own as a tea; also added to Indian or China tea; as a refreshing summer drink.
HEALTH VALUE	Elder flower tea in case of colds; promotes perspiration, etc.
COSMETIC SUGGESTIONS	Elder flower water for eye and skin lotions. Elder flowers (dried) for washing and as a bath addition; also addition to facial steam bath for face packs and face cream; stimulating and tonic.

Fennel (Foeniculum vulgare)

Fennel is one of the earliest known herbs. Its close association with fish is most likely due to its reputation that for many generations it has helped in the digestion of oily fish such as mackerels, eels, and salmon, in boiling and grilling, and that it also grows wild round the coast of Britain. This has probably added to the fact that the fishermen who caught the fish used fennel for flavouring fish and avoiding any digestive difficulties it may cause. It also has the reputation of making fat people lean, already known to the Greeks. Apart from digestive qualities, it is an excellent herb for the eyes, and its cosmetic effect on the skin has also been known throughout the ages.

Fennel is a tall, graceful perennial of bushy growth, with strong shiny stems and leaves divided into feathery segments. The flowers appearing in June, are light yellow and arranged in umbels. As a garden herb it will grow on almost any soil, but thrives best in a sunny well-drained position. Cut down to approximately 4 in. fennel will do well in a pot, even in the smoky atmosphere of window-sills in town or indoors.

The various constituents, apart from the fatty oils which are contained in fennel, give it an anti-spasmodic, anti-inflammatory calming effect. It also stimulates the appetite and is one of the constituents of gripewater for babies. Its main effect is considered to be on the eyes, and compresses steeped in fennel tea, placed on the eyes is suggested for inflamed eyelids, watering eyes, as well as strengthening the eyes and improving the sight. Fennel was used particularly during Lent for its anti-flatulent effect, and it also satisfied the cravings of hunger on fast-days. The reputation for reducing overweight could probably be applied to the wish for slimming. The cosmetic properties, which are recommended against wrinkles, suggest facial packs.

There are many suggestions and recipes for using fennel which come from various countries. One elegant and subtle way is to use fennel with bass or other similar fish. It is centred round the idea of grilling bass on a bed of fennel, then pouring brandy over it; it is set alight and served burning, impregnated with the noble flavour of burnt fennel.

The feathery leaves with their very slight aniseed flavour added to salads, soups, and sauces, make these delicious. Also with soft cheeses, in pickling cucumbers and with cabbage, fennel finds its place. Though it has a hidden tang it can be used lavishly when well known, but at first it is still one to be used WISELY.

Fennel Sauce (page 279)	Mimosa Eggs (page 204)
Bass, Mullet, or Mackerel Flambé au Fenouil (page 226)	Fish Soup (page 221)

Day-to-day dishes for which Fennel is traditionally used:

APPETIZERS	Slimming cocktails; in spreads for canapés, mackerel, crab, snails.
SALADS AND SALAD DRESSINGS	Salads and salad dressings, especially cucumber salad, potato salad, green salads, etc.

SOUPS AND STEWS	For most soups; add to stock and to fish stews; add to water or stock for fish.
FISH	For oily fish like mackerel, eel and salmon. Also for garnishing fish; bass on burnt fennel, etc., in fish-cakes and fish casseroles.
VEGETABLES —	With most vegetables mixed with other herbs; beans, cabbage, cauliflower, tomatoes; young peas instead of mint.
SAUCES	Fennel sauce with fish.
HERB TEAS	Seeds in fennel tea and in seed tea. Reputed to have slimming qualities.
COSMETIC SUGGESTIONS	Face packs for wrinkles. Fennel tea excellent for the eyes.

Lemon Balm (Melissa officinalis)

The sweet lemon-scented lemon balm, or Melissa – to give it its Greek name – is an old and highly valued medicinal, as well as culinary herb. Wholesome and refreshing teas were made from the leaves which, whilst preserving good health, were also delicious to drink. The relaxing effect of this anti-spasmodic tea suggest its use as an early cup of tea or as an after-dinner drink, a custom which has been accepted by an increasing number of people. It was believed to bring long life; for example, Llewellyn, a Prince of Glamorgan, who took melissa tea morning and evening, lived to be 108. At the same time, it adds a refreshing lemon flavour to many other drinks and dishes, particularly to sweets.

Lemon balm is a shrubby perennial growing from 2–3 ft high. It has light green, heart-shaped leaves which are wrinkled and deeply veined, give off a strong lemony scent and have a very distinct flavour. The little flowers are creamy white and grow in tiny loose bundles in the axils of the upper leaves.

Lemon balm can be grown from seed or by dividing the roots in spring or autumn. It is extremely easy to grow anywhere though it prefers fairly rich moist soil in a sunny sheltered position. In fact, it often spreads like a weed and people do not know what to do with it. It grows well indoors or in a window-box, again with rich soil and plenty of moisture. It is one of the first herbs to appear in early spring.

The health-giving properties of lemon balm are many; it has a calming effect on the nervous system which helps relaxation and dispels over-tiredness and incipient headaches and migraine. It also stimulates the heart.

A few lemon balm leaves added to China tea makes a refreshing drink. In the summer it adds its cool fragrant flavour to fruit juices, particularly fresh orange juice, wine cups, and iced teas; on its own as melissa tea it is excellent and has all the refreshing, medicinal effects described above. Freshly chopped or green-dried, the leaves can be used on salads, sauces, egg, and milk dishes. It is also good with chicken and fish dishes where its delicate lemon taste adds a distinctive flavour; it is one of the sugar-saving herbs and together with sweet cicely adds a sweet lemon flavour to all sweet dishes. It can be used LAVISHLY.

Melissa Tea
  (page 46)
Orange Chiffon
  (page 297)

Peach Tart
  (page 296)
Flavoured Salzburger Nockerl
  (page 302)

Day-to-day dishes for which Lemon Balm is traditionally used:

APPETIZERS	Tomato juice. Shrimp and prawn cocktails.
SALADS AND SALAD DRESSINGS	On tomato or cucumber salads; in French dressing. Freshly chopped fresh or green-dried lemon balm (possibly reconstituted) added to fresh tomato or mixed green salad or to their dressings.
SOUPS, STEWS, AND CASSEROLES	Added to asparagus and vegetable soups just before serving. Add to stews.
FISH	With fish baked or boiled.
MEAT	Rub lamb with chopped leaves before roasting.
POULTRY AND GAME	Rub on chicken before roasting. Add to stuffings for poultry and game.

VEGETABLES, POTATOES, With mushrooms.
  RICE, AND PASTA
SAUCES   In herb sauces; fish sauces; cream
                                  sauces; and in marinades.
SWEETS AND DESSERTS   In fruit salads; jellies and custards.
PARTY IDEAS WITH HERBS, In fruit drinks, lemonade, wine cups,
  INCLUDING DRINKS   sherbet, and cooling drinks.
HERB TEAS   Melissa tea, hot.

Lovage (Levisticum officinalis)

Lovage is almost a herb garden in itself. In shape of leaves and
flavour it resembles celery but is much larger and much stronger;
it can replace celery leaves, however, when they are not in season.
Its flavour is reminiscent of Maggi, the famous yeast extract.
Indeed, it is known on the Continent as the 'Maggi herb' and is
widely used in soups, stews, and casseroles.

Lovage is a giant-sized perennial herb which grows 6–7 ft high.
From the straight hollow stem grow dark-green shiny leaves,
themselves stalked and they are divided into narrow ridge-like
segments. Towards the top of the stem the leaves diminish and
the stalks end in the flowerheads which are clusters of greenish-
yellow flowers. The seeds are brown when ripe, resembling those
of caraway and have as strong an aromatic smell and flavour
as the plant itself.

There are few requirements when growing lovage. It prefers
rich, moist soil where the roots can go deep; only heavy clay
soils are less suitable. Propagation can be done by sowing seed,
though germination is slow, by buying plants or by dividing
roots in spring. It flowers from June to August. Though it dies
down in the winter lovage can withstand quite severe weather
and can remain in the same ground for a number of years.

The reputation lovage has for deodorizing both internally and
externally is well known on the Continent. It stimulates the digestive organs and has a diuretic action through its cleansing properties. Lovage was also used as a 'bath herb', a refreshing cleanser
of the skin.

The unique flavour of lovage will give character to vegetable,
meat, and fish dishes and it is most excellent when used in soup.
Its strong yeast-like flavour gives the impression that a complete
soup extract has been added; as it replaces meat and bones in a
soup or casserole it should be used in sufficient quantity to give

strength to such dishes. It is a little spicier than other herbs and until it becomes familiar to the herb cook, it should be used ECONOMICALLY.

Lovage Soup
  (page 216)
Farmer's Omelette
  (page 206)

Ham Lovage Spread
  (page 178)
Lovage Cream Sauce
  (page 280)

Day-to-day dishes for which Lovage is traditionally used:

APPETIZERS	Lovage biscuits; with ham spread.
SALADS AND SALAD DRESSINGS	With tossed green salads, all raw salads. Added to mayonnaise, to kohlrabi, and sauerkraut.
EGGS AND CHEESE	In omelettes.
SOUPS, STEWS, AND CASSEROLES	Any mixed vegetable soup, lovage soup, clear stock; meat stews; fish chowders.
POULTRY AND GAME	Rub birds before roasting.
VEGETABLES	Improves all vegetables; leaves and stems cooked as a vegetable.
SAUCES, DIPS, AND ACCOMPANIMENTS	Lovage cream sauce; fish sauce; meat gravies.
HERB TEAS	Fragrant tisane – more like a broth – can be taken with salt rather than with sugar. Lovage cocktail.

Marigold (Calendula officinalis)

Marigold – a flower which can be found in most gardens – is easy to grow. Only the florets of marigold are used for culinary and cosmetic purposes, though they have also had the reputation of having medicinal value in former times. The flower petals can be used in salads, omelettes, rice, buns, and as a substitute for the expensive and rare saffron. They colour and flavour dishes and the colouring substance, which is similar to that in carrots, has an excellent subtle flavouring quality at the same time.

Marigold is an annual, growing to a height of 20 in. and the simple, boldly coloured flowers in many shades from light yellow to orange red are a pleasant addition to any garden. They grow in any kind of soil, and like a position in full sun. They can be sown straight on to the site in March or April. If the dead flower heads are picked, they will bloom continuously until November.

The petals can be used either fresh or dried and have to be pulled away from the flower centre for drying. If they are dried in thin layers in a low temperature they will retain the beautiful yellow or orange colour. Marigold petals impart a very delicate flavour and a strong colour. A small addition of crushed petals, as well as chopped leaves, give a delightful tang to salads. The dried petals in buns, bread puddings, or any baked sweets make an interesting change. When marigold is used in place of saffron with rice, it provides the look of saffron rice, but a slightly different subtle flavour and is most useful. Also savoury rice with marigold and their use in omelettes, make these dishes much more attractive.

For buns and cakes marigold petals can be soaked in a muslin bag in a small cup of hot milk; then the milk can be used for baking after it has cooled. Marigold petals have been used externally in oils and ointments, in the treatment of wounds, old scars, or other skin troubles. They can be used in quantity, particularly for colouring; indeed at all times they should be used LAVISHLY.

Marigold Rice
  (page 274)
Poultry Pilaf
  (page 254)

Marigold Sweet Buns
  (page 306)

Day-to-day dishes for which Marigold is traditionally used:

SALADS AND SALAD DRESSINGS	For all salads and salad dressings.
EGG AND CHEESE	Omelettes.
FISH	$\frac{1}{2}$ teasp. crushed petals to fish stews and stock in which fish is cooked.
MEAT	Roast beef.
POULTRY AND GAME	Venison or any game stew; chicken broth.
SWEETS AND DESSERTS	Bread pudding.
CAKES	Marigold buns and cakes.
COSMETIC SUGGESTIONS	Soaked in oil or used in ointments for the skin; for scars, particularly old ones. For tired feet.

Marjoram, Sweet (Origanum majorana)

Marjoram has a strong, sweet, yet spicy flavour and is essentially a meat herb. It combines well with made-up dishes such as sausages and meat loaf, adding a very special flavour to them. It is often used together with thyme, to which it is considered a twin. Marjoram has been a popular herb throughout its long history; this was mainly due to the fact that marjoram contains preserving and disinfectant qualities, which – before the days of refrigeration – made it invaluable in the kitchen.

There are several varieties of marjoram; the most important for cooking is sweet knotted marjoram, others are pot marjoram (Origanum onites) which is a perennial and stays with us throughout the winter, but is not as good a flavour as sweet marjoram. Wild marjoram (Origanum vulgare) is a spicier plant, particularly so when grown in hotter climates such as Spain or Mexico and is known as Oregano in North America.

Sweet marjoram is a half-hardy annual in this country because it cannot withstand frost; the bushy plant grows about 8 in. high with very small greyish-green leaves. The knotty flower growth appears at the top of the tough, woody stem, and these green knots eventually become pale mauve. The flowers bloom from June to September and have a strong aromatic scent. Marjoram should be cut when the knots are about to break open.

Marjoram seed should be sown in a frame in March and in May planted out in the warmest most sheltered spot available. The plants need a medium rich, moist soil. In the window-box it needs rich soil and a sunny sill.

For medicinal purposes marjoram was rarely used, though the volatile oil it contains is a good external application for sprains and bruises; also the freshly expressed juice from the leaves sniffed up the nostrils is helpful for headaches and insomnia. The crushed dried leaves were used as a snuff.

Strong meats are all improved by being rubbed with marjoram before roasting. It makes any potato dish more interesting and can be used with most vegetables, especially when stuffed, and above all with all pulses. Its characteristic flavour comes out best when used for stuffings or forcemeat of any kind. However, it is a strong herb and can easily overpower other flavours; those new to this herb should use it JUDICIOUSLY.

Boned Stuffed Chicken
  (page 257)
Marjoram Potato Pie
  (page 271)

Goulash
  (page 236)
Marjoram Liver Dumplings
  (page 247)

Day-to-day dishes for which Marjoram is traditionally used:

APPETIZERS	Cream cheese; stuffed mushrooms.
SALADS AND SALAD DRESSINGS	Very little in French dressing; in chicken salad.
EGG AND CHEESE	In scrambled egg; cheese dishes.
SOUPS AND STEWS	Small sprig or $\frac{1}{4}$ teasp. green-dried, in soups and stews.
FISH	With sea-food and salt fish.
MEAT	Add to beef, pork, lamb, and veal before roasting; with sausages, meat loaves, liver dumplings, rissoles; in stuffings and force-meat.
POULTRY AND GAME	With rabbit; rubbed inside and out for poultry; in poultry stuffings.
VEGETABLES AND POTATOES	Sparingly with carrots, peas, marrows, and mushrooms; with lentils and all pulses; potato dishes; stuffed vegetables.
SWEETS AND DESSERTS	Milk puddings (sparingly).

The Mints: Spearmint (Mentha viridis *or* M. spicata)
Bowles Mint (Mentha rotundifolia) (Bowles variety)
Peppermint (Mentha piperita)

The distinctive and fragrant flavours of mints play an important part in the preparation of many foods and drinks. There are three main varieties used in cooking: Spearmint, Bowles Mint, and Peppermint. Spearmint is the one most commonly used, but bowles mint, though stronger, can be used equally well for the same flavouring purposes and is considered best for mint sauce. Ideally the two should be mixed. Peppermint is used mainly as a beverage – Peppermint tea – and in sweets, but there are many dishes where its extra spiciness can be used with advantage.

Spearmint grows about 1 ft high with a straight stem and long, narrow leaves. The flowers grow in pinkish clusters at the top of the stem. Bowles mint has large round woolly leaves of a lighter green and grows much taller. Peppermint grows about 2 ft high and the leaves are a distinctive reddish-green colour with a strong aroma. As the mints are hybrids and have various strains in their ancestry they cannot be sown. Either plants have to be bought or root divisions or cuttings taken. They grow well in moist rich soils in a warm, sheltered position and the strong roots spread rapidly; they have to be restricted not to encroach on other plants. Spearmint can be grown successfully in a 4 in. pot on a window-sill when the height should be kept to about 6 in.

Mint is most commonly used for mint sauce, but it also improves peas and beans, carrots, beetroot, boiled potatoes, and spinach. It combines well in fruit salad and other fruit dishes, also in cooling drinks. The famous Mint Julep is not only refreshing but is also a 'pick-me-up'. Peppermint is best known as a health-giving tea, refreshing, and settling digestive upsets at the same time, but, as a culinary herb, it adds a delicious flavour to roast meats and vegetables, also to jellies and jams. The mints enhance both sweet and savoury dishes and can be used GENEROUSLY, with the exception of peppermint which has to be used CARE-FULLY.

Mint Sauce with Lemon   Mint Julep
  (page 280)   (page 326)
Mint Syrup   Peppermint Tea and Milk
  (page 328)   (page 46)

Day-to-day dishes for which Mint is traditionally used:

	Mint	*Peppermint*
FRUIT AND VEGETABLE COCKTAILS AND APPETIZERS	Fruit juices	Fruit and vegetable cocktails.
SALAD AND SALAD DRESSINGS	Vegetable salads.	Potato salad.
EGG AND CHEESE	Cream cheese and processed cheeses.	
SOUPS, STEWS, AND CASSEROLES	Pea soup, lamb stew.	Lentil soup.

FISH	Baked, boiled, or grilled fish.	Eels.
MEAT	On roast beef and lamb.	On roast beef and lamb.
POULTRY AND GAME	Rubbed on chicken before roasting.	
VEGETABLES, POTATOES	Carrots, peas, all beans, spinach, cabbage, new potatoes.	Carrots, potatoes, peas and cabbage, cauliflower.
SAUCES	Meat marinades, herb sauces, mint sauce.	
SWEETS AND DESSERTS	Stewed fruit, ice-cream, jellies, custards; mint syrup, pears, melon, and apple sauce.	Add a little to jams and jellies.
DRINKS	In fruit and wine punch, chocolate, iced drinks. Mint Julep. Mint tea.	In hot and iced tea, fruit cups, chocolate drinks.

Nasturtium (Tropaeolum majus *or* minus)

Here is a tasty and health-giving herb which was hardly ever considered a herb at all. Its leaves, petals, and seeds have been used in the East and in Europe for centuries. As it is so simple to grow this attractive flowering plant in every garden, it seems worthwhile to discuss its properties, some of which were only discovered recently. The peppery pungency of the leaves makes nasturtium an excellent substitute for pepper and as there are many people these days who like their food spicy, but should not take too much pepper or salt, nasturtium can become a necessity to them. In addition it is considered a valuable anti-bioticum – a kind of herbal penicillin – and is used as such in German-speaking countries. It is possible that these anti-biotic qualities are connected with the unusually high content of Vitamin C in nasturtium leaves. They have, therefore, become a food which is both attractive and protective and healthy at the same time.

Research has shown that the highest Vitamin C content was found in the leaves before flowering in July.

The custom of eating petals and using them for tea and salads came from the orient. The flowers do not dry well and have to be used while fresh, but the leaves can be dried and used all the year round as garnishes for food and chopped up for canapés.

The plant likes a sandy, moderately rich, soil but will also grow everywhere; it is usually a strong-growing annual climber with orange flowers, but the more recently developed dwarf variety is a non-climber. The colours are usually attractive, and a more colourful border with a background of a hedge or shrubs can hardly be imagined. The leaves are kidney-shaped and the flowers grow in many colours from yellow-orange to browny-red. The best varieties are those of compact habit, while trailers can be left to cover walls and boundaries. All seeds can be sown where the plants are to bloom. Nasturtium also helps to provide an essential prevention to pests because they sometimes attract aphides to themselves and keep roses, soft fruit, etc., free from them. If they are grown in a herb garden amongst other herbs they are often not visited by pests at all. Nasturtium will grow well if sown in a window-box and will not only be an attraction to every window, but provide Vitamin C for the flat-dwellers.

Nasturtium leaves have to be used cautiously because of their strong peppery flavour. In sandwich spreads they provide and retain a spicy flavour. In cream cheese, for instance, 2 teasp. to a ¼ lb. cheese are excellent, but they must not be allowed to stand mixed with the cream cheese for a long time, as nasturtium will turn the cheese bitter. Mixed shortly before serving, they are an excellent addition, as they are for tossed, dressed, or undressed salads and between slices of bread and butter. Both young leaves and flowers are delicious in salads and the seeds, pickled when young and green, are a substitute for capers. When the young leaves are finely chopped they are not only the best substitute for pepper, but in the case of a need for Vitamin C to prevent infections, or as an anti-biotic to combat any existing infection, ways and means will have to be invented in which chopped nasturtium leaves can be used. However, it is not advisable that more than one-third to two-thirds of an ounce should be eaten at one time or one ounce per day should be distributed over several meals. Most of this can be eaten on bread and butter. Use this herb WITH CAUTION.

In the case of 'flu symptoms, such as sore throats, difficulty in swallowing, pains in joints, and general aches and headaches, it has been observed that the finely chopped, green leaves of nasturtium produce a noticeable reduction of symptoms and – if used over longer periods – the symptoms may disappear altogether.

Nasturtium Dressing   Nasturtium Canapé and Sandwiches
  (page 96)   (page 79 and 309)

Day-to-day dishes for which Nasturtium is traditionally used:

APPETIZERS	In canapés; in spreads.
SALADS AND SALAD DRESSINGS	Leaf and flower in green salads; pickled seeds as mock capers; vegetable salads.
EGG AND CHEESE	With cream cheese. (Page 280)
SAUCES	Pickled seeds in nasturtium sauce.
SANDWICHES	Young leaves chopped between bread and butter.
HEALTH VALUE	High Vitamin C content. Antibiotic against colds and other infections.

Onion Green (Allium fistulosum)

The grass-like leaves of the Welsh onion we call 'Onion Green'. While they are stronger than chives, which belong to the same family, they are yet milder than onion. They are a most useful flavouring not only for those who dislike a strong onion flavour, but even in conjunction with onions, for they add something more to a dish which onion alone does not give.

Welsh onion is a hardy perennial and multiplies rapidly through division of roots. They grow on right through the winter so that the leaves or 'grass' are available all the year round. They are, therefore, very useful, providing more of an onion flavour than chives. While onion green form the bulk and the basis of onion flavour in cooking, chives with its more distinguished flavour is preferable in uncooked dishes, like salads, cream cheese, and even in omelettes.

The main qualities of onion green comes out best, however, when using it as a basic flavour for preparing vegetables, soups, stews, casseroles, and fillings. At the very start, after chopped onions are sautéd, onion green and then parsley should be added and sautéd before the vegetables or other ingredients are included. This adds a special punch and a wider range of onion flavour, as well as strength, to such dishes.

A vegetable filling of ravioli should have onion green as a basis to which bread and spinach can be added (Recipe, page 321).

Onion green can also be used for most dishes for which chives are used; it is excellent in cream cheese and egg mixtures to be used as spreads. In all cases onion green can be used freely ACCORDING TO TASTE.

Savoury Onion Green Tart Vegetable-filled Ravioli
  (page 267)   (page 277)
Savoury Bread Mixture
  (page 321)

Day-to-day dishes for which Onion Green is traditionally used:

APPETIZERS, HORS D'ŒUVRES	Can be mixed with nearly any *hors d'œuvres*.
SALADS AND SALAD DRESSINGS	In green salads, mixed vegetables, potato, or cucumber salad; shell-fish salad.
EGG AND CHEESE DISHES, SAVOURIES AND SNACKS	In cottage and cream cheese; omelettes; pancakes; stuffed eggs.
SOUPS, STEWS, AND CASSEROLES	In mixed vegetable soup, minestrone, asparagus, bean, or potato soup; in clear consommé; vichyssoise; in stews and casseroles.
VEGETABLES, POTATOES, RICE, AND PASTA	As a garnish over potatoes, carrots, and other vegetables; add to plain rice just before serving, to bread or meat filling, forcemeat.
SAUCES, DIPS, AND ACCOMPANIMENTS	In white and tomato sauce add before serving; in herb butters.

Parsley (curly) (Petroselinum crispum)

Parsley will go with every dish and cannot be surpassed for its versatility in the kitchen. Also, any dish takes on a party look when garnished with parsley. Its fresh green appearance and fragrant aroma delight the eye and stimulate the appetite. It is, in fact, the main herb in the kitchen and cooking in general can hardly be imagined without parsley.

Parsley is a hardy biennial and the variety most used is curly parsley. The bright green leaves are deeply divided and curled over; it grows about 2 ft high. The delicate greenish-white flower clusters appear during the second year. Parsley is not difficult to grow once it has been realized that it is slow in germinating. The soil needs to be rich and well worked so that the roots can grow deep. Parsley likes a shady position. It is advisable to sow parsley every year to ensure a good crop. It grows successfully sown in pots or boxes indoors and outdoors on the window-sill.

Parsley has always been in demand from ancient times when it was considered a family medicine and all parts of the plant were used. It was mainly used in this country as a diuretic tonic tea and as a help for rheumatism. It has many health-giving properties contained in its vitamins and minerals; particularly its content of Vitamin C makes it an important daily addition to our food.

Parsley emphasizes the flavour of foods without itself adding a strong accent. It even masks the odour of strong vegetables such as onions and carrots. It flavours soups and sauces, salads, and egg dishes while there are special dishes like parsley stuffing and parsley butter for which it is used in quantity. One delicious speciality is fried fresh parsley which is a delicate garnish for fish. Parsley combines well with every other herb and is the basis for most herb mixtures, but whether together or on its own it is such an excellent flavouring and can always be used GENEROUSLY.

Persillade   Lincolnshire Stuffed Chine
  (page 283)   (page 242)
Parslied Chicken
  (page 258)

Parsley can be used with every dish; no list of special uses is therefore added here.

Rosemary (Rosmarinus officinalis)

Perhaps the most fragrant herb of all, rosemary, has a pungent resinous taste which imparts a subtle flavour to foods both sweet and savoury. At the same time it is excellent medicinally, helping a weak digestion, neuralgic pains, and stimulating the circulation and other functions. For these it is taken as a tea and in wine or liqueur. Externally, oil of rosemary is used as a liniment in cases of gout or for sprains and bruises. Water in which rosemary has been boiled is excellent for the skin and, when used in hair-washes, is said to stimulate hair growth.

An evergreen shrub, rosemary grows to about 5 ft. It has succulent leaves green on top and greyish beneath, spiky, which curve slightly, resembling pine needles. The little blue flowers grow in clusters and the whole plant gives off a delicate spicy aroma. It grows best in a light, sandy, dryish soil, requiring a sheltered position even in the south of England. The herb needs more protection in winter than any other herb, and unless it is given this against walls or hedges – it should be grown in pots or tubs and taken indoors during the cold season. Rosemary can be raised from seed or by division of roots or layering. Indoors, it grows most successfully in an enriched loamy soil, but needs to be kept well-watered and restricted in size.

Rosemary has a character very much its own, with its history going back hundreds of years. There are more legends and customs attached to it than to any other herb. One such is the belief that rosemary grew to the height of Our Lord while He was on earth and after His death remained the same height, only growing in breadth.

With its fresh, exciting flavour rosemary can equally well be used for savoury dishes as for jams, jellies, and biscuits; it adds subtlety to fruit salads and cider or claret cup. A few sprigs added to roasting meats, especially lamb, also to poultry, game, and fish, give a delicious taste. It is, however, a strong herb and should at first be used ECONOMICALLY.

Beef Casserole with
    Rosemary
    (page 237)

Rosemary Biscuits
    (page 306)

Rosemary Sauce
    (page 282)

Rosemary Walnuts.
    (page 180)

Day-to-day dishes for which Rosemary is traditionally used:

FRUIT AND VEGETABLE COCKTAILS	In fruit and vegetable cocktails.
EGG AND CHEESE	In omelettes, pancakes, scrambled eggs; with cream cheese.

SOUPS, STEWS, AND CASSEROLES	In meat soups, chicken, pea, spinach soups; in minestrone.
FISH	With strong flavoured fish like eel, halibut.
MEAT	Beef, lamb, pork, and veal roasted.
POULTRY AND GAME	Roast poultry and venison; in stuffings for rabbit, partridge.
VEGETABLES, POTATOES, PASTA	Beans, peas, cauliflower; dumplings; risotto, baked potatoes.
SWEETS AND DESSERTS	Apple jellies, jams; rosemary sugar; fruit salads.
DRINKS	Summer fruit cups – wines and cider cups.
COSMETIC SUGGESTIONS	Rosemary water or tea for skin and hair.

Sage (Salvia officinalis)

In spite of its wide use and popularity sage has lost part of its excellent reputation and its value in the eye of the discriminate user. This can be due to two reasons; firstly, it has been overdone so often and, secondly, if it is badly dried or packed it can spoil dishes with its poor flavour. Only if carefully dried, stored, and packed, and used with discretion, can one begin to understand the tremendous appreciation which the Chinese and Arabs, the Greeks and the Romans, the early Monasteries and the Saxons felt for sage. While other herbs may lose some of their aroma or qualities if badly dried or handled, sage seems to pick up a musty flavour, not originally its own.

Sage is a sub-shrub, about 2 ft high with slender greyish-green leaves, pebbly to the touch; the flowers are spikes of a light purple colour. It will grow almost anywhere, though it will do best, like all herbs, on well-drained soil and grows most luxuriantly in a warm, sunny position. Sage can be increased by division or cuttings and should be renewed every 3 or 4 years for the plants grow woody. They should be planted well apart, otherwise they tend to turn yellow. All sages are good honey plants.

Several old proverbs, Arabian – Old English, testify to the belief that 'sage ensures long life' and sage tea was considered not only a popular drink before tea became well-known but a health-giving one particularly during spring.

Apart from sage and onion stuffing and its use with rich meats such as pork and duck, there are many more ways in which sage can show its particular qualities (with liver, fish, with pulses, game, cottage, or cream cheese; in herb butter, for omelettes, in fritters, pancakes, bean dishes, etc.). Whole leaves, fresh or green-dried, can be wrapped round lamb, veal, and eels for unusual dishes. Sage also gives a surprisingly delicious flavour to summer fruit drinks and cups. But, at all times, sage must be of first-class quality, and as it has a pungent flavour it must be used WITH DISCRETION.

Country-Style Pork (page 242)	Sage Sauce (page 281)
Fresh Eel in Sage Leaves (page 234)	Sage Fritters (page 211)

Day-to-day dishes for which Sage is traditionally used:

EGG AND CHEESE	Cream cheese, herb cheese, soft cheese spreads, fritters, pancakes, omelettes.
SOUPS, STEWS, AND CASSEROLES	Cream soups, meat, vegetable soups, fish chowders, beef, lamb, veal stews, and casseroles.
FISH	In court bouillon or water in which boiling fish (with other herbs) with eels and all fat fish when broiling or grilling.
MEAT	With beef, lamb, mutton, especially pork and veal, when roasted; in stuffings with other herbs. In meat loaves and puddings, with sausage and liver.
POULTRY AND GAME	Chicken, goose, turkey, for rubbing and in stuffing (also with other herbs) sparingly. With hare, rabbit, venison, for rubbing before roasting (also with other herbs).
VEGETABLES	Spinach, beetroot, onions, beans, aubergines, pulses.

SAUCES	With butter sauces for vegetables. In meat gravies.
SANDWICHES AND SNACKS	Sage butter, sage toast, sage stuffing, sage jelly.
DRINKS	Sage tea, sage in 'cups', and apple juice, etc.

Salad Burnet (Sanguisorba minor)

Salad burnet is easy to grow and will stay with us throughout the winter. It provides fresh green foliage all the year round and is therefore suggested to those who grow their own herbs. It has been used since time immemorial but has only been grown in this country since the sixteenth century.

The leaves have a nutty flavour and a slight taste of cucumber. They are suitable in salads – therefore the name salad burnet – and enhance all winter salads. The herb can also be used with other herbs for soups or in all dishes requiring mixed herbs. Like borage it is an excellent herb for flavouring drinks.

The decorative plant grows to a height of 12–15 in. The leaves are pinnate with serrate leaflets and the flowers grow in small round heads, first green and then become reddish. The plant flowers from June to the end of August and is pollinated by wind. When the first flower shoots appear the first cut can be made. The rosette of leaves is a most attractive little bush of greenery during winter in an otherwise dormant herb garden. It even pokes its head through a light fall of snow.

Salad burnet has no special requirements, but likes chalky soil. It should be sown in April and if it is allowed to go to seed it will self-sow. Its broad leaves are always tender and are therefore such a help throughout the winter, and will brighten up in spring. Salad burnet can be cut again and again, therefore only a few plants are needed. A few seeds will grow in a flower-pot for those who have no garden and provide green leaves during the winter.

Salad burnet provides a taste of cucumber for salad mixtures, herb soups and sauces and particularly for claret wine cups and cocktails. It has a similar reputation to borage and can be used as a tonic. Its delicate foliage is an attractive decoration and adds to the appearance of iced drinks as well as to their flavour. All salads with French dressing or mayonnaise, also with asparagus, celery, beans, and mushroom soups benefit by it. The herb should be placed in the soup at the beginning of cooking. Altogether it can be used GENEROUSLY.

Burnet Cocktail   Burnet-Mint Fish Sauce
  (page 325)   (page 288)
Burnet Vinegar
  (page 196)

Day-to-day dishes for which Salad Burnet is traditionally used:

SALADS AND SALAD DRESSINGS	Fresh young tips in vegetable salads; such as in lettuce or mixed-green salads; chopped in French dressing or in mayonnaise. Herb vinegars.
SOUPS, STEWS, AND CASSEROLES	Mushroom, celery, asparagus, and bean soups.
DRINKS	Herb teas; for flavouring iced drinks; in claret cup

Sorrel (Rumex acetosa *and* Rumex scutatus)

Sorrel's contribution to cookery is contained in the slight acidity of its herbage. The best member of the family is French sorrel because of this slightly acid taste which cannot be obtained by any other means. French sorrel soup, made of the leaves, is one of the most excellent soups and is famous in France. The slightly sour flavour stimulates the appetite and is a culinary virtue in itself. It can also be used as a slightly sour seasoning. Care has to be taken that not too much of sorrel is used, and not too often, because part of the plant contains oxalic acid which may be damaging to health if taken in excess; but as a seasoning it can be invaluable with vegetables or any dish which is insipid in itself and for which pepper alone is not the answer.

The Greek and Roman doctors used sorrel leaves for medicinal purposes as a diuretic plant and it has, at times, been recommended for kidney stones. Sorrel is considered to have blood-cleansing and blood-improving qualities, in a similar way to spinach which improves the haemoglobin content of the blood, and sorrel is said to contain Vitamin C and, most likely, iron.

The broad-leafed French sorrel is one of the most frequently cultivated varieties of the sorrels. The leaves are oblong, slightly arrow-shaped at the base and succulent; a slender perennial plant about 2 ft high with spikes of reddish-green flowers from May to July. It grows abundantly and can be easily cultivated. Sorrel can best be propagated by division of the roots in spring or autumn and should be planted out approximately 15 in. apart. It grows best in light, rich soil and full sun, but can also be grown in the shade; if a sheltered position is available it will do well in it. The flowering plants should be cut back to prevent them going to seed and leaves becoming tough. At the end of March, sorrel can be sown like spinach in rows and 4 months after the plants have started to grow they can be cut. Sorrel leaves can also be dried successfully in the same way as other herbs, but colour and flavour must be preserved.

Sorrel, and particularly French sorrel, is excellent if combined with other leaves or herbs as it is sometimes too bitter alone. In a salad sorrel combines well with lettuce and herbs, also sorrel soup with some lettuce added is much improved. For instance, if there is a surplus of lettuce in a garden, lettuce can be cooked and made into a vegetable like spinach by adding sufficient sorrel to make it tasty and valuable. When cooked early in spring as greens, with lettuce and spinach added, sorrel provides a very good vegetable dish. The leaves also feature in a cream soup.

It is an excellent herb with which to experiment and to find out in which of your favourite dishes it will make a difference to the flavour, particularly if used CAREFULLY.

Sorrel Soup
  (page 215)
Potato Salad with Sorrel
  (page 90)

Spinach Purée with Sorrel
  (page 268a)
Sorrel Turnovers
  (page 305).

Day-to-day dishes for which Sorrel is traditionally used:

SALADS AND SALAD DRESSINGS	Tossed green salads; a pinch in French dressing.
EGG AND CHEESE	Omelettes, soufflés.
SOUPS, STEWS, AND CASSEROLES	Sorrel soup, sorrel and lettuce soup.
VEGETABLES	With spinach, cabbage, and lettuce, or young leaves on their own.
PASTRY	Sorrel turnovers.

Summer Savory (Satureia hortensia)

Summer savory is a favourite on the Continent and in America. There it is known as the 'bean-herb' and is widely used for all bean dishes. Underlining the flavour of beans rather than adding a new one, it has a piquant pleasant taste, strong and slightly peppery; it can be used almost as a spice. It can replace both salt and pepper and is a great help to those on a salt-free diet.

A bushy delicate annual, summer savory grows about 1 ft high with sparse dark-green leaves along the stems; the whole plant looks purplish. The pink flowers grow five together in the axils of the leaves and bloom from July to September. It is best to grow from seeds sown in a sunny position. If sown in May or June the herb will be ready for broad, French, runner, and haricot beans. Summer savory can be sown in pots indoors. Its fresh leaves are available throughout the winter.

There is a high content of volatile oil in summer savory which is of medicinal value and, when first brought to this country in the sixteenth century, was infused as a tea for indigestion. This attribute is noticeable when summer savory is added to dishes usually difficult to digest such as cucumber salad, lentils, all the beans, pork, and sausages.

Nowadays beans are available all the year round either fresh, frozen, or tinned, and green-dried summer savory can be bought to go with them. No other dish benefits as much from the addition of summer savory as frozen beans. Any bean flavour lost is recaptured by this addition and their flavour becomes almost that of fresh beans. Besides its excellence with all bean dishes it gives flavour to meat stuffings and vegetables such as cabbage and brussels sprouts. However, it is a pungent herb and until one is familiar with its strength it should be used CAREFULLY.

Chicken with Summer
    Savory
    (page 259)
Broad Beans Sauté
    (page 270)

Bean Salad
    (page 190)

Day-to-day dishes for which Summer Savory is traditionally used:

FRUIT AND VEGETABLE COCKTAILS, APPETIZERS	In vegetable cocktails; cocktail biscuits and rolls.
SALADS AND SALAD DRESSINGS	Raw vegetable salads, bean and tomato salads, pickling cucumbers.
EGG AND CHEESE	In omelettes, pancakes, and soufflés.
SOUPS, STEWS, AND CASSEROLES	In clear broth, bean, lentil, and pea soups; in stews.
FISH	With baked or boiled fish.
MEAT	All roast meats; smoked pork and ham.
POULTRY AND GAME	In stuffings for chicken, duck, and turkey; venison and rabbit stew.
VEGETABLES	For broad beans, French, and runner beans; haricot beans; cabbage, peas, lentils, stuffed marrow, and potatoes.
SAUCES	Savoury butter, tomatoes, and fish sauces. Horseradish sauce and cream.

Sweet Cicely (Myrrhis odorata)

Sweet cicely, unknown to most people for its uses, except in the North of England, is a herb with special qualities in cooking as well as ease of growing. It has a sweetish flavour faintly reminiscent of anise and provides numerous uses as a fragrant herb and as a sugar-saver. It has also a great attraction in the garden because of its beauty as a plant; its charming name and the profusion in which it grows wild as well as cultivated. It is one of the herbs which gives us the longest use during the year as it appears in our gardens in February and is one of the last to go in November; it is therefore a good fresh stand-by almost all the year round; an ever-increasing perennial.

It grows wild in the hilly pastures of the North of England and has been known through the ages among the north-country folk as a useful herb plant. Culpepper assured us: 'It is so harmless you cannot use it amiss.'

Sweet cicely improves all 'bouquets' or mixtures of herbs; it deserves a place in salad dressings, slimming cocktails, in herb butter, delicate soups, and enhances all root vegetables. It tempts children to eat salads or drink juices, particularly when they are not well. It improves sweets, creams, trifles, fruit salads, and is delicious with whipped cream and fruit to which it adds a fresh aromatic flavour.

It has been found most useful as a pleasant way of reducing acidity in tart fruit and in this way helps to save sugar. This is experienced with rhubarb, unripe gooseberries, red or black currants, plums, etc. The large fresh leaves and stalks, or 2–4 teasp. dried sweet cicely perhaps with some lemon balm, added to the boiling water in which fruit is stewed, adds a delightful flavour and helps to save almost half of the sugar needed. This is not only a great help for diabetics but also for the many people who are now trying to save sugar, partly for reasons of slimming, partly because sugar has fallen into disfavour for various health reasons and partly to help children whose sugar intake is usually almost beyond what is good for their health or their teeth.

As sweet cicely is one of the herbs which flavours Chartreuse and therefore suggests many experiments with all kinds of drinks and all kinds of sweets, it has already inspired one or the other new sweets which may go down in culinary history. It is certainly one of the herbs you cannot go wrong with unless its anise flavour is disliked, but this is so slight that it is hardly noticed when used in cooking. Sweet cicely can, in fact, be used as it grows: LAVISHLY.

Hard Sauce (page 291)	Elder-berry Sauce or Soup (page 291)
Plum Salad (page 300)	Orange-Apple Milk Drink (page 329).
	Fruit Cocktail (page 174)

Day-to-day dishes for which Sweet Cicely is traditionally used:

SALADS AND SALAD DRESSINGS	Mixed with other herbs on green salads, with avocado pear dressing.
VEGETABLES	With cabbage and root vegetables.
SAUCES AND ACCOMPANIMENTS	In sweet sauces; in herb butter.
SWEETS AND DESSERTS	In fruit salads; with rhubarb and other tart fruits. In creams, custards, and trifles, and with whipped cream.
DRINKS	In milk drinks, fruit drinks, and fruit cups.

Tarragon (Artemisia dracunculus)

Tarragon is lord of all culinary herbs. The *haute cuisine* of France considers it of supreme importance and bases famous sauces, such as Béarnaise, Hollandaise, or Mousseline on tarragon. Though a strong aromatic herb it has an unusual flavour which is sweet and slightly bitter at the same time. But for all its delicate fragrance it has a hidden tang which only comes out if too much tarragon is used. Tarragon has certainly the most outstanding and distinguished reputation as a herb in sophisticated cookery but has not been used for medicinal purposes.

There are two varieties of tarragon, the French or true tarragon and the Russian which has a less interesting flavour; both are perennial. French tarragon has smoother, shinier and darker leaves, widely spaced on the stems which also carry clusters of whitish woolly flowers. It can never be propagated by seed, plants have to be bought or cuttings obtained. Russian tarragon is said to improve in flavour if grown in the same place for some time; in fact, it is never as excellent as the French tarragon.

For growing, the plants need a dry sunny position in light, well-drained fairly poor soil. The soil should be richer for indoor growing and it should be kept a compact bushy plant, also care must be taken to ensure sufficient drainage; tarragon does not like to have its feet in water.

Chopped tarragon leaves enhance a French dressing and they can be sprinkled on green salads. It is an important ingredient of 'fines herbes', the herb mixture used in omelettes, in marinades for meat, and in stuffings for fish and poultry, in fact in all 'bouquets'. It is excellent on steaks and grilled fish.

Delicate vegetables, such as asparagus and artichokes, are delicious when accompanied by melted butter with chopped tarragon or when the herb is used in fillings for avocado pear. If using good fresh or green-dried French tarragon it can be used GENEROUSLY; otherwise JUDICIOUSLY – beware of hidden tang!

Tarragon Butter
  (page 295)
Sauce Béarnaise
  (page 283)

Chicken with Tarragon
  (page 257).
Tarragon Eggs
  (page 204)

Day-to-day dishes for which Tarragon is traditionally used:

FRUIT AND VEGETABLE COCKTAILS, APPETIZERS	Tomato cocktails, fish cocktails.
SALADS AND SALAD DRESSINGS	In French dressing; on green salads; asparagus and bean salads, chicken salad; tarragon vinegar.
EGG AND CHEESE	In omelettes and scrambled eggs.
SOUPS, STEWS, AND CASSEROLES	Clear broth; chicken, mushroom, tomato, and turtle soups; fish chowders.
FISH	All fish and shellfish baked or boiled.
MEAT	On steaks, sirloin, with veal, sweetbreads; on liver.
POULTRY AND GAME	In stuffings; with chicken, duck, hare, and rabbit.
VEGETABLES	With spinach, courgettes, sauerkraut, salsify, celeriac, asparagus, artichokes.
SAUCES	Herb butter. In marinade for meat. Béarnaise, Hollandaise, Mousseline, and Mayonnaise sauces. In 'fines herbes'.
BREAD, TOAST, AND PASTRY	Yorkshire pudding.

Thyme (Thymus vulgaris)

Thyme is stronger and more 'outspoken' in flavour than any other herb; it is clove-like and pungent and should be used with discretion; it can easily overpower more delicate herbs if too much is used. With tarragon it holds an important place in French cooking. Lemon thyme (Thymus citriodorus), another culinary variety, is not so versatile as garden thyme but can give a most delicious tang and exciting flavour to sweet dishes and drinks.

One of the earliest herbs to reach this country, it became the emblem of courage and soup made of thyme and beer was considered a cure for shyness! Thyme helps in the digestion of fatty food and stimulates the appetite; it also has strong antiseptic qualities in its volatile oil, Thymol. It is this quality which makes it both a part of the Judges posy and the Queen's Maundy Thursday posy which were used as a protection against jail fever and other infectious diseases. Even today the disinfectant and digestive properties of thyme are of great value in sausages, made-up meat and fish dishes. Thyme tea is excellent for coughs and colds, when sweetened with honey. Oil of thyme, distilled from the plant, is used for liniments and in toothpastes and mouth-washes.

Garden thyme is a low perennial evergreen bush and grows about 12 in. high. It has pale mauve flowers which bloom throughout June and the leaves are very small. Lemon thyme is of creeping growth growing only about 6 in. high and is most suitable for rock gardens. The golden leaves have a sharp aromatic scent with a soupçon of lemons.

Thyme flourishes best on chalky but fertile soil; the plants seed themselves and very quickly spread. For indoor growing the plants need to be well trimmed back; when they have recovered from this, they can be transplanted into pots and gradually adapted to indoors.

Thyme helps in the digestion of foods and is the herb to use with fat meats such as mutton or pork and with rich fish such as eels and all shellfish. Thyme is a necessary part of 'bouquet garni' which is called for, and has been adapted to, so many dishes. Such a strong aromatic herb, a little in cooking goes a long way so it should be used with GREAT CARE.

Thyme Jelly   Cheese Logs
  (page 294)   (page 317)
Five Herb Cheese   Cheese Herb Bread
  (page 211)   (page 314)

Day-to-day dishes for which Thyme is traditionally used:

APPETIZERS	Raw vegetable juice; tomato juice; fish and sea-food cocktails; crabs, mussels.
SALADS AND SALAD DRESSINGS	Very small amount in all raw salads.
EGG AND CHEESE	Pancakes; cream cheese; in cheese sauce for eggs.

SOUPS, STEWS, AND CASSEROLES	In thick soups, stews, bean soup, minestrone; split pea soup; jugged hare, rabbit stew.
FISH	With lean and fat, baked and boiled fish, eel.
MEAT	Rub beef, lamb, mutton, fat pork, and veal lightly before roasting. In sausages.
POULTRY AND GAME	In stuffings; over chicken, turkey, pies, ragout.
VEGETABLES AND POTATOES	With beans, beets, carrots; potatoes; mushrooms and other fungi.
SAUCES	Tomato sauce, herb sauce.
SWEETS AND DESSERTS	Lemon thyme in custards and fruit salads and other sweets.

PART THREE

Cookery Recipes

COOKERY RECIPES

SOME RECIPES such as CHERVIL SOUP, FENNEL SAUCE, ROSEMARY BISCUITS, TARRAGON CHICKEN, etc., are based on one main herb; many other recipes, old and new, are collected from this and other countries for various types of dishes, traditionally flavoured with many herbs.

The recipes marked (B) are suggestions for a limited budget.

Cooking Temperatures

The cooking temperatures in this book are all given in degrees Fahrenheit as provided on the settings for electric cookers. Here follows the equivalent in terms for the oven and numbers for the settings of gas cookers. However, the following guide can only be approximate as makes of cookers vary.

Electricity ° F.	Oven Temperatures	Gas Regulo
225 to 250	Cool	0 to $\frac{1}{2}$
250 to 275	Very slow	$\frac{1}{2}$ to 1
275 to 300	Slow	1 to 2
300 to 350	Very moderate	2 to 3
375	Moderate	4
400	Moderately hot	5
425 to 450	Hot	6 to 7
475 to 500	Very hot	8 to 9

Basic Methods of Cooking

Casserole – Cooking slowly in the oven in a covered casserole dish to keep all the juices in.

Deep Frying – Cooking by immersion in a deep pan of smoking hot fat.

Grilling – Cooking and browning quickly under a red-hot grill.

Sauté – Shallow frying in a heavy iron (glazed with enamel) lidded saucepan or heavy frying-pan. The foods are placed into the pre-heated fat (not too hot) and tossed over a low heat until their own juices appear.

Stewing – When they start 'stewing in their own juice', a well-fitting lid should be added and this provides the 'conservative method' of cooking vegetables in their own steam, retaining value and aroma. Shaking and tossing all the time is necessary to prevent burning.

Simmering – Cooking just below boiling point so that the liquid bubbles gently at the side of the pan.

Chapter 1

FRUIT AND VEGETABLE COCKTAILS, APPETIZERS, AND DIPS

Fruit and Vegetable Cocktails

For figure-watchers and those who like the clean taste of fruit and vegetables before a meal.

(a) Fruit Cocktail

Ingredients:

Juice of 1 orange
Juice of ½ grapefruit
1 teasp. lemon juice

½ teasp. fresh chopped or green-dried sweet cicely

Mix ingredients well together.

Leave to stand (covered) for 15 minutes at least. Use honey for sweetening unless preferred unsweetened.

These quantities will provide a 7 oz. 'meal' for the slimming day or several small cocktail glasses for a party. If 1 teasp. nut cream *or* creamed almond emulsified with drops of water is added to the juice, a nourishing 'juice meal' results.

(b) Peach Cocktail

Ingredients (per person):

2 fully ripe, chilled peaches, peeled and pitted
1 egg
½ teasp. fresh chopped or green-dried sweet cicely

½ teasp. fresh chopped or green-dried lemon balm
1 tablesp. orange juice
¼ cup milk
1 teasp. honey

Combine peach with egg, orange juice, and milk, and add herbs. Whirl in a blender or electric mixer until smooth.

(c) Rosemary Cocktail

Ingredients:

Juice of ½ lemon as basis
3 carrots
1 tomato
Leaf of spinach *or* lettuce

Piece of celery
½ teasp. fresh chopped or green-dried rosemary

Method:

1. Squeeze lemon.
2. Peel and put pieces of carrots into juice extractor.
3. Pass tomato through sieve or juice extractor.

4. Put celery and spinach or lettuce leaves into juice extractor.
5. Add rosemary and allow to stand for 10 minutes.
6. Strain, as rosemary should be removed before its flavour becomes too strong.

Note: When no juice extractor is available, root vegetables or such hard vegetables as celery, can be grated, leaves chopped and all squeezed through muslin.

(d) Vegetable Cocktail

Use similar vegetables as for ROSEMARY COCKTAIL passed through juice extractor and flavour with such herbs as:

Parsley	Lemon Balm
Chervil	Tarragon
Fennel	Dill, etc.

and leave standing for a longer period.

Serve strained or with the herbs (finely chopped fresh, or green-dried reconstituted) floating.

All vegetable cocktails can be topped and improved in flavour with a little cream before serving.

(e) Tomato Cocktail

Ingredients:

1 fresh washed tomato
1 teasp. lemon juice per glass
½ teasp. fresh chopped or green-dried lemon balm
¼ teasp. fresh chopped or green-dried basil (according to taste)

Method:

1. Pass the tomato through a sieve.
2. Add the lemon juice and herbs.
3. Allow the herbs to permeate the cocktail by leaving to stand before serving.
4. Strain if preferred.

(f) Tomato Cocktail for the Family

Ingredients:

1 pint plain tomato juice
Pinch salt
Pinch sugar
1 lemon
½ teasp. each fresh chopped or green-dried basil, thyme, marjoram, summer savory, and tarragon
1 teasp. fresh chopped or green-dried chives

Method:
1. Add herbs, salt, and sugar to tomato juice and allow to steep in room temperature for one hour, stirring occasionally.
2. Add juice of one lemon and put into refrigerator and leave until ready to serve, preferably 4–6 hours.
3. Strain before serving.

Caviar from Aubergines

An excellent mixture – can be used as an appetizer on toast, on crunchy biscuits, on wholemeal bread and butter, as a spread, for buffet parties and receptions, and as a dip with potato crisps.

Ingredients:

1 large, whole, undamaged aubergine
Oil
1 teasp. lemon juice (approx.)
Salt
Paprika
1 teasp. finely chopped onions

2 teasp. fresh chopped or green-dried parsley
1 teasp. fresh chopped or green-dried chervil
½ teasp. fresh chopped or green-dried tarragon (if green-dried, reconstitute in lemon juice)

Method:
1. Wash or wipe, whole, aubergine.
2. Bake in its skin in the oven and turn frequently to get it evenly baked.
3. After 30–45 minutes (according to size), it should be soft and can be removed from the oven.
4. In order to retain the light colour, peel carefully with a wooden, horn or plastic fruit knife, removing first all burnt or dark bits of the peel.
5. Then quickly mash the flesh with a wooden spoon (or in an electric blender) – it should retain light green colour.
6. Add oil, approximately half of the quantity of the mashed aubergine, and mix well, lemon juice according to taste – taking into account lemon juice already used for reconstituting the herbs – and add salt and paprika.
7. Add onions and herbs.
8. Will keep in the refrigerator for a few days, but should always be served chilled.

Avocado Appetizers

Highly recommended – to be used as an *hors d'œuvre* on savoury biscuits, as a dip with potato crisps, on wholemeal and French bread, etc.

Ingredients:

½ avocado pear
1 small tomato, very finely diced
1 teasp. onion, finely chopped
1 teasp. each fresh chopped or green-dried basil and chervil
2 teasp. oil and lemon juice, mixed
Pinch of salt

Method:

1. Mash avocado well.
2. Add salt, oil, and lemon.
3. Add tomato and onion.
4. Add basil and chervil.

Celery Sticks with Cheese

Clean celery sticks and choose long and flat ones. Leave on some leaves. Pass cream cheese through sieve, add top of the milk until smooth and fluffy, but the mixture should remain thick. Add freshly chopped or green-dried celery leaves according to taste or until mixture looks fairly green.

Either serve as a dip with celery sticks or arrange small heaps of cream cheese on the lower white base of the celery stick.

Celery sticks can be served in the same way with roquefort. For this purpose mash cheese with a fork and mix well with butter until a smooth but thick mixture is obtained. Add celery leaves according to taste and serve small heaps on celery sticks.

Cheese and Horseradish Paste

This paste can also be served on celery sticks as an appetizer or on bread and canapés, and, if thinned a little with extra cream, as a dip.

Ingredients:

4 oz. cream cheese
2 oz. butter
1–1½ heaped tablesp. finely grated horseradish (varies whether horseradish is very hot and according to taste)
1 tablesp. lemon juice
2 level *or* 1 heaped tablesp. fresh chopped or green-dried tarragon
Pinch of sugar and salt
1 teasp. double cream

Method:
1. Cream butter.
2. Pass cheese through a sieve and blend with butter.
3. Add tarragon, sugar, salt, and lemon juice.
4. Add horseradish.
5. Add double cream.
6. Mix all well to a firm paste.

Pâté de Foie Gras (made with Chicken Liver)

A delicate paste for the not so health-conscious but more gourmet-minded of your guests.

Ingredients:

½ lb. chicken liver
2 tablesp. cream cheese
½ teasp. fresh chopped or green-dried marjoram
1 tablesp. fresh chopped or green-dried chives
Pinch of fresh chopped or green-dried rosemary (crushed)

¼ lb. butter
1 tablesp. brandy, sherry, or wine
Salt
Paprika } According to taste
Nutmeg

Method:
1. Cook livers slowly in covered pan with tablesp. of butter – DO NOT BROWN.
2. Remove pan from the heat, take out liver and pass it through a sieve or mash in liquidizer.
3. Add the wine to the liquid left in the pan; stir well.
4. Mix the remaining butter, cream cheese, herbs, and seasoning with the liquid from the pan to a smooth consistency.
5. Add sieved liver and whisk well.
6. Put into covered dish and keep cool until needed.
7. Serve on thin dry toast or Vita-Weat.
   Note: Becomes better when kept for a day or two in the refrigerator.

Ham Lovage Spread (*makes ⅔ cup*)

Served on small biscuits, wholemeal bread, or Ryvita as an appetizer.

Ingredients:

½ lb. minced cooked ham
6 oz. butter
Pinch of paprika

2 tablesp. fresh chopped or green-dried lovage (if green-dried, reconstitute in lemon juice)

Method:

1. Blend ham with butter and lovage.
2. Add paprika.
3. Mix well.
4. Use on canapés or as sandwich spread.

   Note: If available, the spread can be made from lovage seed or any other herb seeds, such as dill seed, celery seed, or poppy seed.

Herb Canapés

There are many recipes elsewhere in the book which are suitable for Canapés, Those for sandwich fillings in Chapter 11, page 309; 'Herb Cheese', Chapter 3, page 211, and other recipes in this chapter. Here follow three Herb Canapés in particular:

Nasturtium

Blend ¼ lb. cream cheese with 2 teasp. chopped tender leaves and stems of nasturtium. Decorate with nasturtium flowers. This spread should be eaten at once as it becomes bitter if left standing mixed with the nasturtium for any length of time.

Rosemary

To ¼ lb. finely chopped walnuts, add 2 oz. finely chopped green olives and 2 teasp. crushed fresh or green-dried rosemary.

Tarragon

Place asparagus tips on bite-size pieces of buttered wholemeal bread. Sprinkle liberally with fresh chopped or green-dried tarragon, reconstituted in lemon juice.

Garnish with dabs of mayonnaise to which a little tarragon has been added.

Bachelor Toast with Herbs (*serves 4*)

Substantial starter or T V snack.

Ingredients:

1 clove garlic, minced or crushed
2 tablesp. butter
½ teasp. each fresh chopped or green-dried marjoram and chives

4 slices French bread
Grated Cheddar cheese

Method:
1. Mix crushed garlic with butter.
2. Add herbs.
3. Spread garlic butter on French bread slices and sprinkle heavily with grated cheese.
4. Place in hot oven (400°) until bread assumes a rich yellow-brown colour.
5. The cheese, too, should have melted and mingled into the bread with the butter.

Shrimp Toast (*serves 6–8*)

A delicately flavoured *hors d'œuvre* or snack.

Ingredients:

8 oz. shrimps
4 oz. fat raw pork
2 tablesp. onion, minced
1 tablesp. cornflour
1 egg, beaten
¼ teasp. oil
1 teasp. sugar
1 teasp. salt
2 tablesp. fresh chopped or green-dried parsley

½ teasp. fresh chopped or green-dried fennel
1 teasp. fresh chopped or green-dried dill
½ teasp. fresh chopped or green-dried marjoram
6 slices stale bread
Oil for cooking

Method:
1. Finely mince together shrimps, pork, and onion.
2. Mix cornflour, egg, and oil together, and add to shrimp mixture.
3. Add sugar, salt, and herbs, blending well.
4. Spread mixture on to bread slices.
5. Heat oil in heavy frying-pan and slide in bread slices, shrimp side down.
6. Fry until the bread is a golden brown; it takes about 10–15 minutes.

Rosemary Walnuts

Serve as an unusual appetizer – also excellent for sherry parties and other wine parties.

Ingredients:

1 tablesp. melted butter
1 teasp. crumbled rosemary
½ teasp. salt

¼ teasp. paprika
1 cup walnut halves

Method:
1. Mix together the melted butter, rosemary, salt, and paprika with the walnuts.
2. Pour into a shallow pan, spreading nuts in a single layer.
3. Roast until richly brown in a moderate oven 350°, shaking occasionally.
4. Takes about 10–15 minutes.
5. Serve hot or re-heat in the oven as an appetizer.

Various Dips

Everyone likes an occasional snack, but it is extremely difficult for the figure-watchers to find something which will not add to their calorie intake. The following snacks can be offered as *hors d'œuvres* or can be served when the family watches a TV show or they are particularly good for the weight-conscious teenager who will appreciate them when coming home from school.

Raw Fruit and Vegetables with Various Dips

Arrange a variety of raw vegetables, such as tomato slices, cucumber sticks, sliced raw turnips, cauliflower rosettes, green pepper strips, carrot sticks, celery strips, suitably cut chicory, etc.

Wrap apple slices or small celery or cucumber sticks with a narrow band of boiled ham, salami, or other luncheon meat. Secure with a cocktail stick and serve on a flat tray.

Top carrot, cucumber, or celery sticks with ripe olives, securing with a cocktail stick and serve in a bowl of crushed ice.

All these are intended to be used for dunking in special 'dips'.

(*a*) Herb and Yoghourt Dip

Ingredients:

2 cups sour cream *or* yoghourt
1 teasp. caraway seeds
2 teasp. minced onion
2 teasp. fresh chopped or green-dried onion green *or* chives

Salt
½ teasp. fresh chopped or green-dried summer savory
A dash of fresh chopped or green-dried thyme

Method:
Blend sour cream or yoghourt with all the other ingredients, allow to permeate and then chill for several hours.

(b) Herb Mix Dip

Ingredients:

1 cup yoghourt *or* sour cream
½ teasp. fresh chopped or green-
dried lovage

1 teasp. each fresh chopped or
green-dried rosemary, thyme,
parsley, dill, tarragon, sage, and
basil

Method:

Mix ingredients well together and season with a little salt and a
little paprika.

(c) Rainbow Cheese Bowl

Ingredients:

½ lb. cottage cheese
1 teasp. salt
1 tablesp. fresh chopped or
green-dried chives
or 1 teasp. fresh chopped or
green-dried summer savory *or*
nasturtium

½ cup coarsely grated carrot
½ cup sliced radishes
½ cup sliced spring onions
or ¼ cup chopped onions and fresh
chopped or green-dried onion
green

Method:

1. Mix cheese with salt and herbs and add a vegetable to each
   part, thus making three different flavours and colours (carrot,
   radish, onion).
2. Spoon into shallow bowl in three segments.
3. Separate segments with long sticks of any large vegetable,
   eg celery.
4. Decorate each segment with the appropriate vegetable.

Note: Alternate apple wedges of red and green apples can be
arranged around the bowl of these various cheese dips.

The apples can be used in place of biscuits or potato crisps,
but a variety of apple should be chosen such as Cox's which will
not turn brown quickly.

Horseradish Cheese Spread
   (page 117)
Tomato Cottage Cheese Spread
   (page 108)
Red Radish Spread
   (page 109)
Carrot Cheese Spread
   (page 109)

} Can be used for other dips.

Dip for Shellfish

Something tasty and different for the imaginative party-giver.

Ingredients:

1 cup mayonnaise
½ cup curd *or* cottage cheese
¼ cup chopped onions
3 tablesp. fresh horseradish, (grated) *or* the equivalent of dried horseradish, according to strength and taste
Salt ⎱ According to taste
Paprika ⎰
1 tablesp. fresh chopped or green-dried parsley

Tarragon ⎫
Chervil ⎪ See GUIDE,
Celery leaves ⎬ page 127,
Lovage ⎪ for
Rosemary ⎪ proportions
Summer savory ⎭

A pinch of each, fresh chopped or green-dried marjoram, thyme, basil
1 tablesp. butter
1 tablesp. breadcrumbs
½ apple
1 teasp. lemon juice

Method:

1. Sauté horseradish and onions until golden.
2. Add breadcrumbs and sauté until golden.
3. Remove from heat and allow to cool.
4. Add ½ grated apple, 1 teasp. lemon juice, the herbs, and seasoning.
5. Mix well with curd and mayonnaise.

Avocado Pear with Horseradish Cream

An elegant starter to a dinner or luncheon.

Cut ripe avocado pears into halves; if the avocados are large, cut into quarters. Remove stone and fill with the following mixture:

Horseradish Cream:
(Quantities given are only approximate according to taste and strength of the horseradish available.)

½ horseradish stick, grated
Fresh breadcrumbs
1 tablesp. butter
1 dessertsp. yoghourt
1 teasp. lemon (approx.)
Pinch of salt
Pinch of sugar

1 teasp. fresh chopped or green-dried chervil
½ teasp. each fresh chopped or green-dried tarragon and dill
1 apple
3–4 tablesp. double cream

Method:

1. Peel and grate horseradish.
2. Grate bread, and clean grater by making the breadcrumbs from stale bread.
3. Melt butter, add horseradish and breadcrumbs and fry until golden brown.
4. Take away from heat and grate apple into the mixture.
5. Add yoghourt, lemon juice, salt, sugar, and herbs.
6. Put aside to cool, uncovered if horseradish is very hot, otherwise cover.
7. Allow to permeate until cold, then chill in refrigerator.
8. Whisk double cream to stiff consistency and chill in refrigerator.
9. Gently fold cream into the mixture, shortly before serving.
10. Arrange generously on halves or quarters of avocado pears.
   Serve with lettuce leaves or curly endive, radishes, quartered tomatoes, etc.

Stuffed Tomatoes with Basil (*serves 3*)

An attractive and substantial *hors d'œuvre*.

Ingredients:

3 good ripe tomatoes
2 oz. cream cheese
1 triangular processed cheese
1 teasp. sunflower oil
Lemon juice

1 tablesp. fresh chopped or green-dried chives
½ teasp. fresh chopped or green-dried basil, or according to taste
Paprika

Method:

1. Cut lid off tomatoes.
2. Scrape out insides.
3. Pass contents through a sieve.
4. Mix well with cream cheese and all other ingredients.
5. Fill tomatoes with this mixture.
6. Put lid back and serve.

Herb and Orange *Hors d'œuvre*

Equally good at the beginning or end of the meal.

Ingredients:

4 tablesp. double cream
Grated rind of ½ orange
Juice of whole orange
1 teasp. each fresh chopped dandelion and spinach

1 teasp. each fresh chopped or green-dried parsley and lemon balm
Lettuce leaves

Method:
1. Whip double cream until stiff.
2. Add grated orange peel and the juice, mixing carefully.
3. Mix dandelion, spinach, parsley, and lemon balm together.
4. Add herbs to the orange mixture and serve on lettuce leaves.

Pineapple Yoghourt Appetizer

A healthy and attractive way to begin a meal.

Ingredients: (per person)

2 tablesp. yoghourt	Finely diced or crushed pine-
Sweet cicely	apple

Method:
1. Put yoghourt in sherbet dish.
2. Add layer of pineapple and sprinkle with sweet cicely.
3. Repeat layers. Use yoghourt for top layer; garnish with pineapple.
4. Serve chilled.

Cucumber Herb Rings

A cool, nourishing beginning to a meal on a hot summer's day.

Ingredients:

1 cucumber	Paprika
4 oz. cream cheese	1 tablesp. each, fresh chopped or
1 teasp. mayonnaise	green-dried parsley, chives, and
A few drops of lemon juice	dill

Method:
1. Cut cucumber into several pieces and take out the centre.
2. Mix all other ingredients together.
3. Fill the cucumber with the cheese mixture and put in refrigerator until required.
4. Before serving, cut into thick slices, sprinkle each cucumber ring with salt and the whole slice with paprika.
5. Serve on lettuce leaves.

SALADS AND SALAD DRESSINGS

SALADS SHOULD BE made in good time before a meal – though not too long before – so that herbs, dressing, and the salad foods can have at least half an hour to permeate; after that the salad can be placed in the refrigerator where this process will go on, but to a lesser degree. However, too long a period in the refrigerator will reduce the flavour of the uncooked parts of a salad, although dressings can be kept for several days. The ingredients should be carefully washed, roots scrubbed and peeled, then drained well in a salad basket.

If a salad is to be served in a salad bowl, much depends on arranging it so that the colours and the shapes do not get mixed, but are arranged, as in a garden, in separate beds, perhaps surrounded by green leaves such as lettuce and watercress. If salads are served individually as is suggested in some of these recipes, the salad is arranged on top of a layer of leaves, perhaps garnished with egg, tomato or olives. In this case the ingredients of the salad should be well mixed with the dressing in the salad bowl and then be arranged on plates.

The salad bowl should be a wooden one with the exception of fish salads or salads flavoured with anchovy – these must be made in a glass or china bowl, otherwise the fish flavour will remain in the wood. The best way to serve all salads – other than fish – is in a wooden bowl, preferably a shallow one for those salads arranged in strips. Wooden servers should be used.

Macaroni and Shrimp Salad (*serves 8*)

An unusual and very tasty salad.

Ingredients:

4 cups elbow macaroni
Water
Salt
1 lb. cooked shrimps cut in pieces *or* small whole shrimps
1 cup fresh chopped *or* ¼ cup green-dried onion green
1 cup fresh chopped *or* ½ cup green-dried celery leaves
6 chopped hard-boiled eggs
Enough mayonnaise to bind (about 1 pint) (see Recipe, page 84)
Lettuce

Method:

1. Cook macaroni in salted water until just tender.
2. Drain, rinse, and cool.
3. Combine with cooked shrimps.
4. Add onion green, celery leaves, hard-boiled eggs.
5. Bind with mayonnaise.
6. Add more salt for seasoning, if necessary.
7. Serve cold on beds of lettuce.

Sausage Salad (*serves 6*)

A concentrated salad – add diced potatoes if liked.

Ingredients:

6 Frankfurters
3½ oz. Gruyère cheese, diced
Good quantity of fresh chopped
  or green-dried chives
1 tablesp. lemon juice

2 tablesp. oil
1 teasp. fresh chopped or green-
  dried mint
Salt

Method:

1. Cut Frankfurters into thin slices.
2. Mix Frankfurters, cheese cubes, and chives.
3. Stir well together, the lemon juice, oil, mint, and salt.
4. Add this mixture to sausages, cheese, and chives.
5. Allow to permeate half an hour before serving.
6. Serve on salad leaves.

Niçoise Salad (cooked salad) (*serves 4*)

For buffets and cold meals.

Ingredients:

5 boiled potatoes
4 tomatoes
Radishes
Olives
Gherkins
3 hard-boiled eggs
3 tablesp. oil
2 tablesp. lemon juice
Salt

1 tablesp. green-dried bouquet for
  salad
or 1 teasp. each fresh chopped or
  green-dried chives and chervil
1½ teasp. fresh chopped or green-
  dried parsley
½ teasp. fresh chopped or green-
  dried basil
Cabbage lettuce leaves

Method:

1. Slice vegetables and eggs.
2. Prepare salad dressing with the herbs.
3. Mix dressing with vegetables and eggs.
4. Add lettuce leaves to the salad shortly before serving.

Raw Carrot and Horseradish Salad (*serves 6*)

Can be served as *hors d'œuvre*, but is best as accompaniment to
cold meat.

Ingredients:

½ lb. grated carrots
1 tablesp. grated horseradish
1 tablesp. lemon juice
4 tablesp. top of the milk or single cream
1 tablesp. oil
1 tablesp. yoghourt

1 tablesp. fresh chopped or green-dried salad burnet
or 1 tablesp. green-dried bouquet for salad
Pinch of sugar
Salt according to taste

Method:

1. Mix carrots and horseradish immediately after grating, with lemon.
2. Mix other liquid ingredients well.
3. Add herb, sugar, and salt, and stir.
4. Mix this with grated roots.

Potato Salad

A substantial salad, suitable for many occasions.

Ingredients:

2 lb. potatoes (approx.)
1 cup (10 oz.) vegetable stock
3 tablesp. sunflower oil
2 tablesp. lemon juice
2 tablesp. cream
1 tablesp. chopped onion

1 tablesp. each fresh chopped or green-dried onion green and chives
Salt
Nutmeg

Method:

1. Boil potatoes and peel while they are still hot.
2. Slice potatoes and cover immediately with hot vegetable stock.
3. Leave to stand for some time.
4. Make a dressing of oil, lemon juice, herbs, and cream, and mix well together.
5. Mix with potatoes while still warm.
6. Add seasoning to taste.

Note: Decorate with watercress, or cornsalad (in autumn), or gherkins. Can be served and decorated with hard-boiled eggs or Frankfurters.

Radish Lettuce Salad (*serves 4–6*)

Serve with cold poultry.

Ingredients:

2 cabbage lettuces
1 small head curly endive (use inner leaves only) *or* chicory
1 sweet Florence fennel (if available)
½ cup thinly sliced radishes *or* grated large white radish
2 tablesp. oil

1 tablesp. lemon juice
1 dash of paprika
1 teasp. finely chopped onion
1 teasp. each, fresh chopped or green-dried fennel, chervil, tarragon, and chives
¼ teasp. fresh chopped or green-dried summer savory

Method:

1. Tear lettuce and endive leaves into bite-size pieces, place in a large salad bowl.
2. Trim the head of the fennel and thinly slice the heart.
3. Add, with radishes, to salad bowl.
4. Pour oil into a small bowl.
5. Add lemon juice, all the herbs, paprika, and onion, blend until smooth, and pour over salad.
6. Toss lightly with wooden salad spoon or fork until mixture is evenly coated.
7. Divide between 4 or 6 salad plates.

Salmon Salad (*serves 4*)

An easy but substantial salad for an outdoor meal.

Ingredients:

1 lb. cold boiled salmon
3 sliced hard-boiled egg yolks
Salt to taste
1 dessertsp. each, fresh chopped or green-dried chervil and dill

1 teasp. each, fresh chopped or green-dried parsley and summer savory
1 tablesp. mayonnaise
1 medium-sized crisp lettuce

Method:

1. Skin, bone, and flake salmon (or use tinned salmon).
2. Place in a mixing-bowl with the egg yolks, herbs, salt, and mayonnaise.
3. Toss ingredients lightly together with wooden salad servers.
4. Line 4 cold salad plates with washed and dried lettuce leaves.
5. Divide salad equally between plates.

Bean Salad (*serves 4*)

A very good salad with cold poultry.

Ingredients:

1 lb. string beans
2 tablesp. sunflower oil
1 tablesp. lemon juice
1 medium-sized onion
1 minced clove garlic
1 teasp. each, fresh chopped or

green-dried parsley and summer savory
Some lettuce leaves
1 chopped hard-boiled egg
Grated Parmesan cheese to taste

Method:

1. String and slice beans.
2. Cook in boiling salted water until crisp but tender; drain and cool thoroughly.
3. Place in a wooden salad bowl.
4. Gradually beat the oil into the lemon juice.
5. Peel and slice onion thinly.
6. Stir the onion and garlic into the oil mixture.
7. Add herbs and salt and stir until thoroughly blended.
8. Pour dressing over the beans.
9. Mix slightly with wooden salad servers.
10. Cover and chill in refrigerator.
11. When ready to serve, garnish with egg and Parmesan cheese. Can be served on plates with lettuce leaves.

Curly Endive Salad (*serves 6*)

A summer salad.

Ingredients:

1 peeled clove garlic
1 head curly endive
2 cups sliced cold boiled potatoes
4 hard-boiled eggs, in quarters
¼ cup sunflower oil

Juice of 2 lemons
½ teasp. each fresh chopped or green-dried marjoram, salad burnet, chervil, and tarragon
Salt to taste

Method:

1. Halve garlic and rub inside of wooden salad bowl.
2. Tear the endive into bite-size pieces.
3. Place the endive, potatoes, and egg in the bowl.
4. Blend in the oil with the lemon juice and herbs.
5. Toss lightly with wooden salad servers.
6. Season to taste with salt and toss lightly again.
7. Divide equally between 6 salad plates and serve at once.

Aubergine Salad (*serves 6*)

Nourishing and refreshing – an excellent main salad dish.

Ingredients:

2 medium-sized aubergines
1 tablesp. lemon juice
½ teasp. finely minced onion
1 cup shredded celery
½ cup chopped nuts
Salt to taste
1 teasp. each fresh chopped or green-dried tarragon and

chervil
½ teasp. fresh chopped or green-dried summer savory
1½ tablesp. oil
1 dessertsp. lemon juice
Crisp lettuce leaves
6 quartered hard-boiled eggs
Spanish stuffed olives (optional)

Method:
1. Peel and cut aubergines into 1-in. cubes, place in a saucepan.
2. Cover with boiling salted water and add lemon juice.
3. Cover and boil until tender, then drain, chill, and place in wooden salad bowl.
4. Add onion, celery, nuts, salt, and herbs.
5. Mix the oil with the lemon juice, and add to the salad bowl. Mix well.
6. Divide into 6 equal portions.
7. Serve on salad plates lined with lettuce leaves.
8. Garnish with eggs and olives.

Basic French Dressing (*makes ½ pint*)

Enough for 4 medium-sized salads.

Ingredients:

¾ cup olive *or* salad oil
¼ cup lemon juice
½ teasp. salt
½ teasp. castor sugar
¼ teasp. each fresh chopped or green-dried tarragon, summer savory, and chervil

¼ teasp. paprika
Freshly ground black pepper to taste
1 saltsp. dry mustard

Method:
1. Place all the ingredients in a glass jar with a tightly-fitting screw top.
2. Shake until thoroughly blended, then chill
3. Shake well each time before using.

Piquant French Dressing (*makes 8 oz.*)

Ingredients:

1 dessertsp. salt
¼ teasp. castor sugar
1 saltsp. freshly ground black pepper
1 saltsp. paprika
½ teasp. made mustard
2 teasp. fresh chopped or green-dried tarragon

¼ teasp. onion juice *or* minced onion
½ clove garlic, crushed
1 dessertsp. boiling water
¼ cup olive *or* salad oil
1¾ tablesp. lemon juice *or* wine vinegar

Method:

1. Mix the seasonings in a bowl with a small wooden spoon.
2. Add tarragon, onion, and garlic.
3. Stir in boiling water.
4. Gradually stir in the oil and lemon, or vinegar.
5. Beat till blended, then beat again before using or serving.

Mayonnaise (see Part One – Salad Dressings, page 84)

Horseradish Mayonnaise

Ingredients:

2 tablesp. grated horseradish, or according to taste

1 cup mayonnaise (see Recipe, page 84)

Method:

Simply blend ingredients well together.

Green Mayonnaise

To serve with lobster.

Ingredients:

2 tablesp. fresh chopped or green-dried parsley
1 tablesp. each fresh chopped or green-dried chives and tarragon

1 teasp. each fresh chopped or green-dried chervil and dill
2 cups mayonnaise (see Recipe, page 84)

Method:

Blend all ingredients well together; allow to stand an hour before serving.

Herb Salad Dressing (*makes 8 oz.*)

For any mixed salad to be served with cold lamb or duck.

Ingredients:

1 teasp. each fresh chopped or green-dried mint and lemon balm

½ teasp. each fresh chopped or green-dried marjoram and summer savory

2½ tablesp. oil
1 tablesp. lemon juice
1 clove garlic
1 lightly beaten egg
Salt and pepper to taste

Method:

1. Mix the herbs with the oil and the lemon juice in a small basin.
2. Chop or crush garlic finely and add with egg.
3. Stir, till blended, with a small wooden spoon.
4. Season to taste with salt and freshly ground black pepper.
5. Stir thoroughly before using with any salad.

Yoghourt Dressing (*about ½ pint*)

A salad accompaniment especially to a green salad.

Ingredients:

½ clove garlic
¼ cup finely chopped onion
¼ cup each fresh chopped or green-dried celery leaves and parsley
1 tablesp. fresh chopped or green-dried basil

½ teasp. salt
1 teasp. castor sugar
¾ tablesp. tomato purée
1 cup yoghourt

Method:

1. Peel and finely mince the garlic.
2. Mix all ingredients, in order given, in a small basin.
3. Stir till smoothly blended.

Avocado Dill Dressing

This light-green, speckled dressing, delightful to look at, is a delicious accompaniment to any delicate vegetable salad, goes well with fruit salads and is excellent with asparagus.

Ingredients:

1 medium sized avocado
Salt
1 tablesp. honey
⅓ cup sunflower *or* other good
    salad oil
4 tablesp. lemon juice
1 teasp. each fresh chopped or
green-dried sweet cicely and
    lemon balm
2 teasp. fresh chopped or green-
    dried dill
¼ cup water

Method:

1. Halve avocado, discarding the stone.
2. Scoop the flesh out of the skin and cut directly into blender.
3. Add salt, honey, salad oil, herbs, lemon juice, directly to the
   blender, add the water, turn on blender and blend about 2
   minutes on No. 2 or 3 or until smooth.
4. Store the dressing in the refrigerator.

Note: This salad dressing is lower in calories than mayonnaise
or even French dressing and looks so attractive served with
salads, particularly for a buffet. When using it, some additional
water may have to be used to thin the dressing. It makes about
2 cups.

Remoulade Dressing (*makes 1⅓ cups*)

Almost a sauce to go with salads, asparagus, vegetable fritters,
and grilled meat.

Ingredients:

1 cup freshly made mayonnaise
    (see Recipe, page 84)
¼ cup finely chopped gherkins
1 dessertsp. finely chopped
    capers (optional)
½ teasp. made mustard
½ teasp. each fresh chopped or
    green-dried chervil, parsley, and
    tarragon

Method:

1. Place mayonnaise in a small mixing-bowl.
2. Stir in remaining ingredients in order given.
3. Blend till smooth.

Chiffonade Dressing (*about ¾ pint*)

A thin dressing for any mixed or tossed salad.

Ingredients:

1 cup sunflower oil
¼ cup lemon juice
½ teasp. salt
½ teasp. castor sugar
1 teasp. fresh chopped or green-dried basil

½ teasp. fresh chopped or green-dried summer savory
½ teasp. paprika
½ teasp. minced onion
¾ tablesp. diced green pepper
1 finely chopped hard-boiled egg

Method:

Mix all ingredients thoroughly together, in order given, in a mixing-bowl or electric blender, until blended.

Herb Vinegars

The acid in salad dressings can be supplied either with lemon juice, yoghourt, or vinegar, but the vinegar should be preferably wine or cider vinegar, and can often be a vehicle for herbs. Here follow various suggestions for Herb Vinegars – 1 tablesp. of any of the following herbs – chervil, chives, mint, parsley, salad burnet, can be added to the vinegar. Pour it into a porcelain jar, cover with a cheese cloth, allow to stand for 2–3 weeks and strain off into bottles and cork tightly.

(*a*) Burnet Vinegar

Ingredients:

½ pint white wine vinegar
½ pint dry white wine
½ cup fresh chopped burnet leaves
or 1½ tablesp. green-dried leaves

½ chopped shallot
Lemon verbena leaves (optional)
or lemon thyme (optional)

Method:

1. Mix vinegar and wine in a deep enamel pan.
2. Add burnet leaves.
3. Add shallot and (if desired) a pinch of lemon verbena or lemon thyme.
4. Simmer the mixture for 30 minutes.
5. Strain through filter papers or a wet linen cloth.
6. Pour into sterilized bottles and cork them tightly.
7. When the vinegar has mellowed for 2 weeks, pour it into smaller bottles in which fresh sprigs of burnet have been placed.

(b) Tarragon Vinegar

Ingredients:

Fresh tarragon leaves *or* shoots *or* 1 tablesp. green-dried tarragon

Rind of ½ lemon (without white pith)
2–3 whole cloves
White wine *or* cider vinegar

Method:

1. Fill a quart glass bottling jar with fresh tarragon leaves or shoots, putting them in loosely, or with the green-dried tarragon.
2. Place rind and cloves into the jar and fill up with vinegar.
3. Screw cover down tightly, allow to stand in the sun for 2 weeks.
4. Strain through pressing liquid from the leaves.
5. Pass through filter paper and pour into small bottles and cork tightly.

(c) Nasturtium Vinegar

Ingredients:

Nasturtium blossoms
1 shallot, peeled
⅓ clove garlic

½ red pepper, thinly sliced
Cider vinegar
1 teasp. salt

Method:

1. Fill a quart bottling jar loosely with full-blown nasturtium blossoms.
2. Add shallot, garlic, and red pepper.
3. Fill jar to the top with cold cider vinegar.
4. Cover closely and stand for 2 months in a shady spot.
5. Dissolve salt in the vinegar, then strain and pass through filter paper.
6. Pour into small bottles and cork tightly.

To all these vinegars, 1 or 2 sprigs of the herb in question can be added.

Sweet Dressing for Fresh Fruit Salad (*makes ½ pint*)

Ingredients:

1 tablesp. lemon juice
½ cup thick cream
Pinch of salt
1 dessertsp. fresh chopped or green-dried sweet cicely
1 teasp. fresh chopped or green-dried lemon balm

1 pinch fresh chopped or green-dried lemon thyme
A dash of ground ginger
1½ tablesp. sifted icing sugar
1 avocado pear

Method:

1. Place the lemon juice, cream, herbs, salt, ginger, and sugar, in a bowl or an electric blender.
2. Peel and stone pear, then cut into fine dice.
3. Blend until smooth and fluffy, either with a wooden spoon or in blender.
4. Chill thoroughly.

Note: To make a fluffier dressing, fold in an additional half cup double cream, whipped till thick, just before serving.

Lemon Cream Dressing (*makes ½ pint*)

Delightful accompaniment to any fruit salad.

Ingredients:

1 teasp. lemon juice
2 egg yolks
1 teasp. honey
1 teasp. each fresh chopped or green-dried sweet cicely and lemon balm

1 pinch fresh chopped or green-dried lemon thyme
1 cup cream, *or* sour cream, *or* yoghourt

Method:

1. Blend the lemon juice with the egg yolks.
2. Stir in honey, herbs, and cream.
3. Beat with a wooden spoon until smoothly blended.
4. Use with fruit salad.

Chapter 3

EGG AND CHEESE DISHES, SAVOURIES, SNACKS

Eggs in Casserole

Ingredients:

2 teasp. lovage
Pinch of summer savory
½ cup of double cream
½ cup of sour cream
(*or* all double cream)
¾ cup soft sharp Cheddar cheese
6 beaten eggs
2 teasp. fresh chopped or green-dried herbs consisting of bouquet for omelettes

or a mixture of
1 teasp. fresh chopped or green-dried chervil
1 teasp. fresh chopped or green-dried chives and parsley
1 pinch each of fresh chopped or green-dried lemon thyme and marjoram

Method:
1. Add lovage and summer savory to cream and allow to stand for a while.
2. Pour half the seasoned cream into a buttered shallow baking-dish.
3. Crumble cheese into the mixture and dot with butter.
4. Add herbs to beaten eggs and pour eggs carefully over the cream and cheese mixture.
5. Bake in a moderate oven (350°) 20–30 minutes, or until the eggs have formed a light crust but are still soft.
6. Pour the remaining cream carefully over the eggs and return the dish to the oven and bake for a further 10 minutes, or until the eggs have golden-puffed crust but are not dry.
   Note: Any left over could be diced and served in clear soup.

Cold Egg Ring with Green and Red Sauce

A most decorative dish, excellent for a cold lunch or buffet with mixed raw salad and hot 'Herb-Buttered French Loaf' (Recipe, page 313).

Ingredients:
8 eggs

Green Sauce	Red Sauce
1 tablesp. each chives, parsley, tarragon, chervil (fresh chopped or green-dried)	1 cup mayonnaise (Recipe, page 84)
½ lemon (juice only)	1 dash paprika
⅔ cup mayonnaise (page 84)	1 small tin (5 oz.) tomato purée
Salt	1–2 teasp. fresh chopped or green-dried basil
	Pinch of sugar
	Salt

Method:
If green-dried herbs are used, reconstitute them in the lemon juice in a small bowl and, if necessary, add a little water. There should be just enough liquid for the herbs to soak up until fully reconstituted – no liquid should remain.

1. Oil well a small ring mould or tin (approx. 6½ in. diam.).
2. Break eggs carefully into it.
3. Place into larger pan filled with boiling water.
4. Bake in moderate oven (350°) for 15 minutes or until set. (No longer as eggs should not become hard-cooked.)

5. Turn out on to a round plate (larger than the ring) when cold.

Green Sauce

6. Chop herbs finely or reconstitute in lemon juice.
7. Add lemon juice to herbs if fresh herbs are used.
8. Whirl in a blender with mayonnaise or whirl herbs by themselves and then add to mayonnaise.
9. Add a little salt.

Red Sauce

10. Mix well together mayonnaise, paprika, tomato purée, basil, a pinch of sugar, and salt.
11. Coat egg-ring with green sauce, allowing surplus to flow to the outside.
12. Fill centre with red sauce.

Herb Omelette

Individual omelettes are easier to make than larger ones.

Ingredients (per person):

2 large eggs
1 teasp. cold water
¼ teasp. salt
Fresh ground pepper to taste
2 tablesp. butter

1 tablesp. green-dried bouquet for omelette
or
½ teasp. fresh chopped or green-dried tarragon
½ teasp. fresh chopped or green-dried chervil
1 teasp. fresh chopped or green-dried chives
1 teasp. fresh chopped or green-dried parsley

Method:

1. Beat eggs slightly with the cold water and salt.
2. Heat a 6-in. omelette pan; add the butter and tilt the pan so that butter covers the bottom.
3. Pour in eggs all at once.
4. Stir with a fork 2 or 3 times through the bottom and round the sides, shaking pan constantly.
5. When omelette is set but still moist on top, sprinkle the herbs over it.
6. Fold it in half and place on a hot plate.
7. Keep warm until the required numbers are done.

Chervil Soufflé

Excellent, light yet substantial dish.

Ingredients:

3 tablesp. butter
2 tablesp. finely milled dry breadcrumbs
2 tablesp. cornflour
1 teasp. fresh chopped or green-dried chives
1 teasp. strong stock

1 cup milk
½ cup grated mild Cheddar cheese
4 eggs
2 tablesp. fresh chopped or green-dried chervil
Pinch of summer savory
Salt

Method:
1. Butter bottom and side of 3-pint casserole, using 1 tablesp. butter (going up 1 in. at the side).
2. Melt remaining 2 tablesp. butter in a saucepan and stir in the breadcrumbs and the cornflour.
3. Mix chives, stock, and milk, and add to the butter mixture.
4. Add the cheese and stir until thick and smooth.
5. Separate eggs, beat yolks.
6. Pour hot sauce slowly over egg yolks, return to pan.
7. Cook over low heat, stirring constantly until sauce begins to bubble and is thickened again.
8. Stir in chervil and pinch of summer savory.
9. Add salt to egg whites and beat until stiff, but not dry.
10. Fold egg whites carefully into sauce.
11. Pour into casserole and bake for 30 minutes in oven (375°).
12. Soufflé should be browned and well done.
13. SERVE AT ONCE.

Lentils with Eggs

A new taste to add to the humble lentil.

Ingredients:

½ cup lentils
1 onion
2 eggs
Oil
Garlic

A sprig of mint or ½ teasp. green-dried mint
½ teasp. fresh chopped or green-dried marjoram
½ teasp. fresh chopped or green-dried lovage

Method:

1. Fry the chopped onion, garlic, and lentils in oil for a few minutes.
2. Add a pint of water and the herbs and boil for 30 minutes.
3. Let it cool.
4. Meanwhile, hard-boil two or more eggs.
5. Cut eggs in quarters and serve with the lentils, leaving pieces of eggs for decoration.

   Note: Serve hot or cold.

Herb Eggs

From the cold table to the big reception, from the family supper to the garden party – a most excellent dish.

Ingredients:

4 eggs	1 tablesp. oil
1 tablesp. lemon juice	1 oz. softened butter
1 tablesp. grated cheese	A little salt

2–3 tablesp. of a mixture of the following fresh chopped or green-dried herbs (see GUIDE, page 127, for proportions):

Parsley	Chives	Onion green
Lemon balm	Tarragon	Marjoram
	Thyme	

or 2–3 tablesp. bouquet for omelettes

Method:

1. Hard-boil eggs.
2. Shell and halve.
3. Remove yolks and mash well with a fork or pass through a sieve.
4. Add lemon juice and oil to the mashed yolks and mix well until smooth.
5. Add the herbs; the mixture should look more green than yellow when finished.
6. Add salt and grated cheese and the softened butter to smooth.
7. Let the mixture stand for 10 minutes.
8. Pile mixture into halved whites and smooth dome with a knife.
9. Serve eggs on lettuce leaves on a flat dish decorated with parsley.

Mimosa Eggs

Ingredients:
4 hard-boiled eggs
1 small tin tuna fish
Home-made mayonnaise
  (see page 84)
Salt
Little paprika
4 lettuce leaves
Fresh chopped or green-dried fennel

Sauce:
A little tomato purée
1 carton single cream
Castor sugar

Method:
1. Halve eggs and remove yolks.
2. Mash the tuna fish and mix with mayonnaise, season with salt and paprika.
3. Fill egg whites with the mixture.
4. Put a lettuce leaf on each plate and place half egg on it.
5. Grate the yolks over the eggs and sprinkle the eggs with plenty of fennel.
6. Surround with tomato sauce made in the following way:

   Sauce:
   Add a little sugar and enough tomato purée to the cream to colour it pink.

Tarragon Eggs

Ingredients:
5 eggs
2 tablesp. vegetable oil
1 tablesp. fresh chopped or green-dried parsley
1 tablesp. fresh chopped or green-dried tarragon
Salt

Method:
1. Boil the eggs for 8 minutes, shell and halve.
2. Remove the yolks and mash with a fork.
3. Blend in the yolks with the oil (slowly) and herbs.
4. Add salt to taste and blend well together.
5. Fill the whites with the mixture.
6. Serve on lettuce with quartered tomatoes.

Picnic Omelette (*serves 4–6*)

This omelette is a good (hearty) dish for a family meal, but can also be taken cold for fork-supper in the garden or to a picnic.

Ingredients:

1 tin (15½ oz.) butter beans
1 onion, finely chopped
Sunflower oil
Salt
½ teasp. fresh chopped or green-dried sage
½ teasp. fresh chopped or green-dried basil

½ teasp. fresh chopped or green-dried summer savory
Pinch of thyme
6 eggs
Knob of butter

Method:

1. Rinse butter beans well in cold water and drain them well.
2. Sauté the beans with finely chopped onion in just enough oil to prevent the beans from sticking.
3. When they begin to take on colour add all the herbs and salt, if necessary.
4. Heat enough butter in a large omelette pan to cover the bottom.
5. Beat 6 eggs with 2 tablesp. cold water.
6. Pour two-thirds of the eggs into the pan.
7. When the eggs have just set spread the bean mixture on them.
8. Pour over this the remaining eggs and set the pan under the grill under a low heat until the surface of the omelette is formed.
9. Cover the omelette and chill in the refrigerator.

Poor Knight Fritters

This savoury snack is quick and easy.

Ingredients:

1 egg
Salt, according to taste
1 teasp. fresh chopped or green-dried basil
½ teasp. fresh chopped or green-dried summer savory

2 slices of bread
½ oz. fat or oil
2 tomatoes
2 rashers bacon

Method:
1. Beat the egg well, adding salt and herbs.
2. Cut 3 or 4 half-slices of bread and remove crust.
3. Coat with the egg.
4. Melt the fat in a heavy saucepan and when very hot lay the bread in the fat.
5. Turn almost immediately to set the egg on both sides.
6. Brown under grill.
7. Garnish with grilled half-tomatoes, sprinkled with basil or chopped grilled bacon, if liked.

Farmer's Omelette (*serves 4–6*)

A hearty omelette as its name implies.

Ingredients:

1 small cabbage
2 boiled potatoes
either
1 cup grated cheese
1 oz. oil
  or
  5 oz. coarsely chopped bacon
  1½ oz. melted bacon fat

1 tablesp. fresh chopped or green-dried lovage
1 teasp. fresh chopped or green-dried basil and tarragon, mixed
1 pinch nutmeg
3 eggs beaten up with 3 tablesp. double cream
Oil for frying

Method:
1. Boil quickly one small cabbage in salted water.
2. Drain well and press out liquid.
3. Chop up finely.
4. Grate boiled potatoes and mix with cabbage.
5. Add to this grated cheese and oil, or bacon and melted bacon fat.
6. Add eggs beaten up with cream, basil, tarragon, nutmeg, and lovage.
7. Pour the well-beaten mixture into a frying-pan and cook over low heat.
8. Turn omelette and fry well on both sides; turn over with the help of a lid.

Note: Farmer's omelette can be made either with cheese or bacon.

Cream Cheese Custards (*serves 6*)

Light and delicious with any vegetable.

Ingredients:

½ lb. cream cheese
½ cup, half milk and half cream
¼ cup sauterne wine
1 tablesp. fresh chopped or green-dried onion green
4 eggs
1 teasp. fresh chopped or green-dried rosemary

½ teasp. salt seasoned with paprika
1 teasp. fresh chopped or green-dried tarragon
Butter
Fresh herb sprigs or watercress

Method:

1. Thoroughly blend cheese with cream and wine.
2. Add onion green, rosemary, and tarragon.
3. Beat eggs with seasoned salt and combine with cheese mixture.
4. Butter bottom of 6 ramekins or custard cups and fill.
5. Set in a pan of hot water, half depth of custards.
6. Serve hot from ramekins,
   or
7. Let stand 5 minutes and turn out on serving dishes.
8. Garnish each with a sprig of herb or watercress.
9. Serve at a luncheon or as a savoury dish for dinner.

Cheddar Ring with Brussels Sprouts (*serves 6*) (B)

Brussels sprouts are the natural accompaniment to this light but satisfying ring; any other vegetables, prepared in a similar way, can be used instead.

Ingredients:

¼ cup melted butter *or* margarine
1¾ cups hot milk
1 cup soft bread cubes
3 cups (about ¾ lb.) shredded mild or medium sharp Cheddar cheese
2 cups cooked rice
3 eggs, beaten
1 tablesp. chopped onion
1 teasp. salt
3–4 cups hot cooked and flavoured brussels sprouts

1 tablesp. fresh chopped or green-dried marigold
1 teasp. fresh chopped or green-dried summer savory
1 teasp. fresh chopped or green-dried basil
1 teasp. fresh chopped or green-dried parsley
1 teasp. fresh chopped or green-dried chives
or
4 teasp. bouquet for omelettes

Method:

1. Combine butter, milk, bread, cheese, rice, eggs, onion, herbs, salt.
2. Mix thoroughly.
3. Pour into well buttered 3–4 pint size ring-mould. Set in a pan of hot water and bake in a moderately hot oven (350°) for 1 hour or until surface is brown.
4. Loosen edges with a knife and turn out on to a warm, flat serving dish.
5. Fill centre with hot cooked brussels sprouts.
6. Brussels sprouts to be cooked with onions, onion green, lovage, and parsley (Recipe, page 269).

Cheese Soufflé

This is a delicate savoury which could be served as an accompaniment to vegetables for lunch or dinner and is also a substantial protein supplying dish for the family.

Allow one egg per person; therefore the ingredients are given per egg.

Ingredients (per egg):

1 oz. grated Cheddar *or* Gruyère cheese

½ oz. butter

2 tablesp. of cream; *or* top of the milk; *or* sour cream; *or* half yoghourt and half cream

1 teasp. fresh chopped or green-dried chives

or

1 teasp. bouquet for omelette

½ tablesp. plain flour

Method:

1. Cream the butter well with a little salt and a pinch of paprika and gradually add one yolk after the other, the grated cheese, the cream, and the flour, beating all the time. When well mixed, gently add the stiffly beaten whites of eggs.
2. Fill mixture into well-buttered dishes lined with breadcrumbs and bake in a temperature of 350°. If baked in individual dishes, 20 minutes may be enough, but if baked in one dish, at least 30–40 minutes are necessary.

Note: If a soufflé of 6 eggs is used for a festive occasion, the flour can be omitted and 8 tablesp. of full-cream, well whipped, should be gently folded in before baking.

If 5 or 6 eggs are used, a teasp. of one or the other (up to 5–6 teasp.) of the following fresh chopped or green-dried herbs can be used:

Parsley	Lemon balm	Chives
Tarragon	Onion green	Marjoram
	Thyme	

(See GUIDE, page 127, for proportions)
or
5–6 teasp. of bouquet for omelette.

Bread and Cheese Pie (*serves 3–4*) (B)

A savoury edition of the well-tried bread-and-butter pudding.

Ingredients:

5 slices fairly thin dry bread	A little butter
1 large tomato	6 oz. grated Cheddar cheese
1 large onion, cooked	½ pint milk
1 dessertsp. fresh chopped or green-dried celery leaves	2 eggs
	Salt and pepper

Method:

1. Lightly butter and cut bread into approximately 1-in. squares, put half in greased pie-dish.
2. Slice tomato and place layer over bread (need not be completely covered).
3. Slice onion and place layer over tomato and bread.
4. Place a layer of bread squares over onion.
5. Sprinkle over celery leaves.
6. Heat milk, beaten egg, and cheese until cheese has melted, stirring all the time.
7. Pour over contents of pie-dish and leave to soak through.
8. Bake in a hot oven (400° F.) for about 20 minutes until set and top is golden brown.

Cheese Popovers (*serves 6*)

Delicious served with Frankfurter green sauce *or* Spring sauce (Recipes, page 285).

Ingredients:

½ cup grated Cheddar cheese
2 eggs
½ pint milk
4 oz. flour
½ teasp. salt

½ teasp. fresh chopped or green-dried thyme
1 teasp. fresh chopped or green-dried chives

Method:

1. Grease 6 ramekin dishes.
2. Divide the grated Cheddar, placing it in the bottom of each dish.
3. Beat together well the eggs and the milk.
4. Mix flour, salt, and herbs.
5. Make a well in centre of flour and gradually add milk mixture, stirring all the time.
6. When batter is smooth and free from lumps, pour into ramekin dishes.
7. Bake in a hot oven (425° F.) for about 20–30 minutes, or until they are puffed and brown.

Cheese Savoury (*serves 4*) (B)

This makes a good luncheon dish. A slice of tomato and a strip of crisp bacon can be placed on the cheese.

Ingredients:

1 tablesp. flour
1 tablesp. butter
¾ cup milk
Pinch of salt
¼ teasp. fresh chopped or green-dried basil
¼ teasp. fresh chopped or green-dried summer savory

2 tablesp. tomato sauce
6 oz. grated Cheddar cheese
1 cup cooked vegetables such as peas, string beans, or spinach
Paprika

Method:

1. Blend flour and butter in a saucepan over a low flame.
2. Smooth out with milk, add salt, herbs, tomato sauce.
3. Add cheese, and stir until it is melted and smooth.
4. Add the cup of vegetables and stir in well.
5. Serve on toast with a dash of paprika over each.

Sage Fritters

Ingredients:

Batter:

Fresh whole or green-dried whole sage leaves
Batter (page 312)
Frankfurter green sauce (page 285);
or
   Spring sauce (page 285);
or
   Remoulade dressing (page 195);
or
   Tomato sauce (page 286)

4 tablesp. flour
Salt
6 tablesp. water
1 yolk of egg
1 white of egg
(Method, page 312)

Method:
1. Use fresh sage leaves, 1 or 2 per fritter, according to size. (If green-dried sage leaves are used, they should be reconstituted in water and then drained on a sieve.)
2. Dip sage leaves into batter.
3. Deep fry fritters in vegetable oil or butter until golden brown.
4. Drain and serve dry accompanied by one of the four sauces.

Cheese Snack (B)

For a one-woman lunch (takes 10 minutes).
   For Sunday supper round the fire.

Method:
1. Put 1 slice of cheese between 2 slices of bread which have been lightly buttered on both sides.
2. Sprinkle either chives or bouquet for omelettes on both inner-buttered sides facing the cheese, or chives on one side and bouquet for omelettes on the other.
3. Grill on both sides of sandwich until bread is golden brown and cheese is softened.

Five Herb Cheese (*makes about 1 cup*)

For your cheeseboard – excellent for snacks.

Ingredients:

½ lb. Cheddar cheese, shredded   2 tablesp. whipped cream
1 dessertsp. each fresh chopped   4 tablesp. sherry
   or green-dried parsley, chives,
   thyme, sage, and summer savory

Method:

1. Blend well by hand (or with electric mixer) the cheese, herbs, cream, and sherry.
2. Refrigerate for several days, or use immediately.

SOUPS

Vichysoisse (*serves 6*)

Traditionally a creamy-cold soup, but equally good served hot in winter.

Ingredients:
6 leeks, finely chopped
1 onion, finely chopped
2 oz. butter
1½ pints chicken stock
4 potatoes, peeled and sliced
Salt

1 pint milk
⅛ teasp. mace
¼ pint cream
¼ cup chopped chives, fresh or
  green-dried

Method:

1. Gently sauté the leeks and onion in butter.
2. Cover and cook, but do not brown.
3. Add the stock, and potatoes, and salt.
4. Cook until all vegetables are tender.
5. Put the vegetables through a sieve.
6. Heat the milk with the mace.
7. Add to vegetable mixture.
8. Chill.
9. Beat for 2 minutes; add cream and beat again.
10. Serve very cold topped with a liberal amount of chopped chives.

Note: If chives are green-dried they should be reconstituted in a little stock before using.

Cold Cucumber Soup (*serves 6*)

The crunchy cucumber pieces make this an unusual soup for summer parties.

Ingredients:

2 cups milk
3 beaten eggs
2 tablesp. finely chopped fresh onion green
or 1 tablesp. green-dried onion green
or the same quantity of chives
1 tablesp. finely chopped fresh or green-dried celery leaves
1 cup sour cream
1 cup chicken broth
½ cup white table wine
1½ cups finely chopped peeled cucumber
½ teasp. paprika
1 teasp. salt
1 teasp. fresh chopped or green-dried dill

Method:

1. Heat milk over direct heat in top part of double boiler.
2. Gradually stir in beaten eggs and onion green and celery leaves.
3. Place over hot water, and cook, stirring, until mixture coats a spoon.
4. Remove from heat and cool.
5. Fold in sour cream.
6. Stir in broth, wine, cucumber, paprika, salt, and dill.
7. Chill thoroughly.

Chervil Soup (*serves 4*)

Best of all soups.

Ingredients:

2–3 tablesp. butter *or* oil
2 tablesp. flour
3 tablesp. fresh chopped or green-dried chervil

1 pint hot vegetable stock
Salt
1 tablesp. cream, fresh or sour

Method:

1. Sauté chervil in butter, or oil.
2. Add the flour and sauté again.
3. Smooth with a little cold water or stock.
4. Add the hot stock and salt.
5. Cook for 20 minutes.
6. Lastly, add the cream, shortly before serving.

Sorrel Soup (*serves 6–8*)

One of the most popular French soups.

Ingredients:

1 oz. butter *or* oil
1 lettuce (large)
2 tablesp. fresh chopped or green-dried sorrel, reconstituted
4 potatoes, quartered
1 onion *or* ½ leek, chopped

1 cup spinach *or* equivalent in lettuce
2 quarts boiling stock *or* water
1 tablesp. fresh chopped or green-dried chervil
(4 slices buttered toast, if liked)

Method:

1. Sauté onion or leek in hot butter or oil, without browning, in large saucepan.
2. Add sorrel, chopped up lettuce, and spinach, and sauté.
3. Add potatoes and stock.
4. Simmer gently for 45 minutes.
5. Mash potatoes or pass through a coarse sieve.
6. Add chervil and simmer for five minutes.

Note: If the soup is wanted to be more substantial, serve over buttered toast.

Lovage Soup (*serves 4*)

A full-bodied nourishing soup.

Ingredients:

2 onions
½ oz. butter
½ oz. flour
1 pint stock
½ pint milk

Salt
2 tablesp. fresh chopped or green-dried lovage
1 tablesp. chopped parsley

Method:

1. Peel and slice onions.
2. Sauté onions in the butter until soft but not brown.
3. Add the lovage and sauté.
4. Add flour and cook for a further few minutes.
5. Add stock and salt. Stir until it comes to the boil.
6. Simmer for 20 minutes.
7. Add milk.
8. Put through a sieve or blender.
9. Heat again, and serve sprinkled with chopped parsley.

Herb Soup (*serves 6*)

A delicately flavoured soup to be made all-the-year-round.

Ingredients:

3 tablesp. flour
2 tablesp. butter *or* oil
2 pints stock
2 tablesp. cream
2½ tablesp., mixed fresh chopped or green-dried tarragon, chervil,

parsley, lovage, and basil (for proportions, see GUIDE, page 127)
or
2½ tablesp. herb bouquet for soups and stews

Method:

1. Sauté 3 tablesp. flour in butter or oil.
2. Add stock, and cook for 20 minutes.
3. Put herbs and cream into a large bowl.
4. Add thickened hot stock and mix well.
5. Allow to stand for ½ hour.
6. Reheat and serve.

Note: This soup could also be made with chives only.

Herb Soup (2nd version)

This version is particularly suited when using green-dried herbs.
The same ingredients as the above Herb Soup.

Method:
1. Sauté the flour in butter or oil.
2. Add all the herbs and sauté.
3. Smooth with stock and then add all the stock.
4. Cook for 20 minutes.
5. Add cream shortly before serving.

Green Soup (*serves 6*)

A substantial soup which also makes a good main course for
lunch or supper.

Ingredients:

3 pints beef, ham, or strong vegetable stock

8 oz. minced raw spinach

4 oz. fresh chopped onion green *or* ½ oz. green-dried onion green (= 8 tablesp.)

4 oz. mixed greens (kale, brussels, or beet tops, etc.), chopped

1 teasp. fresh or green-dried sorrel

Bouquet of parsley, celery leaves, and rosemary, *or* 1 teasp. green-dried each of parsley and celery leaves

¼ teasp. rosemary

1 tablesp. flour

5 tablesp. sour cream

2 tablesp. top of the milk

3 hard-boiled eggs

Method:
1. Bring the stock slowly to the boil.
2. Add the spinach, onion green, mixed vegetable greens; and the herbs tied together.
3. Simmer for 1 hour.
4. Remove pan from fire and take out the herbs, if in a bunch.
5. Mix flour with sour cream, gradually adding a little of the hot soup at the same time, until the mixture is fairly thin and smooth.
6. Add mixture to soup-pan, return it to the fire and stir until it thickens slightly and just comes to a boil.
7. Serve with slices of hard-boiled egg in each soup-bowl.

Thick Vegetable Soup (*serves 6–8*)

Ingredients:

1 tablesp. vegetable fat
1 tablesp. chopped onion
½ leek, shredded
¼ celery, shredded
1 small carrot, diced
2–3 cabbage leaves, shredded
1–2 diced potatoes
Some spinach beet leaves
1 handful cooked beans
2 ripe tomatoes *or* 1 teasp. tomato purée, diluted
4 pints water
1 teasp. fresh chopped or green-dried chives

1 teasp. fresh chopped or green-dried parsley
1 teasp. fresh chopped or green-dried lovage
1 tablesp. mixed of: summer savory; celery leaves; basil; onion green; marjoram, (pinch); thyme, (pinch); sorrel, (pinch); rosemary, (pinch)
or
2½ tablesp. bouquet for soups and stews

Method:

1. Melt fat and sauté onions in it.
2. Add all vegetables and sauté together.
3. Add tomatoes, or purée, and sauté again.
4. Then add water, herbs, and salt and simmer for 1 hour.

Note: This soup can be made more substantial and thus becomes like the Italian Minestroné, if the following ingredients are added:

    5½ oz. noodles, spaghetti, *or* rice
    1 tablesp. butter
    2 tablesp. grated cheese (Parmesan or other)

Method:

5. Add noodles or rice and cook with the mixture for the last 15 minutes.
6. When cooked, put butter and grated cheese into a tureen or bowls and pour soup.

Thick Lentil Soup (*serves 6–8*)

Quite a good meal in itself, with or without smoked sausage or Frankfurters.

Lentils are not only one of the most nourishing foods, but also are more easily digested than either beans or peas. They are an important substitute for meat, fish, or poultry. In spite of their reputation as 'a poor man's meat' they have a delicious flavour, if properly cooked, particularly with herbs.

Two kinds of lentils are available in this country; the browny-green German lentils and the reddish-yellow small Egyptian lentils. The German lentils are 'whole' while the Egyptian lentils are sold without a seed coat, looking more like split peas.

Ingredients:
½–1 lb. pink *or* green lentils (select, rinse, and soak overnight)
1 large onion, chopped
1 clove garlic, chopped
2 leeks, cut up in slices
1 celery, cut up in small pieces
1 small carrot, small strips
2 small potatoes, in dices

2 teasp. fresh chopped or green-dried lovage } *or* 2 tablesp. bou-
¼ teasp. fresh chopped or green-dried marjoram } quet for soups and
1 tablesp. fresh chopped or green-dried parsley } stews, with a little
extra marjoram

3 pints water *or* stock
1 oz. flour
1 oz. butter *or* dripping
½ pint stock *or* water
Salt
1 ring of smoked sausage or a round of thick small smoked sausages
or
1 pair of Frankfurters per person

Method:
1. Sauté onions and garlic.
2. Add and sauté vegetables and herbs.
3. Add soaked lentils and their water.
4. Add diced potatoes and salt.
5. Boil until tender (1 hour or more) or cook for 15 minutes in the pressure cooker.
6. Melt the butter, add the flour and sauté.
7. Smooth with water or stock.
8. Allow to boil for 2–3 minutes.
9. Add to the lentil soup and allow to boil.
10. If sausage is served, add it now and allow to simmer for 10 minutes (or less if small sausages are used).

Chicken in Vegetable Soup

Ingredients:

1½ lb. bony chicken parts (such as wings and backs)
2 pints water
6 carrots, cut in halves
3 sprigs parsley *or* 1 tablesp. green-dried parsley
1 medium-sized onion, sliced
1 small stalk celery
1 bay leaf
¼ teasp. fresh chopped or green-dried thyme
¼ teasp. fresh chopped or green-dried marjoram
1 teasp. fresh chopped or green-dried tarragon
1 teasp. fresh chopped or green-dried summer savory
1½ teasp. salt
Chopped chives

Method:

1. In a large saucepan put the chicken, water, carrots, parsley, onion, celery, bay leaf, thyme, marjoram, tarragon, summer savory, and salt.
2. Bring to a boil, cover, and simmer for 2 hours.
3. Strain and chill stock; when cold, discard fat layer.
4. Force carrots through a wire strainer and add to stock.

Chicken Vegetable Soup

This same soup can have its flavour heightened by adding minced chicken to stock.

5. Put meat and skin from chicken through the mincer; add to stock.
6. Heat and serve, sprinkling each serving with chopped chives.

Court Bouillon – Stock in which to Boil Fish

Ingredients:

2 shallots
6 tiny onions
1 shredded carrot
1 bay leaf
Small strip of lemon rind
1 teasp. fresh chopped or green-dried parsley
1 teasp. fresh chopped or green-dried summer savory
1 tablesp. fresh chopped or green-dried lovage
1 teasp. fresh chopped or green-dried thyme
1 teasp. fresh chopped or green-dried basil
½ teasp. salt
4 peppercorns
Equal quantities of water and dry white wine *or* cider to cover

Method:
1. Put all ingredients into a large saucepan.
2. Bring to the boil, cover and allow to simmer for half an hour.
3. When tepid, put in prepared fish and simmer until cooked, about 15 minutes.
Note: If the fish is to be served cold, allow to cool in the court bouillon.

Fish Soup (*serves 4*)

An appetizing and unusual soup.

Ingredients:

2½ lb. mixed boned fish
2 large onions
2 tomatoes
2 cloves garlic
½ cup corn oil
4 teasp. fresh chopped or green-dried fennel

2 teasp. fresh chopped or green-dried parsley
A pinch of marigold petals
1 bay leaf
Salt and pepper to taste
Bread
Butter
2 pints water

Method:
1. Pound garlic, chop onions, and tomatoes, and place in stew-pan with seasoning, herbs, and olive oil.
2. Set over heat and bring to simmering point.
3. Simmer for 5 minutes, add 2 pints water and fish, and bring back to simmering point and cook until all is tender.
4. For each person, fry a slice of bread in butter, lay in the bottom of a hot plate and pour soup over this.

Alternatively – serve the whole contents in a tureen; remove bay leaf.

Tomato Soup with Herbs (*serves 4*)

A delicate summer soup.

Ingredients:

1 teasp. fresh chopped or green-dried basil
1 teasp. fresh chopped or green-dried lovage
Fresh chopped or green-dried chives

2 lb. ripe tomatoes
Salt
1 teasp. sugar
2–3 tablesp. thin *or* sour cream
1 teasp. lemon juice

Method:
1. Chop tomatoes finely, add salt, sugar, basil, and lovage.
2. Bring to the boil, then simmer slowly until tomatoes are pulpy.
3. Sieve.
4. Add lemon juice and cream and serve at once piping hot, garnished with chives.

A number of soups gain a special flavour and strength by the addition of herbs. In many cases this avoids using salt or seasonings for those who should not have them or at least reduce the use of salt in cooking and eating. Apart from this purpose, the herbs often replace meat and bones; vegetable broth and yeast extracts can be used instead as the herbs strengthen the soup.

Rice Soup (*serves 4–6*)

So good – and yet so simple to make.

Ingredients:

1½ oz. brown rice
1 tablesp. butter *or* oil
1 small onion, finely chopped
1 leek, finely chopped
Some celery *or* celeriac, finely chopped
1 small carrot, sliced
2–2½ pints stock
2 teasp. parsley, fresh chopped or green-dried

1 teasp. fresh chopped or green-dried chervil
1 teasp. fresh chopped or green-dried basil
1 teasp. fresh chopped or green-dried lovage
Nut of butter

Method:
1. Rinse rice in a sieve under running warm water; allow to drain.
2. Sauté onion in butter or oil; add vegetables and sauté; add rice and sauté.
3. Add boiling stock and allow to cook until rice is tender.
4. Add all the herbs and leave to stand in warm place for 15 minutes.
5. Before serving add nut of butter.

Cauliflower Soup (*serves 6*)

Ingredients:

1 small cauliflower
1 bay leaf

1 teasp. fresh chopped or green-dried chervil

1 tablesp. butter *or* oil
3 tablesp. flour
4 pints vegetable stock
Salt
1 tablesp. fresh chopped or green-dried parsley
1 teasp. fresh chopped or green-dried basil

1 teasp. fresh chopped or green-dried salad burnet (if available)
½ teasp. fresh chopped or green-dried lemon balm
1 teasp. lemon juice
Nut of butter
2 tablesp. cream

Method:
1. Cook cauliflower florets carefully in salted water with a bay leaf.
2. Cut uncooked stalks into small pieces.
3. Heat fat and sauté flour.
4. Add small pieces of stalk and sauté together.
5. Add stock, salt and herbs and cook for ¾ hour.
6. Put all through a sieve.
7. Add cooked florets, lemon juice, cream, and butter shortly before serving.
8. Heat through but do not allow to boil again.

Semolina and Leek Soup (*serves 4–6*)

Ingredients:
1 oz. semolina
1 dessertsp. wholemeal flour
1 small onion, finely chopped
2 dessertsp. butter *or* oil
2 leeks, finely chopped
2–2½ pints stock
Salt
½ teasp. fresh chopped or green-dried basil

½ teasp. caraway
1 teasp. fresh chopped or green-dried lovage
1 teasp. fresh chopped or green-dried lemon balm
2 tablesp. cream (optional)

Method:
1. Sauté onion in butter or oil until golden.
2. Add leeks and sauté.
3. Add semolina, and flour, and sauté.
4. Smooth with a little stock; then add remaining stock and allow to cook for about 20 minutes.
5. Add salt, caraway, and all the herbs.
6. Leave in a warm place for 15 minutes.
7. Add cream before serving.

Curly Kale Soup (*serves 6*)

Ingredients:

½ lb. curly kale
¾ lb. potatoes, peeled and diced
1 large onion, finely chopped
Some celery *or* celeriac, finely chopped
1 small carrot, sliced
1 teasp. tomato purée
1 oz. butter *or* oil

2½–3 pints stock
½ teasp. mixed fresh chopped or green-dried marjoram and sage
½ teasp. fresh chopped or green-dried basil
1 teasp. fresh chopped or green-dried lovage
Butter (size of a nut)

Method:

1. Strip curly kale off stalks and ribs; wash and drain.
2. Cook, covered, with a little addition of stock for 5 minutes; chop finely.
3. Sauté onion in butter or oil; add all other vegetables and sauté.
4. Add boiling stock; mix this with curly kale; allow to cook until tender.
5. Add the herbs and allow to stand in warm place for 15 minutes.
6. Add a nut of butter before serving.

Spring Soup

Ingredients:

1 tablesp. butter *or* oil
4 tablesp. flour
3½ pints water *or* stock
Salt
1 small onion, sliced
1 small carrot, sliced
1 teasp. fresh chopped or green-dried celery leaves

1 teasp. fresh chopped or green-dried lovage
Some young spinach leaves, young nettle, and/or dandelion, sorrel, and lovage leaves, chopped finely

Method:

1. Heat fat, add flour, and cook gently for a few minutes.
2. Add stock, salt, vegetables, chopped leaves, and herbs.
3. Simmer for half-hour.
4. Add milk, heat through again, and serve.
5. Put cream into bowl, or divide into individual bowls, and pour soup over.

Chapter 5

FISH

Chilled Salmon (*serves 10–12*)

An attractive party dish.

Ingredients:

4 lb. fresh salmon
1 pint milk
1 pint boiling water
1 tablesp. salt
2 bay leaves
1 cup mayonnaise
1 grated carrot

1 teasp. bouquet for fish
or 1 teasp. mixed fresh chopped or green-dried dill, fennel, and parsley
½ teasp. fresh chopped or green-dried basil
1 hard-boiled egg

Method:

1. Wrap salmon in cheese cloth to hold it together.
2. Place milk, boiling water, salt, bay leaves, herbs, in a saucepan large enough to hold the whole piece of salmon.
3. Boil for 5 minutes.
4. Add fish and cook gently for 35 minutes.

5. Allow fish to cool in water.
6. Remove and drain, remove skin.
7. Chill, covered, in the refrigerator.
8. Blend mayonnaise and spread over cold salmon on a serving platter.
9. Decorate with slices of hard-boiled egg and grated carrot and sprinkle with bouquet for fish or parsley, fennel, and dill, and the basil.

Bass, Mullet, or Mackerel Flambé au Fenouil (*serves 4*)

An exquisite dish well known in France – for a dinner party.

Ingredients:

2 bass at approx. 1 lb. each
Little salt
3 teasp. fresh chopped or green-dried fennel leaves, *or* 4 tablesp. green-dried fennel
1 sprig fresh chopped sage, *or* 2 teasp. green-dried sage
Large bunch of fennel (stalks and leaves), green-dried straight from the plant, *or* 2 handfuls of green-dried fennel from a jar
4 tablesp. oil
1 lemon, cut in slices
Parsley for garnish
1 glass brandy

Method:

1. Wash and prepare the fish, dry and salt inside and out.
2. Fill the fish with the chopped fennel and sage.
3. Arrange a bed of green-dried fennel in the bottom of the grill-pan.
4. Brush fish on both sides with oil and place on wire rack of grill-pan above the fennel.
5. Grill fish, turning once, and brushing with oil from time to time.
6. Warm brandy.
7. When fish is grilled, remove fennel bed to flat fireproof serving dish.
8. Place fish on fennel bed and decorate with lemon and parsley.
9. Pour warmed brandy over, light, and serve while burning.

Spanish Halibut Casserole (*serves 4–6*)

Substantial, yet tasty family dish.

Ingredients:
2 lb. cooked halibut
1 medium-sized onion, finely chopped
¼ cup chopped green pepper
1 cup chopped celery
2 tablesp. sunflower oil *or* butter
1 tin (10½ oz.) condensed tomato soup
1 soup tin water
Salt
1 teasp. curry powder
2 teasp. lemon juice
1 tablesp. bouquet for fish
or
   1 teasp. each fresh chopped or green-dried tarragon, basil, and celery
     leaves; ½ teasp. each fresh chopped or green-dried marjoram and
     summer savory; ¼ teasp. fresh chopped or green-dried thyme
¼ lb. shredded sharp Cheddar cheese
1 cup dried breadcrumbs

Method:
1. Sauté onions, green pepper, and celery in oil until soft, but not
   brown.
2. Add tomato soup and the can of water.
3. Add all other ingredients but halibut, cheese, and breadcrumbs.
4. Let this simmer for 15 minutes.
5. Flake halibut into a large bowl and add previous mixture,
   together with breadcrumbs.
6. Blend well.
7. Place into greased casserole and bake in a medium oven (350° F.)
   for about 30 minutes, until heated through.
8. Add grated cheese topping and put casserole under the grill
   until cheese is slightly browned.

Fillet of Sole Rolls with Egg Sauce (*serves 6*)

Ingredients:
6 fillets of sole, approx. same
  size

Egg Sauce Ingredients:
2 tablesp. butter
2 tablesp. flour

2 teasp. butter
1 small onion, chopped
½ cup breadcrumbs, soaked in milk and then squeezed
15 cooked shrimps (about ½ lb.), finely chopped
½ teasp. each fresh chopped or green-dried parsley, dill, chervil
½ teasp. fresh chopped or green-dried summer savory
1 hard-boiled egg, finely mashed
Salt
1 egg white, beaten stiff

½ teasp. salt
½ cup stock
½ cup dry white wine
2 hard-boiled eggs
2 tablesp. double cream
1 teasp. each fresh chopped or green-dried parsley and summer savory
1 teasp. chopped capers

Method:

1. Melt butter in saucepan and sauté onion until cooked, but not brown.
2. Add squeezed breadcrumbs, shrimps, herbs, mashed egg, and salt.
3. Cook gently for 3 minutes and remove from heat.
4. Add egg white and fold in.
5. Fill fillets with this mixture, roll, and fix with tooth-picks.
6. Arrange in a greased shallow baking-dish; cover with foil.
7. Bake in a moderate oven (350° F.) for 20 minutes or just until sole flakes with a fork. DO NOT OVERCOOK.
8. Remove tooth-picks and serve with egg sauce.

Egg Sauce

1. Melt the butter in saucepan.
2. Add the flour and salt, and stir until smooth.
3. Whip with a wire whisk.
4. Add the stock and the wine.
5. Simmer for 5 minutes.
6. Add hard-boiled eggs, finely chopped, and double cream.
7. Heat again but do not bring to the boil; then remove from heat.
8. Add parsley, summer savory, and capers.
9. Serve hot with sole rolls.

Scallops and Shrimps with Herbs (*serves 6*)

The delicate herbs cooked together with the shellfish make it an
excellent dish.

Ingredients:

½ lb. scallops
3 tablesp. butter
½ teasp. green-dried tarragon
1 teasp. green-dried chervil or
freshly chopped parsley
2 teasp. chopped onion
¼ lb. shelled shrimps
1 tablesp. flour

½ cup, equal portions, milk and
cream
¼ cup chicken broth *or* dry white
table wine
Salt and pepper
Toasted buttered croutons

Method:

1. Melt butter slowly in a frying-pan, together with tarragon,
chervil, and chopped onion.
2. Add scallops, and cook over medium-high heat for 3–4
minutes, stirring constantly.
3. Stir in shrimps.
4. Blend in flour, cream, milk, and chicken broth.
5. Cook, stirring constantly, until sauce is thickened, season to
taste.
6. Divide into 6 scallop shells or serve on a flat fireproof dish.
7. Top with breadcrumbs and dots of butter and brown under
the grill.
8. Serve with hot thin toast.

Halibut in Wine and Lemon (*serves 6*)

An elegant dish for a dinner party. The halibut steaks should be
marinated in a mixture of lemon and wine to which is added a
mixture of the following herbs (or those which are available):

1 tablesp. mixed of parsley,
tarragon, chervil, dill
1 teasp. mixed of basil, marjoram,

thyme, summer savory: and a
bay leaf, or the equivalent in
shredded bay leaves

This marinade becomes the basis of the sauce served with the
halibut.

Ingredients:

6 halibut steaks (about 2 lb.)
1 egg
2 tablesp. lemon juice
1¼ cups dry white wine
Salt

A dash of paprika
4 tablesp. butter *or* margarine
1 tablesp. fresh chopped or green-
dried parsley

Method:

1. Arrange fish steaks in a single layer close together in a shallow dish.
2. Beat together egg, lemon juice, 1 cup of the wine, salt, and
all the herbs.
3. Pour mixture over the fish.
4. Cover lightly.
5. Allow to chill for 1 hour.
6. Lift fish from marinade and drain well.
7. Heat 2 tablesp. butter in a wide frying-pan.
8. Add fish steaks and brown on both sides, until cooked.
9. Place fish on a heated platter in a warm place.
10. Melt the remaining 2 tablesp. of butter in the frying-pan.
11. Add 1 cup marinade and ¼ cup of wine.
12. Bring to rapid boil.
13. Pour some of the sauce over the fish.
14. Serve remaining sauce in a sauce-boat at the table to add to
each serving.
15. Sprinkle fish with chopped parsley and garnish with lemon
slices.

Fish Steaks (*serves 4*) (B)

A succulent way to serve fish for the family.

Ingredients:

4 cod steaks
2 tablesp. oil
1 tablesp. butter
1 teasp. fresh chopped or green-
dried basil
½ teasp. fresh chopped or green-
dried thyme
2 teasp. fresh chopped or green-
dried parsley
1 teasp. fresh chopped or green-
dried celery leaves

Salt and pepper
1 clove garlic, finely chopped
or ¼ teasp. concentrated garlic salt
2 pints stock
6 oz. rice, long grained
1 stalk celery, chopped
1 onion, sliced
A knob of butter
4 tomatoes, thickly sliced
Chopped parsley for garnish

Method:
1. Dust fish steaks with flour.
2. Brown quickly in hot oil and butter.
3. Place in a fireproof dish.
4. Sprinkle over herbs, seasoning and garlic.
5. Add ½ cup stock and put in slow to moderate oven (350° F.) for 15–20 minutes.
6. Bring rest of stock to boil, add rice, celery, and onion.
7. Boil till just tender, about 15 minutes; drain.
8. Stir knob of butter into the rice.
9. Fry quickly the sliced tomatoes.
10. Arrange fish steaks on the rice garnished with tomatoes and chopped parsley.
11. Serve very hot.

Blushing Cod (*serves 4*) (B)

A tasty yet satisfying way of serving everyday fish.

Ingredients:

2 lb. cod on the bone	1 clove garlic
2–3 bay leaves	1 lb. peeled tomatoes *or* 1 large
Salt	tin tomatoes
1 oz. butter	2 teasp. fresh chopped or green-
1 onion, finely sliced	dried basil

Method:
1. Place fish in saucepan with water to cover well; add bay leaves and salt.
2. Bring slowly to the boil, cover and simmer until cooked – about 20 minutes.
3. Melt butter in a saucepan and sauté gently onion and garlic, do not let them get brown.
4. Add the tomatoes, ½ teasp. salt, and the basil, stir well, simmering gently.
5. Remove skin and bones from fish.
6. Add fish to tomato mixture, cover and leave on very low heat for 5 minutes.
7. Serve very hot surrounded by broccoli spears (when available).

Baked Halibut (*serves 4*)

A very good main dish; also makes a good barbecue meal.

Ingredients:

2 lb. halibut in one piece
¼ cup soy sauce
½ cup dry white wine
1 tablesp. lemon juice
1 clove garlic, minced
¼ cup salad oil

1 tablesp. fresh chopped or green-dried rosemary
3 tablesp. fresh chopped or green-dried parsley
½ lb. mushrooms, chopped
3 oz. butter

Method:

1. Mix together soy sauce, wine, lemon juice, garlic, and salad oil.
2. Pour this mixture over fish and marinate 2–3 hours.
3. Pour off marinade; save.
4. Rub fish with rosemary and parsley.
5. Place in baking-tin and cover with foil.
6. Place in a hot oven (450° F.) for about 40 minutes, basting fish twice with its own juices.
7. Sauté mushrooms in butter, add marinade and heat through.
8. Pour over fish and serve.

Note: To barbecue fish, put small pieces of it on skewers, grill over low heat coals; cook till fish flakes when tested, about 15 minutes.

Fish Soufflé (*serves 6–8*) (B)

A light fish dish, good for supper.

Ingredients:

3 lb. cod *or* haddock
2 tablesp. butter
2 tablesp. flour
1 pint milk
4 eggs, separated
Salt and pepper
1 tablesp. fresh chopped or green-dried fennel

1 teasp. fresh chopped or green-dried tarragon
½ teasp. fresh chopped or green-dried thyme
2 tablesp. fine breadcrumbs

Method:

1. Place fish in steamer over boiling water and steam for 10 minutes.
2. Remove skin and bones and flake fish.
3. Melt butter in a saucepan and stir in flour.
4. Cook a few minutes then add milk.
5. Stir until smooth and cook for 5 minutes, remove from heat.
6. Beat egg yolks and add with fish to saucepan.
7. Season with salt, paprika, and herbs.
8. Beat egg-whites until stiff; gradually fold into fish mixture.
9. Grease soufflé dish or casserole and sprinkle bottom with breadcrumbs.
10. Pour in fish mixture and place in pan of boiling water.
11. Bake in moderate oven (350° F.) for 30 minutes.

Stuffed Haddock (*serves 4*)

Makes a substantial family meal.

Ingredients:
2½ lb. haddock
3 tablesp. bacon fat
4 oz. mushrooms, chopped
A little flour
1½ cups court bouillon
   (Fish Stock, page 220)

Stuffing:
1 tablesp. chopped onion
1 oz. butter
6 tablesp. fresh breadcrumbs
1 tablesp. fresh chopped or green-dried parsley
1 teasp. fresh chopped or green-dried summer savory
Grated rind and juice of ½ lemon
1 egg beaten
Salt and paprika

Method:

1. Wash and dry the fish.
2. Sauté the onions lightly in the butter until soft, but not brown.
3. Mix with breadcrumbs, herbs, lemon rind, and juice.
4. Season with salt and paprika and bind with egg.
5. Stuff the haddock with this mixture and tie securely.
6. Heat the bacon fat in baking-pan, put in fish and baste.
7. Cover with foil, then cook in a moderate oven (350–400° F.) for about 40 minutes, basting once or twice during cooking.

8. Remove fish on to a hot dish.
9. Leave a tablesp. of fat in tin, cook the mushrooms in this.
10. Add flour, cook for a few minutes then add stock.
11. Serve the sauce with the fish.

Fresh Eel in Sage Leaves (*serves 4–6*)

A most delicate outcome of an unusual combination; eels and sage.

Ingredients:

2 medium-sized young fresh eels
¼ cup lemon juice
½ cup vegetable oil
1 large finely chopped onion

Bacon slices
Whole fresh or green-dried sage leaves

Approx. 1 tablesp. of a well-blended herb mixture of:

Fresh chopped or green-dried parsley, tarragon, dill *or* fennel, pinches of basil, marjoram, thyme, sage, summer savory, bay leaves
or 1 tablesp. bouquet for fish dishes

See GUIDE (page 127) for proportions

Method:

1. Skin eels and cut into pieces 2–3 in. long, according to thickness, and pour over the following marinade:

   Mix well lemon juice, oil, onion, and herbs, and if there is not enough liquid to cover the pieces of eel in a bowl, add a little water or stock to the marinade.

2. Set aside to marinate for about 1–2 hours.

3. Wrap each piece of eel in a slice of bacon and then cover with sage leaves and tie with thread.

   (If green-dried whole sage leaves are used for the wrapping, they should be reconstituted in water or marinade for ½–1 hour.)

4. Place wrapped pieces of eel in a flat fireproof dish and pour the marinade over them.

5. Bake in the oven uncovered for at least half an hour.

Chapter 6

MEAT

Braised Silverside (*serves 6*)

An unusual way to serve this succulent piece of beef.

Ingredients:

2 lb. unsalted silverside
½ lb. pork rind
3 onions
3 shallots
1 clove garlic
1 teasp. fresh chopped or green-dried thyme
1 tablesp. fresh chopped or green-dried parsley

1 teasp. fresh chopped or green-dried tarragon
1 teasp. fresh chopped or green-dried basil
¼ pint red wine
Salt and pepper
½ pint water
1 lb. carrots, sliced

Method:

1. Chop onions, shallots, and garlic.
2. Put them in a basin with beef, wine and ½ pint water.
3. Add the herbs.
4. Leave the meat to marinate 8–12 hours, if possible.
5. Cut pork rind into pieces to cover bottom of large heavy saucepan.
6. Put everything, save the carrots but including the marinade, into the pan. Season well with salt.
7. Bring to the boil with pan uncovered.
8. Lower heat to gentle simmering point and cover the pan tightly, first with aluminium foil and then with the lid pressed down.
9. Simmer for 3 hours or until tender, adding more wine or water if necessary.
10. After 2 hours, add sliced carrots.
11. Serve with the gravy from the pan.

Goulash (*serves 4*)

Egg noodles or risotto can accompany this goulash 'with a difference'.

Ingredients:

1 lb. chuck steak
1 large onion, sliced
2 or 3 tomatoes, chopped
1 tablesp. butter *or* bacon fat
1 clove garlic, chopped
3 potatoes, peeled and chopped
Salt
Paprika
½ teasp. bay leaf, shredded

1 teasp. fresh chopped or green-dried marjoram
1 cup red wine *or* water
1 green pepper chopped
2 oz. sour cream (optional)
Parsley, fresh chopped or green-dried

Method:
1. Cut meat into 1½-in. cubes.
2. Melt butter in saucepan and brown beef slowly.
3. Add onions and continue to cook until onions are tender.
4. Add seasoning, garlic, tomatoes, herbs, green pepper, and half the wine.
5. Cover and cook slowly (without boiling) for 3 hours.
6. Stir occasionally, adding more wine if necessary.
7. Add chopped potatoes and cook for a further 30 minutes.
8. Stir in sour cream and heat again.
9. Serve sprinkled with parsley.

Beef Casserole with Rosemary (*serves 4*)

Rosemary gives the beef casserole its exciting flavour.

Ingredients:

2 lb. topside *or* silverside
Some bacon for larding
Salt
A little flour
Oil
2 oz. butter *or* oil
1 clove garlic, chopped

4 cloves
2 teasp. fresh chopped or green-dried rosemary
1 teasp. fresh chopped or green-dried sage
¾ pint red wine

Method:
1. The prepared and salted meat is larded; in case larding is too difficult the beef can be wrapped in slices of bacon which are tied round the meat.
2. Dust the meat with flour and pour oil in drops on to meat.
3. Put the butter in a very heavy saucepan or fireproof casserole.
4. Add garlic, rosemary, sage, and a few cloves.
5. Cover well and allow the meat to simmer gently for 2 hours in low oven (300 F.°).
6. Add stock or water from time to time.
7. Add wine after 2 hours.
8. Allow to stew gently for another hour.
9. Any gravy which is left should be passed through a sieve and poured back over the meat.

Beefsteak Pie (*serves 4*)

To make this dish go farther, add a few small peeled potatoes.

Ingredients:

2 lb. chuck steak
1 tablesp. cooking oil *or* fat
¾ teasp. salt
A pinch of pepper
2 cups boiling water
2 teasp. fresh chopped basil *or* 1
    teasp. green-dried basil

2 teasp. fresh chopped thyme *or* 1
    teasp. green-dried thyme
1 medium sized onion, sliced
2 teasp. flour
A pinch of nutmeg
½ lb. flaky pastry

Method:
1. Cut steak into squares.
2. Heat fat in fireproof casserole placed over medium heat.
3. Add meat and brown quickly on all sides to seal in juices.
4. Season with salt and pepper.
5. Add boiling water, cover and simmer 10 minutes.
6. Add basil, thyme, and onion, and simmer 10 minutes more, or until meat is almost tender.
7. Blend flour in cup with very little cold water; add enough hot liquid from casserole to make smooth, thin mixture.
8. Pour mixture into casserole, stirring well.
9. Sprinkle ingredients lightly with nutmeg.
10. Cover with pastry and bake in moderate oven (375° F.) for 30 minutes (page 312*f*) .

Dill Meat Cakes (*serves 4*)

A good supper dish.

Ingredients:

1 lb. minced meat
1 large onion
2 oz. grated cheese
2 teasp. fresh chopped or green-dried dill

3 eggs
Salt
3–4 oz. cooked rice
Oil for frying

Method:
1. Mix well together the rice, meat, seasoning, dill, cheese, and chopped onion.

2. Add yolks of 2 eggs and knead well.
3. Form mixture into round flat cakes.
4. Roll the cakes in egg, then flour.
5. Fry in oil.

Mutton Hot-Pot (*serves 6*) **(B)**

A simple-to-make, substantial family dish.

Ingredients:

2 lb. breast of mutton
1 pint stock
4 onions, chopped
A few bacon bones
1 small cabbage, shredded
Salt and pepper
¼ lb. mushrooms
6 carrots, sliced

1 tablesp. fresh chopped or green-dried celery leaves
1 tablesp. fresh chopped or green-dried parsley
1 teasp. fresh chopped or green-dried thyme
1 bay leaf
6–8 potatoes

Method:

1. Trim the meat and cut into pieces.
2. Slice the potatoes and mushrooms and cabbage.
3. Put the meat, bacon bones, vegetables, herbs, and seasonings into a casserole, topping it with a layer of potatoes.
4. Add the stock.
5. Cover and cook in a moderate oven (350° F.) for about 2 hours.
6. Remove lid for last 20 minutes to brown the potatoes.

Note: If it is found to be too fatty, cook the day before required; take off layer of fat and reheat.

Lamb and Pork Roll Roast (*serves 6*)

An unusual combination for a Sunday lunch.

Ingredients:

1 small leg of lamb, boned
1 lb. pork tenderloin
Salt and pepper
1 teasp. fresh chopped or green-dried marjoram

1 teasp. fresh chopped or green-dried thyme

Method:

1. Rub the inside of lamb with the herbs.
2. Roll the lamb round the pork tenderloin.

3. Tie with string or use skewers.
4. Roast in a slow oven 300–325° F. for 30–35 minutes per pound.
5. When cooked remove lamb and make gravy from juices in the pan.
6. Serve at once.

Lamb Stew in Foil Packets (*serves 4*)

An elegant and tasty way of serving lamb chops.

Ingredients:

4 double lamb chops
4 potatoes, diced
4 carrots, sliced
4 onions, sliced in rings
1 teasp. fresh chopped or green-dried celery leaves
1 teasp. fresh chopped or green-dried rosemary
4 tablesp. sherry
Seasoning

Method:

1. Cut 4 large squares of heavy tinfoil.
2. Rub the lamb chops on both sides with the herbs.
3. Place one double chop on each square.
4. On top of each place an equal quantity of onion, potato, and carrot.
5. Season with salt and pepper.
6. Pour one tablesp. sherry over each portion.
7. Fold foil so it is sealed and put on baking sheet.
8. Bake in a slow oven (300° F.) for 1½–2 hours.

Sweetbreads New Style (*serves 3*)

A light supper dish served with toasted garlic bread and a green salad.

Ingredients:

1 lb. sweetbreads (lamb *or* calf)
½ lb. mushrooms
3 oz. butter
½ cup fresh chopped or 4 tablesp. green-dried chives
¼ cup fresh chopped or 2 tablesp. green-dried parsley
Salt and pepper
¼ teasp. fresh chopped or green-dried marjoram
½ lb. cooked peas
¾ pint lovage cream sauce (Recipe, page 280)
Grated Parmesan cheese

Method:
1. Blanch the sweetbreads in salted water for 30 minutes.
2. Drain, cover with fresh water and simmer for 10–12 minutes.
3. When cooked, remove membranes and cut into pieces.
4. Cut up mushrooms and sauté in butter with chives and parsley.
5. Season with salt, pepper, and marjoram.
6. Add this mixture to sweetbreads and put in a greased oven-proof dish.
7. Add peas and sauce and mix thoroughly.
8. Sprinkle with Parmesan cheese.
9. Bake in moderate oven (350° F.) for 20 minutes.

Kidney Margot (*serves 2*)

For an unusual supper dish – not too heavy, but tasty and quickly prepared.

Ingredients:

4 lambs' kidneys
2 oz. butter
4 oz. mushrooms
4 oz. tomatoes
1½ gill of stock
2 tablesp. fresh chopped or green-dried chives
1 tablesp. fresh chopped or green-dried basil
1 tablesp. sherry
Salt and pepper

Method:
1. Skin kidneys and cut in two, lengthwise.
2. Melt butter in deep frying-pan and brown kidneys quickly on both sides – about 4 minutes; remove.
3. Sauté sliced mushrooms and tomatoes with the chives and basil. Cook about 5–6 minutes.
4. Stir in stock and sherry.
5. When this boils, replace kidneys, add salt and a dash of pepper.
6. Cover pan and allow to simmer gently 15–20 minutes.
7. Remove lid and continue simmering for a further 5 minutes. Serve.

Country-Style Pork (*serves 8*)

A good dish for a cold day – elegant enough to serve for dinner.

Ingredients:

3½ lb. chump end loin of pork, boned
6 sage leaves
2 lb. pork sausage meat
¼ cup oil
1 dessertsp. fresh chopped or green-dried sage

1 dessertsp. fresh chopped or green-dried thyme
Salt and pepper
2 cloves of garlic, chopped

Method:

1. With a sharp knife insert the sage leaves in the pork a day before cooking.
2. Spread sausage meat inside pork, roll up, and tie up with string or skewers.
3. Place in a roasting-tin.
4. Pour over oil then sprinkle with sage and thyme.
5. Season well and put garlic on top.
6. Roast on middle shelf in a very hot oven 445° F. for 40 minutes.
7. Reduce heat to moderate 355° F. for further 2 hours.

Lincolnshire Stuffed Chine (*serves 8–10*)

Useful for picnics or a sandwich lunch.

Ingredients:

3 lb. *green* bacon collar (not smoked)
Sufficient fresh chopped parsley to tightly fill a pint basin or the green-dried equivalent (approximately 6 tablesp. or more), reconstituted in half lemon juice, half water

Method:

1. Cut bacon into ½-in. strips right up to, but not into, the rind.
2. Fill the cut strips as full as possible with parsley and tie joint tightly with string.

3. Put into a cloth such as muslin, and tie round again (cloth must completely cover bacon).
4. Boil for 2½ hours with lid on saucepan.
5. Take out when nearly cold but do not unwrap.
6. Place weight on top and leave for some hours.
7. Take off cloth but leave on rind.
8. Cut across top of bacon so that each slice has ½ in. of bacon and its quota of parsley.
9. Serve with sprinkling of lemon juice.

Pork Chops Madeira (*serves 4*)

A rich-tasting party dish – so easy to prepare.

Ingredients:

4 pork chops
Pinch of salt
Dash of pepper
A little crushed garlic
1 tablesp. fresh chopped or green-dried parsley
1 tablesp. fresh chopped or green-dried onion green

1 teasp. fresh chopped or green-dried marjoram
½ pint condensed mushroom soup
3 tablesp. water
2 tablesp. madeira

Method:
1. Thoroughly brown the pork chops in frying-pan.
2. Season with salt, pepper, and garlic.
3. Combine rest of ingredients.
4. Pour over chops.
5. Simmer until tender (30–40 minutes), turning chops once.
6. Pour sauce from the pan over the chops.

Note: Serve with green bean salad (page 190) and Piquant French Dressing with Tarragon (see page 193).

Sauerkraut Spareribs (*serves 6*)

A rare but tasty combination; can also be served with toasted wholemeal bread and garlic butter or Herb Butter Loaf (page 313).

Ingredients:

2 lb. best end neck of pork (spareribs)
4 cups water
1 teasp. salt
3 bay leaves
1 onion, chopped
1 tablesp. fresh chopped or green-dried celery leaves

1 clove
2½ lb. sauerkraut
1 cup white wine
1–2 teasp. caraway seeds
3 bay leaves
2 cups pork broth

Method:

1. Put spareribs in water with salt, 3 bay leaves, onion, and celery leaves.
2. Bring to boil and simmer until meat is tender (about 1½ hours).
3. Leave to cool then skim off fat, remove spareribs from broth.
4. In a large saucepan put sauerkraut, wine, 3 other bay leaves, caraway, and 1–2 cups of the pork broth.
5. Place meat on top, cover and cook very slowly for 1½ hours.

Ham in a Crust (*serves 8*)

An ideal dish for unexpected guests, if there is a tin of ham in the larder.

Ingredients:

2 cups short pastry mixture (see page 310)
1 teasp. dry mustard
3 teasp. fresh chopped or green-dried basil

⅓ cup milk
3 lb. boneless cooked ham

Method:

1. Mix the mustard, basil, and pastry mixture together.
2. Add the milk and knead into a dough.
3. Roll out dough on lightly floured board to a large rectangle.
4. Put ham in centre and fold long ends of pastry over ham, overlapping each other.
5. Turn over and carefully tuck in other ends of pastry, making a parcel.
6. Brush all the pastry with milk and place on greased baking-pan.

7. Bake in moderately low oven 325° F. for about 40 minutes until crust is golden brown.
8. Allow crust to cool slightly before cutting.

Veal Tarragon (*serves 6*)

One of the most excellent ways of serving veal.

Ingredients:

1½ lb. veal, thinly sliced	Salt and pepper
1 tablesp. butter	2 teasp. fresh chopped or green-dried tarragon
Juice of lemon	

Method:

1. Pound veal slices very thin; cut into serving pieces.
2. Sauté in butter very quickly on both sides.
3. Add lemon juice, salt, and pepper to taste, and tarragon.
4. Cook until tender about 7–10 minutes.
   Note: Serve with peas or asparagus.

Veal Olives (*1–2 olives per person*)

For one of those dinners when you want to show your skill.

Ingredients:

Fillet of veal, cut into thin slices
Chopped fat bacon
Chopped onion
Fresh chopped or green-dried herbs mixed of:

Tarragon	Rosemary	
Lovage	Chervil	For proportions
Lemon balm	Mint	see GUIDE (page 127)
Summer savory	Marjoram	
Thyme	Basil	

or
The equivalent quantity of bouquet for meat dishes
1 cup sour cream
½ teasp. cornflour

Method:

1. Beat and salt slices of fillet of veal and spread out on a flat board.

2. Put some finely chopped fat bacon, onion, and parsley on each piece.
3. Sprinkle the whole surface generously with mixed herbs or bouquet for meat dishes.
4. Roll each piece and tie with thread.
5. Fry these olives in butter in a heavy pan until golden brown on both sides.
6. Mix sour cream with cornflour.
7. Add this to the meat, cover and simmer until tender.
8. Before serving add some top of the milk if the sauce is too salty.
9. Remove thread from olives and serve sauce separately.

Veal Casserole (*serves 4*)

A good family meal; also an easy party dish for a buffet which can be prepared well beforehand.

Ingredients:

1½ lb. stewing veal
4 oz. mushrooms, chopped
4 oz. tomatoes, chopped
4 oz. button onions, chopped
⅜ pint stock
A little salt and pepper
1 green pepper, medium size, chopped
1 tablesp. flour
1 oz. butter

1 tablesp. mixed fresh chopped or green-dried herbs: parsley; mint; tarragon; chervil; sage; marjoram; thyme; basil.
For proportions see GUIDE, page 127)
or
1 tablesp. bouquet for meat dishes

Method:

1. Cut veal into small pieces and roll in a little seasoned flour.
2. Sauté meat in butter in deep frying-pan and remove.
3. Sauté onions, mushrooms, tomatoes, and green pepper, then remove.
4. Add flour, cook gently for a few minutes, then add stock and herbs.
5. Put all in a casserole dish.
6. Cover closely and cook in a slow oven (300° F.) for 3–4 hours.

Liver Casserole (*serves 4*)

This quick-to-make liver dish goes well with creamed spinach and dill potatoes (page 271).

Ingredients:

1 lb. calves' liver, thinly sliced
2 oz. butter
1 medium onion, chopped
1 clove garlic, crushed
¼ lb. mushrooms, chopped
2 carrots, sliced
Salt and a dash of pepper
1 teasp. fresh chopped or green-dried parsley
1 teasp. fresh chopped or green-dried thyme
1 teasp. fresh chopped or green-dried basil
1 bay leaf
1 dessertsp. cornflour
¼ cup water
¼ cup wine

Method:
1. Sauté the liver gently in butter with onion and garlic.
2. Place alternate layers of onion, garlic, liver, mushrooms, and carrots in a pie-dish.
3. Sprinkle well with the herbs and seasoning.
4. Blend the wine and water with the cornflour and pour over the dish.
5. Top with a bay leaf and bake for 30 minutes in moderate oven (350° F.).

Marjoram Liver Dumplings (*serves 4*) (B)

Marjoram adds a special flavour to this traditional dish from German-speaking countries.

Ingredients:

½ lb. (in one piece) calves' or pigs' liver
2 tablesp. butter *or* 1 tablesp. suet
Grated rind of 1 lemon
1 cup flour (approx.)
¼ cup water
½ teasp. fresh chopped or green-dried marjoram
¼ teasp. salt
⅛ teasp. white pepper
1 clove garlic, chopped (optional)

Method:
1. Dip liver in boiling water. Simmer for 2 minutes.
2. Remove from water.

3. Grate or mince liver, removing all fibres.
4. Blend liver, butter or suet, lemon rind, and seasonings, and marjoram in large bowl.
5. Gradually add sufficient flour until mixture can be formed into small round dumplings, not too firm (less than 1 cup of flour is usually enough).
6. Cook dumplings in boiling bouillon, consommé, or chicken broth for 10 minutes. Serve broth and dumplings immediately.

Note: Or remove from broth after cooking; drain, top with melted butter and fried onions, and serve with any vegetables or sauerkraut.

Chapter 7

POULTRY AND GAME

Chicken Casserole (*serves 4–6*)

This casserole with its vegetable makes a complete meal.

Ingredients:

2¼ lb. chicken, jointed
3 oz. butter
½ lb. sliced mushrooms
3 oz. (⅔ cup) flour
2 teasp. salt
A little paprika
1 teasp. each fresh chopped or green-dried sage and lemon thyme

1 teasp. poultry bouquet (optional)
1 lemon, cut in half
½ teasp. ground ginger
1 lb. fresh green beans, sliced, *or* 1 large frozen packet, thawed
½ cup stock

Method:

1. Melt butter in frying-pan and sauté mushrooms for 5 minutes; remove.

2. Mix flour, salt, paprika, and herbs together.
3. Rub chicken with cut lemon and coat lightly with flour mixture.
4. Melt remaining butter in pan and brown chicken well.
5. Remove to large casserole and sprinkle with ginger.
6. Coat beans with flour mixture and lightly brown in pan.
7. Mix beans with mushrooms and spoon over chicken.
8. Add the stock and bake, covered, in hot oven (400° F.) about 30–40 minutes.

Marjoram Chicken (*serves 6*)

This delicately-flavoured chicken makes an out-of-the-ordinary party dish.

Ingredients:

2½–3 lb. chicken, jointed
3 tablesp. butter
⅛ cup oil
1 teasp. salt
Paprika
½ clove garlic, finely chopped, *or* ¼ teasp. garlic salt

1 teasp. grated lemon peel
½ teasp. fresh chopped or green-dried summer savory
2 teasp. fresh chopped or green-dried marjoram

Method:

1. Melt butter in shallow baking-pan.
2. Coat chicken pieces in the melted butter and arrange in a single layer in the pan.
3. Pour oil over the chicken.
4. Season with salt, paprika, and garlic.
5. Sprinkle over the lemon peel, summer savory, and marjoram.
6. Cover with foil and bake in moderate oven (350° F.) for 15 minutes.
7. Turn chicken pieces over and bake 15 minutes longer.
8. Remove foil. Increase temperature to 400° F.
9. Bake 15 minutes more, turning chicken once again during that time.
10. The juices in the pan make an excellent gravy.

Herbed Turkey

This recipe, using foil, produces not only the most succulent but also the most tasty turkey.

Ingredients:
12–14 lb. turkey
lemon juice
Butter for brushing bird
Salt
2–3 tablesp. (or more) bouquet for poultry and game
or more of the same herbs as for stuffing
(to rub the bird inside and out)
¼ pint white wine
¼ pint giblet stock
Flour
Cream (if liked)

Stuffing:
8 oz. butter
8 oz. breadcrumbs
Grated rind of 2 lemons
Juice of 1 lemon
2½ dessertsp. fresh chopped or green-dried parsley
1 teasp. each fresh chopped or green-dried thyme, lemon thyme, and marjoram
or 4 dessertsp. bouquet for poultry and game
Paprika
½ medium-sized onion, minced
1 clove garlic, crushed
3 large eggs

Method for Stuffing:
1. Reconstitute the herbs in juice of one lemon.
2. Blend herbs well with grated rind, minced onion, and minced garlic.
3. Cream the butter and add eggs and herbs.
4. Add breadcrumbs and mix well.

Method for Turkey:
1. Rub the bird inside and out with a cut lemon, sprinkle and rub with salt.
2. Rub the bird inside with the herbs.
3. Brush the outside with softened butter and sprinkle with the herbs.
4. Stuff the body and crop of the bird.
5. Sew the openings together with white thread.
6. Weigh the prepared bird and allow 15 minutes per pound for birds up to 14 lb., and 10 minutes per lb. for larger birds.
7. Wrap in buttered foil and seal well.
8. Lie the bird on its back on a rack in a baking-tin.
9. Place in pre-heated oven (400–425° F.).
10. Half-way through cooking, turn the bird.
11. 30 minutes before the end, remove the foil, turn the bird breast upwards for browning.
12. When cooked, pour off the juices into a saucepan.
13. Add the white wine and giblet stock to the juices and herbs.

Note: If the sauce should be thickened, sauté the flour in butter until golden, then smooth with cold water, add giblet stock, mix in the gravy from the pan, add the wine and bring to the boil; then add cream (if liked) before serving.

Rabbit Casserole

Ingredients:

1 large young jointed rabbit	Salt
1 rabbit liver	4–6 juniper berries
4 oz. bacon	1 bay leaf
Some small shallots	1 teasp. each fresh chopped or
1 finely chopped onion	green-dried lemon balm, rose-
1 chopped garlic clove	mary, summer savory
Flour	½ teasp. lemon peel
1 pint stock	½ bottle red wine

Method:

1. Melt bacon in heavy casserole.
2. Brown the joints on all sides.
3. Add the rabbit liver and the chopped onion and garlic.
4. When meat is well browned, sprinkle with flour, stir well and add gradually 1 pint boiling water or stock.
5. Season with salt, juniper berries, and herbs.
6. Add lemon peel, and pour half of the red wine over it.
7. Cover and allow to simmer on low heat until the meat is quite tender.
8. Add remaining red wine and allow to stew thoroughly.
   Note: Serve with noodles or rice.

Herb Chicken (*serves 6–8*)

Very easy to make and yet a surprising success!

Ingredients:

4 lb. roasting chicken, jointed	¼ pint red wine
2 bay leaves	1 tablesp. oil
6 sprigs, or 1 teasp. each, green-dried tarragon and thyme	1 oz. butter
4 leaves fresh sage, *or* ½ teasp. green-dried sage	¼ pint stock
	Cream

Method:

1. Cover the herbs with the red wine and leave for 1½ hours.
2. Brown the chicken in the oil and butter in a deep pan.

3. Pour over the wine and add stock.
4. Cover and put into a fairly hot oven, centre shelf (400° F.), for 30–40 minutes.
5. Lift bird on to a hot dish.
6. Strain wine sauce into another pan and reduce a little by boiling, then add a little cream.
7. Pour over the chicken.

Hasenpfeffer with Marinade (*serves 6*)

The marinade ensures that the hare is tender and tasty.

Ingredients:

2 small hares or rabbits, jointed
Marinade (recipe follows)
½ cup flour
½ teasp. salt
1½ teasp. fresh chopped or green-dried thyme
½ cup dripping

1 cup stock
1 teasp. sugar
2 tablesp. sour cream
1 tablesp. cream
If sauce is too thick, add another ¼ cup of stock

Method:

1. Marinate the joints for 2 days.
2. Drain, saving marinade, and then dry the meat.
3. Coat pieces with flour mixed with salt and 1 teasp. thyme.
4. Sauté in dripping.
5. Drain off fat.
6. Strain marinade and add the stock.
7. Pour over meat. Cover and simmer 45 minutes, or until tender.
8. Season, if necessary, and add the sugar.
9. Arrange joints on a dish.
10. Thicken the sauce with flour, if desired; add the remaining thyme; allow to boil and then add cream.

Marinade (can be used for other game – makes about ¾ pint)

Ingredients:

1 cup red wine
3 tablesp. lemon juice
½ cup oil
1 small chopped onion
½ clove garlic
6 juniper berries
4 cloves
Salt

1 tablesp. poultry and game herb bouquet *or*
1 tablesp. mixed fresh chopped or green-dried parsley, tarragon, celery, thyme, marjoram, sage, basil, bay leaves, rosemary (see GUIDE, page 127, for proportions)

Method:

1. Mix all the above ingredients, cover well and allow to permeate overnight at room temperature.
2. Then marinate poultry, and especially game, in it for 24 hours.
3. Use for tenderizing and preserving and for basting.
4. If used in the cooking, the marinade should be strained.

Note: This can be strained and kept in the refrigerator for several weeks.

Poultry Pilaff (*serves 6*)

This dish originated from Eastern countries, such as Egypt and Turkey, and can be made of fish, poultry, and rice. This is a suggestion for PILAFF made of chicken or any other fowl.

Ingredients:

1 young bird
2–3 pints stock
2 oz. almonds
3 onions
1 clove of garlic, crushed
3 tablesp. butter
3 oz. stoneless raisins
1 cup rice
2 tablesp. marigold

1 teasp. each fresh chopped or green-dried summer savory and tarragon
½ teasp. fresh chopped or green-dried thyme
¼ teasp. cinnamon
Paprika
Salt

Method:

1. Put the bird, trussed, for boiling into the stock and cook until half tender.
2. Blanch almonds.
3. Peel onions and cut into rings.
4. Sauté onions and garlic in butter, but do not brown them.
5. Sauté raisins and almonds lightly.
6. Wash and dry rice and sauté in the butter until golden; add herbs and sauté.
7. Put rice mixture into deep saucepan and add onions, raisins, and almonds.
8. Make a well in the centre and put the bird into it.
9. Cover rice and bird with 2½–3 cups of stock and simmer slowly until the chicken and rice are cooked and the rice has absorbed the stock (25 minutes).
10. Place the chicken on a hot dish and arrange the rice around it.

Cherry-garnished Duckling

An excellent party dish, well worth the trouble for a special occasion.

Ingredients:

1 3–4 lb. duck
3 oz. butter
1 carrot
1 onion
¾ pint stock
1 bay leaf
1 teasp. each fresh chopped or green-dried celery leaves and marjoram
1 teasp. fresh chopped or green-dried parsley

1 pinch of fresh chopped or green-dried thyme
or 1 teasp. bouquet for poultry and game
¼ pint wine
Salt and pepper
1 teasp. cornflour
2 tablesp. water

Garnish:

Strained juice of 1 orange
Pinch of grated orange peel
1½ oz. castor sugar
¼ pint port *or* less
10 oz. tin Morello cherries, stoned

Stuffing:

Duck's liver
Flour
1 oz. butter
Breadcrumbs
Salt and pepper
1 teasp. fresh chopped or green-dried marjoram
1 egg

Method for Stuffing:

1. Toss the duck's liver in seasoned flour.
2. Melt the butter in a pan and sauté the liver for 3 minutes.
3. Remove from pan and chop finely.
4. Mix with breadcrumbs, salt, pepper, marjoram, and bind with the egg.

Method for Duck:

1. Stuff the duck with this mixture and rub with 1 oz. butter.
2. Prepare and dice vegetables and sauté in remaining butter until brown.
3. Put vegetables into a casserole and place duck on top.
4. Sprinkle duck with marjoram and celery leaves and add stock and other herbs.
5. Cover with tight-fitting lid and cook on centre shelf of moderate oven (355° F) for 1½ hours.
6. Remove duck from casserole and keep hot.

7. Strain liquid from casserole into a pan, adding wine; season if necessary.
8. Blend cornflour with water and add to wine mixture; return to heat and stir until thick.

Method for Garnish:
1. Mix orange juice, orange peel, sugar, and port in a pan and heat gently until sugar is dissolved.
2. Add drained cherries and heat through.
3. Serve the duck surrounded by the garnish, and hand the wine sauce separately.

Chicken Pie (*serves 6*)

Another way of serving a satisfying yet tasty chicken dish.

Ingredients:

3 lb. boiling fowl
1½ pints stock
3 medium onions, sliced
1 carrot, sliced
Salt and paprika
1 tablesp. fresh chopped or green-dried celery leaves
1 tablesp. poultry and game mixture
or 1 teasp. each fresh chopped
or green-dried lemon balm, tarragon, basil, rosemary
½ oz. semolina
Small wineglass white wine
1 oz. butter
1 egg yolk
1 teasp. lemon juice
3 rashers bacon, cut in strips
1 lb. easy pastry (page 312)

Method:
1. Joint the chicken into small pieces. Put into pan with stock and vegetables.
2. Add seasoning and all herbs.
3. Simmer for 1 hour.
4. Add semolina, wine, and butter, and simmer for further 15 minutes.
5. Blend egg yolk and lemon juice with ½ pint of the hot broth.
6. Place chicken in pie-dish, add strips of bacon.
7. Pour over thickened broth.
8. Cover with pastry.
9. Cook in the middle of the oven (400° F.) for 1 hour or until pastry is golden.

Chicken with Tarragon (*serves 4*) **(B)**

A simplified version of the traditional French dish.

Ingredients:

1 chicken
2 tablesp. fresh chopped or green-dried tarragon

A nut of butter
½ pint stock or water
Some cream (optional)

Method:

1. Rub chicken inside and out with 1 tablesp. tarragon.
2. Put chicken and giblets in a casserole with the butter and the stock or water, and cook until tender.
3. Take chicken out of casserole and add 1 tablesp. tarragon to the liquid.
4. Cook for 10 minutes, adding a little flour if the sauce is too liquid, and cream.
5. Pass the sauce through a sieve, if liked; and season, if necessary.

Boned Stuffed Chicken (*serves 10–12*)

Although a lengthy recipe, it is well worth the trouble for a cold buffet or picnic.

Ingredients:
To stuff a 2 lb. chicken.

Stuffing – 1
1 lb. sausage meat
2 slices chopped bacon
1 egg
1 clove garlic, finely chopped
1 glass of sherry
1 chicken liver, minced
1 tablesp. fresh chopped or green-dried marjoram
or 1 tablesp. bouquet for poultry and game

Stuffing – 2
2 oz. sliced mushrooms
1 hard-boiled egg, sliced
2 Frankfurter sausages, sliced
Chopped meat off chicken bones

Chicken Jelly
Chicken bones
¾ pint water
¼ oz. gelatine
½ teasp. each fresh chopped or green-dried chives, lovage, and parsley
Parsley for garnish

Method:
1. Bone the chicken or ask the butcher to do it for you.
2. Place the chicken, skin side down, to make an even layer of meat.
3. Combine all ingredients of Stuffing No. 1 into a thick mixture.
4. Spread half of Stuffing No. 1 on chicken.
5. Over this place a layer of the ingredients of Stuffing No. 2.
6. Cover with the remainder of Stuffing No. 1.
7. Form a smooth compact roll of chicken.
8. Sew skin together to hold in filling.
9. Oil top of the chicken roll, put in a roasting-tin with plenty of fat.
10. Cover with foil and seal well.
11. Place on lowest shelf of the oven at 350° F. for 1–1½ hours.
12. Remove foil for the last 10 minutes to brown the top.
13. Place on a dish and leave to cool.

Method for Jelly:
1. Boil the bones in the water with the herbs added.
2. Remove the bones, add gelatine, and stir until dissolved.
3. Pour into shallow bowl and leave to set.
4. Serve chicken cold with chopped chicken jelly around it, and garnish with parsley.

Parslied Chicken (*serves 4–8*)

An attractive and unusual way to serve chicken.

Ingredients:
2 small chickens
A large bunch of parsley, chopped
or 6 tablesp. green-dried parsley
3 tablesp. soft butter
¼ cup butter
2 cups chicken stock
Fresh or green-dried parsley for garnish

Sauce:
2 tablesp. butter
2 tablesp. flour
1 tablesp. fresh chopped or green-dried tarragon
½ cup cream
Salt

Method:
1. Wash and dry chickens.
2. Mix parsley with the soft butter.

3. Stuff each chicken with half of this mixture and fasten openings with skewers, or sew.
4. Truss, tying legs and wings close to the body.
5. Melt ¼ cup butter in a large, heavy frying-pan.
6. Add chickens and brown lightly on all sides.
7. Put chickens in a large casserole, pour over the brown butter and add two cups of chicken stock.
8. Cook uncovered in a moderate oven (350° F.) for 30 minutes or until tender, basting 4 or 5 times.
9. Arrange on a dish and garnish with parsley.

Method for Sauce:
1. In a small pan, melt butter for sauce and stir in flour.
2. Strain the chicken stock and stir in gradually.
3. Add tarragon and simmer for at least 8 minutes.
4. Stir in cream and salt, then heat again for 1 minute.
5. Pour this sauce over the chicken or serve it separately.

Chicken with Summer Savory (*serves 4*)

The sauce is the important part of this lunch and supper dish; it can also be served with other poultry and game.

Ingredients:
2 lb. chicken pieces
1½ pints water
1 carrot, chopped
1 clove garlic, crushed
1½ teasp. salt
1 teasp. each fresh chopped or green-dried parsley and celery leaves
2 teasp. fresh chopped or green-dried summer savory

Sauce:
2 tablesp. butter *or* oil
4 mushrooms
1 dessertsp. fresh chopped or green-dried summer savory
1 teasp. each fresh chopped or green-dried lemon balm and parsley
or 1 tablesp. bouquet for poultry and game
2 oz. flour
½ glass white wine
2 tablesp. sour cream
1 tablesp. top of the milk

Method:
1. Put chicken pieces into a large saucepan with water, carrot, garlic, salt, and the herbs.
2. Bring to the boil and simmer gently until chicken is cooked.

3. Remove, then bone chicken.
4. Strain the stock and save for the sauce.

Method for Sauce:
1. Heat butter or oil, then sauté mushrooms and herbs.
2. Add flour and cook gently for a few minutes.
3. Smooth with a little cold water.
4. Add all chicken stock and wine.
5. Cook for 20 minutes, stirring until it thickens.
6. Add sour cream and top of the milk.
7. Put chicken pieces back and heat well (but do not boil).
8. Serve in a rice ring.

Braised Pheasant with Chestnuts (*serves 4*)

An excellent game bird, enhanced by herbs.

Ingredients:

1 pheasant
1 tablesp. mixed of fresh chopped or green-dried parsley, tarragon, lemon balm, basil, bay leaves, and rosemary (see GUIDE, page 127, for proportions)
or 1 tablesp. bouquet for poultry and game

2 tablesp. butter
1 medium onion, sliced
4 carrots, sliced
1 lb. peeled chestnuts
½ pint marinade (see Recipe, page 253)
or ½ pint game stock
¼ pint cream

Method:
1. Prepare pheasant for the oven and rub well inside and out with the herbs.
2. Melt butter in a deep pan and brown bird on all sides.
3. Add the sliced onion, sliced carrots, and peeled chestnuts.
4. Moisten well with marinade or stock.
5. Cover the pan and braise in a slow oven for 1½–2 hours.
6. Remove bird and chestnuts on to a warm serving-dish.
7. Strain the sauce, add the cream, and pour over pheasant.

Note: Can be served with marjoram jelly (see Recipe, page 293).

Wrapped Partridge

The foil retains, and the herbs underline, the flavour of this tasty partridge.

Ingredients:
1 bird to 2 persons
For each bird:
1 piece celery
¼ teasp. fresh chopped or green-dried sage leaves
1 tablesp. onion, finely chopped
1 teasp. fresh chopped or green-dried basil
1 pinch each of fresh chopped or green-dried summer savory and thyme
1 slice toast
1 slice bacon
Parsley for garnish

Sauce:
¼ cup red wine
¼ cup stock
1 teasp. lemon juice
3 oz. cooked mushrooms, sliced
Salt to taste
1 tablesp. cream

Method:
1. Cut celery piece to fit inside bird.
2. Put sage in channel of celery and place this inside the bird.
3. Cut foil large enough to wrap bird in.
4. Place onions and herbs in centre of foil.
5. Place bird on top covered with slice of bacon on breast.
6. Wrap tightly, put in roasting-pan and place in moderate oven (375° F.).
7. Bake for 20–25 minutes.
8. Remove bird from foil and brown it in the oven or under the grill for 5 minutes.
9. Meanwhile, in a saucepan, combine the juices from the foil with wine, stock, and lemon juice, and reduce slightly.
10. Add mushrooms and salt, if necessary.
11. Continue cooking sauce until it thickens and then add cream.
12. Serve birds on slice of toast, covered with the sauce, and garnish with parsley and the bacon and celery, chopped.

Pot Pigeon (*serves 4–6*)

Served with rice and carrots – a delicious, yet economical dish.

Ingredients:

4 pigeons
Salt
1 large onion
1 clove garlic
1 carrot, sliced
1 bay leaf
1 teasp. each fresh chopped or green-dried thyme and celery leaves, or lovage
4 peppercorns
1 pinch of ground ginger
½ cup white wine
2 tablesp. lemon juice

2 tablesp. green-dried bouquet of poultry and game
or 2 tablesp. mixed fresh chopped or green-dried parsley, tarragon, summer savory, and basil (see GUIDE, page 127, for proportions)
3 oz. butter
2 tablesp. breadcrumbs
1 tablesp. fresh chopped or green-dried tarragon
2 teasp. flour
2 teasp. cream *or* top of the milk

Method:

1. Halve the prepared pigeons lengthways.
2. Rub with salt and the bouquet or the mixed herbs on both sides.
3. Put into a saucepan with slices of the onion and the carrot, all the seasonings and the herbs, and add sufficient water or stock almost to cover the pigeons.
4. Add the wine and lemon juice.
5. Cover and allow to simmer until tender (1½–2 hours).
6. Remove pigeons and keep warm.
7. Strain liquid and reduce slightly by simmering.
8. Smooth flour with cold water, add to the liquid, and cook until thickened.
9. Add cream shortly before serving.
10. Fry breadcrumbs with the tarragon in melted butter and spoon over the pigeons.
11. Serve gravy separately.

Chapter 8

VEGETABLES, POTATOES, RICE, AND PASTA

Tomato Casserole (B)

This is an economical yet very good dish for a family when tomatoes are not too expensive; it has to be started early in the day.

As the casserole should be made according to the size of the family, onions, tomatoes, and potatoes should be washed and sliced as required.

Ingredients:
Onions, tomatoes, and potatoes, cut into really thin slices
Grated cheese
Paprika
Rosemary
Onion green   ⎫   Fresh chopped
Parsley and basil   ⎬   or
Parsley, fennel *or* dill, marjoram, thyme   ⎭   green-dried
Caraway (optional)
½ cup sour cream, *or* cream, *or* top of the milk

Method:
1. Place a layer of grated cheese at the bottom of the casserole and sprinkle with a little paprika and rosemary over each layer of cheese.
2. Add next a layer of onion slices, sprinkled with onion green.
3. A layer of sliced tomatoes, sprinkled generously with parsley and some basil.
4. Then a thick layer of thinly sliced potatoes, sprinkled with some parsley, fennel or dill, marjoram, thyme, and caraway.
5. Repeat these layers until casserole is filled. Last layers should be potatoes and cheese.
6. Pour over sour cream, cream or top of the milk.
7. Cover with well-fitting lid, and place in oven at 350° F. for 1 hour at least (according to size of casserole). Then turn to 300° F. for about 2 hours. Remove lid and brown for further 15–30 minutes before serving.

Note: Onions and potatoes must be tender.

Ratatouille – A Southern Vegetable Stew

Ingredients:

2 large onions
1 clove garlic, chopped
8 tablesp. oil
2 green peppers, carefully cleaned inside and diced
2 large aubergines, diced
Salt
1 tablesp. fresh chopped or green-dried parsley

1 tablesp. mixed fresh chopped or green-dried marjoram, basil, rosemary, lemon thyme, and tarragon
2 large courgettes, thickly sliced
6 tomatoes, peeled, and each cut into 8 sections

Method:

1. Sauté onions together with garlic in oil until transparent.
2. Add peppers and aubergines, herbs, and a little salt.
3. Cover and cook for 15 minutes.
4. Add courgettes and cook for a further 15 minutes.
5. Add tomatoes, and allow to cook together for 1 hour.
6. If there is too much liquid, leave off cover for a short time before serving.

Haricot Beans with Tomatoes

An excellent winter vegetable dish which can be used as a main course.

Ingredients:

1 lb. haricot beans
½ stick celery, diced
½ carrot
¼ leek, sliced finely
1 to 2 juniper berries
4 shallots *or* 2 onions, finely chopped
2 cloves of garlic, crushed
1 tablesp. fresh chopped or green-dried onion green *or* chopped leek
2 oz. oil

1 lb. tomatoes, peeled and chopped
1 tablesp. mixed fresh chopped or green-dried lovage, basil, summer savory, thyme, tarragon, and rosemary (see GUIDE, page 127, for proportions)
Salt
4 tablesp. fresh chopped or green-dried chervil
or 2 tablesp. fresh chopped or green-dried parsley
1 oz. butter

Method:

1. Pour boiling water over the beans and soak overnight.
2. Simmer in slightly salted water together with the celery, carrot, leek, and juniper berries until soft (about 2 hours) or cook in pressure cooker.
3. Drain.
4. Sauté onions with garlic and onion green in the heated oil, and simmer gently until soft.
5. Add the tomatoes and the tablesp. of mixed herbs.
6. Add salt, and cook a little longer, then add this purée to the beans and heat well.
7. Heat chervil or parsley in melted butter and add just before serving.

Note: This dish can be made more nourishing by topping with grated cheese and buttered breadcrumbs and browning in the oven, or by adding fried lean bacon or sliced sausages.

Herb-Fried Tomatoes

A tasty accompaniment to a main course.

Ingredients:

4 or 5 large firm tomatoes	tarragon, thyme, and summer
Salt to taste	savory (see GUIDE, page 127,
3 tablesp. mixed fresh chopped	for proportions)
or green-dried basil, parsley,	*or* 3 tablesp. bouquet for salads
	6–8 tablesp. flour
	4 tablesp. butter

Method:

1. Cut unpeeled tomatoes into ½-in. thick slices.
2. Season both sides with salt.
3. Cover both sides with herbs.
4. Dip each slice in flour.
5. Sauté tomato slices on both sides in butter until golden brown – about 7 minutes.

Savoury Stuffed Onions (*serves 6*)

A good self-contained dish for lunch or supper.

Ingredients:

6 large onions
1 cup cooked rice
¼ cup tomato sauce *or* purée
2 tablesp. oil
¾ cup grated cheddar cheese
1 teasp. fresh chopped or green-
   dried basil

Pinch of each, fresh chopped or
   green-dried thyme and summer
   savory
Salt

Method:

1. Peel onions and cut slice off stem end of each one.
2. Cook uncovered in salted water for 30 minutes or until tender
   but firm.
3. Drain and cool.
4. Remove centres of onions (these can be used for sauce or
   stuffing for another dish).
5. Mix together rice, sauce, oil, ½ cup grated cheese, herbs and
   seasoning to taste.
6. Fill onions with this mixture.
7. Sprinkle remaining cheese over the onions.
8. Arrange onions in greased casserole.
9. Bake in hot oven (425° F.) for 20 minutes.

Savoury Onion Green Tart

This quiche can be made from freshly chopped onion tops or
green-dried onion green.

Ingredients:

3 cups thinly sliced green onion
   tops
or ¾ cup green-dried onion green
3 tablesp. butter or margarine
8-in. flan tin lined with pastry
   (see page 310)

3 eggs
¼ cup single cream
1 teasp. salt
½ teasp. fresh chopped or green-
   dried summer savory
Nutmeg

Method:

1. Sauté onion green tops in butter for 5 minutes (if green-dried
   onion green used, reconstitute the ¾ cup in a ¼ cup water with
   a few drops of lemon juice and wait until the liquid has been
   soaked up and the onion green reconstituted. Do not use more
   water than absolutely necessary).
2. Turn into pastry-lined tin.

3. Beat eggs until well blended and add to them the cream, salt, summer savory, and nutmeg.
4. Pour egg mixture over onions.
5. Bake in a very hot oven (425° F.) for 30 minutes or until custard is just set.

Note: Serve either hot or cold; cut into wedges as a hot appetizer, or for cold buffets and picnics.

Courgettes or Baby Marrows

An easy to prepare, unusual vegetable dish – good enough for a special occasion.

Ingredients:

2 lb. vegetable courgettes	1 tablesp. fresh chopped or green-dried parsley
3 tablesp. oil	
Salt	Vegetable stock, if necessary
½ teasp. each fresh chopped or green-dried rosemary and dill	Grated cheese
	Sour cream

Method:

1. Select small courgettes or young marrows (4–6-in. long), wash and cut off both ends.
2. Halve and put on a shallow fireproof dish.
3. Pour oil over and sprinkle with herbs.
4. Bake in a moderate oven.
5. Add a little vegetable stock if too dry.
6. Sprinkle with grated cheese and dot with sour cream.
7. Allow to brown in the oven.

Spinach Recipes

(*a*) Spinach Purée

Ingredients:

2 lb. spinach	1 teasp. fresh chopped or green-dried peppermint leaves (if available)
1 tablesp. oil	
1 onion, chopped	
1 clove garlic, chopped	1 tablesp. fresh chopped or green-dried parsley
1 heaped tablesp. flour	
1 cup (10 oz.) vegetable stock	1 teasp. or more sorrel (if liked)
Salt	1 teasp. nettles, dandelion (if liked)
Nutmeg	2 tablesp. cream or milk
2 oz. raw spinach	

Method:

1. Pick over spinach and remove any thick stalks, if spinach beet is used.
2. Place the washed spinach in a saucepan, cover and cook over low heat until the water collects.
3. Drain well.
4. Mince or chop spinach finely.
5. Sauté onion, garlic, and parsley in heated fat.
6. Add flour and sauté.
7. Add stock, smooth, and cook for 15 minutes.
8. Add spinach and seasoning.
9. Chop raw spinach or put through a liquidizer.
10. Add this and the herbs to the cooked spinach just before serving. Do not allow to boil again.
11. Add cream or milk.

(b) Spinach Pudding

Ingredients:

1½ oz. butter *or* margarine	1 onion, chopped
6 oz. bread (French loaf or wholemeal)	1 tablesp. fresh chopped or green-dried parsley
3 eggs	Salt
1 soup plate of left-over spinach purée (see previous recipe)	Nutmeg

Method:

1. Cut the bread, take off crusts and soak in water.
2. Meanwhile, sauté onions in heated fat until golden.
3. Cream the butter.
4. Add sautéd onions, parsley, 3 yolks of eggs, and the spinach.
5. When the bread is soft, squeeze the water out and add to the mixture.
6. Mix well and add salt and nutmeg.
7. Beat the egg whites stiffly and mix in lightly.
8. If the mixture becomes too moist, add some breadcrumbs.
9. Fill into a well-greased ring or angel cake tin and bake in the oven at 375° F. for at least an hour.

Brussels Sprouts with Herbs

Herbs make this everyday vegetable surprisingly different and delicious.

Ingredients:

2 lb. brussels
1 medium onion
1 tablesp. each fresh chopped or green-dried onion green and parsley
2 teasp. each fresh chopped or green-dried chives and lovage

Pinch of grated nutmeg
Salt
½ pint stock
2 tablesp. oil

Method:

1. Chop onions finely.
2. Sauté until golden.
3. Sauté onion green and other herbs.
4. Add brussels and shake.
5. Add nutmeg and salt.
6. Then add stock.
7. Cover well.
8. Allow to simmer until tender or cook in a pressure cooker for 3–5 minutes.
9. Serve in cheddar ring page 207 or as an accompanying vegetable.

Note: Another version – use a little garlic, marjoram, lovage, and tarragon, and 2 tablesp. sour cream; also breadcrumbs sautéd in oil can be sprinkled over brussels before serving.

Broad Beans Sauté

Ingredients:

1½–2 lb. broad beans
1 large onion, finely chopped
1 clove garlic, finely chopped
1 tablesp. oil
1 tablesp. fresh chopped or green-dried parsley
1 teasp. fresh chopped or green-dried summer savory

½ teasp. fresh chopped or green-dried lovage
½–1 pint stock
Salt
1 tablesp. sour cream (optional)
Nutmeg

Method:

1. Sauté onions and garlic in the heated oil until transparent.
2. Add all the herbs and sauté.
3. Add broad beans and sauté.
4. Add stock depending on size of the beans and cooking time.
5. Add seasoning.
6. Cover well and cook until tender, or in the pressure cooker.
7. Add sour cream just before serving.

Chive Potato Cakes

Ingredients:

4 medium boiled potatoes
2 tablesp. butter *or* margarine
Salt

1 tablesp. green-dried chives reconstituted in 1 tablesp. warm milk
1 beaten egg

Method:

1. Mash potatoes while still hot.
2. Mix well with butter and salt.
3. Add chives.
4. When cool, add well-beaten egg.
5. Shape into flat cakes and fry in butter.

Dill Potatoes

Goes well with fried or other dishes when served without a sauce.

Ingredients :

2 lb. potatoes
1 onion, finely chopped
1½ oz. oil *or* butter
2 tablesp. flour
¼ pint stock

Salt
2 tablesp. fresh chopped or green-dried dill
6–8 tablesp. sour cream *or* milk

Method:

1. Boil potatoes, peel, and cut into fairly thin slices.
2. Sauté onion in the fat until golden.
3. Add flour and sauté.
4. Smooth with cold water stirring well, then add stock, salt, potatoes, and bring to the boil.
5. Add the dill and allow to simmer.
6. Shortly before serving, add cream or milk, and reheat.
   Note: If liked, a little crushed garlic can be added to the onion.

Marjoram Potato Pie

Ingredients:

2 lb. peeled boiled potatoes
Oil *or* butter
Salt
1 teasp. fresh chopped or green-dried marjoram leaves

½ teasp. each fresh chopped or green-dried parsley, tarragon, and celery leaves
¼ pint sour cream
¼ pint yoghourt

Method:
1. Sauté diced potatoes in butter until golden.
2. Add herbs and sauté again.
3. Place into well-buttered casserole.
4. Pour over yoghourt and cream.
5. Bake in oven (375° F.) about 1 hour or until golden.

Baked Potatoes with Chervil Sauce

Ingredients:

4 large potatoes
1 cup sour cream
1 tablesp. chopped onion
1 tablesp. fresh chopped or green-
    dried chervil

½ teasp salt
½ teasp. fresh chopped or green-
    dried summer savory

Method:
1. Scrub potatoes, brush skin with oil.
2. Bake in hot oven (400° F.) until done.
3. Combine sour cream with all other ingredients.
4. Split potatoes lengthwise and spoon on sauce.

Potato Recipes – Using Herbs

For ringing the changes and making attractive dishes when flavouring and serving the everlasting potato.

(*a*) Sauté Potatoes

Ingredients:

Old *or* new potatoes (if they are
    new, brush, wash and dry them
    and use unpeeled; otherwise
    peel potatoes)
Onions, chopped

Butter *or* oil
Fresh chopped or green-dried
    parsley
Fresh chopped or green-dried
    marjoram

Method:
1. Cut potatoes and onions into slices.
2. Sauté onion in butter or oil.
3. Add a generous quantity of parsley.
4. Then add potatoes and a little marjoram and turn over several times.
5. Cover with lid until almost tender.
6. Remove lid and sauté until golden-yellow.

(b) Potato Snow

Ingredients:

Boiled potatoes in their skins
Fresh chopped or green-dried
  parsley
Fresh chopped or green-dried
  chives
Butter

Method:

1. Peel potatoes while hot.
2. Immediately pass through a potato press on to a hot dish.
3. Sprinkle with parsley and chives.
4. Add a little fresh butter.

(c) Potato Croquettes

Ingredients:

1 lb. potatoes (not new ones)
  boiled, peeled, mashed, cooled
1 oz. butter *or* margarine
1 egg (small)
Salt
1 tablesp. fresh chopped or green-
  dried chives
1 teasp. fresh chopped or green-
  dried marjoram
3–3½ oz. flour
Breadcrumbs
Oil

Method:

1. Cream butter and egg.
2. Add salt and herbs.
3. Mix in potatoes and flour, working until smooth.
4. Shape small sausages to the thickness of a thumb, and roll in breadcrumbs.
5. Deep fry in hot oil.

(d) Parsley Potatoes

Ingredients:

2 lb. small potatoes cooked in
  their skins
1 oz. butter
3 tablesp. fresh chopped or green-
  dried parsley

Method:
1. Peel potatoes while hot.
2. Put immediately into frying-pan with heated butter and finely chopped parsley.
3. Cover and toss well.
4. Serve on hot dish immediately.

(*e*) Sage Potatoes

Ingredients:

2 lb. boiled potatoes, peeled and diced

Oil *or* butter

2 teasp. fresh chopped or green-dried sage

½ teasp. each fresh chopped or green-dried parsley and tarragon

4 oz. cream cheese

or 4 oz. curd mixed smooth with a little top of the milk

Method:
1. Sauté potatoes in oil or butter until golden.
2. Add herbs and sauté again.
3. Put into well-buttered casserole.
4. Pour over cheese and milk.
5. Bake in oven (350°) for about 1 hour or until golden.

Marigold Rice (*serves 4–6*)

An excellent accompanying dish; serve instead of potatoes.

Ingredients:

1 chopped onion

1 tablesp. oil

½ lb. rice

1 pint vegetable stock

Salt

A little fresh chopped or green-dried rosemary

2–3 teasp. marigold petals

Grated cheese

A little butter

Method:
1. Sauté onion in fat.
2. Add rice and sauté again.
3. Add vegetable stock, salt, and rosemary.
4. Cook until tender.
5. Add marigold petals, dissolving in hot stock first.
6. Sprinkle with grated cheese and dot with a little butter.

Rice Soufflé with Tomatoes and Vegetables

A satisfying, yet tasty savoury rice dish.

Ingredients:

1 onion, chopped
1 tablesp. oil
7 oz. rice (preferably whole)
2 pints hot stock *or* water
Salt
Fresh chopped or green-dried rosemary
½ cup carrots, diced (cooked)

Marigold petals
1 tablesp. each fresh chopped or green-dried onion green and celery leaves
4–6 tomatoes, sliced
Fresh chopped or green-dried basil
2 tablesp. grated cheese
½ oz. butter

Method:

1. Sauté onion in heated oil.
2. Sauté rice until transparent.
3. Add stock, salt, and rosemary.
4. Mix rice with carrots, marigold petals, onion green, and celery leaves.
5. Place alternate layers of rice mixture and tomatoes into a well-buttered fireproof dish.
6. Sprinkle basil over each layer of tomatoes.
7. Finish with grated cheese and dot with the butter.
8. Bake in a moderate oven (375°) for about 10 minutes.

Genoese Spaghetti

This is a way of cooking spaghetti or any pasta as it is done in Genoa with the Genoese Basil Paste (Chapter 9, page 289). When using this for pasta, boil spaghetti, macaroni, noodles, etc., in salted water until cooked but still firm. Drain pasta well and rinse with cold water in a sieve or colander.

Ingredients:

1–2 tablesp. of Pèsto alla Genovese
2 tablesp. cooking water in which the pasta has been boiled

Finely grated Parmesan cheese
Pine kernels (optional)

Method:

1. Dilute Pésto in the 2 tablespoons of cooking water in a heavy frying-pan.
2. Turn pasta in it until covered with green specks.
3. Serve with additional finely grated Parmesan cheese in a separate bowl, if liked.
4. If a genuine Genoese flavour is wanted, sprinkle with a few whole pine kernels.

Spaghetti with Tomato-Meat Sauce (*serves 4–6*)

One of the most delicious ways of serving spaghetti.

Ingredients:

Spaghetti:
1 lb. spaghetti
1 cup olive oil
1 clove garlic, chopped
1 onion, finely chopped
1 teasp. fresh chopped or green-dried basil
Salt and pepper to taste

Sauce:
3 oz. fat bacon, diced
¾ lb. minced steak
1 clove garlic, minced
1½ cups red wine
4 large tomatoes, peeled and diced
4 oz. mushrooms, sliced
1½ cups water
2 teasp. fresh chopped or green-dried basil
1½ tablesp. finely chopped parsley
½ teasp. fresh chopped or green-dried rosemary
Pinch of ground cinnamon
1 tablesp. sugar
5 oz. tin condensed tomato purée
Salt and pepper to taste
Grated Parmesan cheese

Method:

Spaghetti:

1. Boil spaghetti for 20 minutes, drain, and dry quickly over heat.
2. While spaghetti is cooking, place olive oil, garlic, onion, and basil in a large heavy saucepan over medium heat, and heat the oil, but not to smoking temperature.
3. Toss the drained spaghetti in the oil, turning with two forks until it is thoroughly coated with the hot oil mixture.
4. Season to taste with salt and pepper.

Sauce:

1. Cut bacon into small pieces and cook in a heavy saucepan over a low flame until fat is melted out.
2. Discard pieces of bacon and add steak to hot fat and brown quickly.
3. Add garlic and cook until golden coloured.
4. Add wine and allow to simmer for about 10 minutes.
5. Add all other ingredients and simmer for 1 hour, stirring frequently.
6. Pour sauce over hot spaghetti and serve with grated Parmesan cheese.

Ravioli (vegetable filled) (*makes about 30*)

Ingredients (pastry):

5 oz. flour	1 tablesp. oil
1 egg	1 tablesp. water
Salt	

Method:

1. Work into a smooth paste and allow to rest for 15 minutes.
2. Roll out as thinly as possible, making 2 large rounds.
3. Allow to dry on a clean tea-cloth.
4. Spread the filling over the whole surface or make little heaps at small distances. Brush between fillings with water.
5. Cover with the second half of the paste and press down.
6. Then cut with a pastry wheel in squares or oblongs.
7. Allow to dry a little more on a pastry-board.
8. Cook ravioli in small quantities in a saucepan full of salted boiling water.
9. Simmer until they come to the surface.
10. Take out with perforated ladle.

Note: They can be served in clear broth as a substantial soup or in layers sprinkled with grated cheese, topped with melted butter or with tomato sauce.

Filling:

For Ravioli filling, halve the quantity of savoury bread mixture (Chapter 11, page 321). It can be used well-mixed with a larger quantity of onion green approx. $\frac{1}{2}$–$\frac{3}{4}$ cup (reconstituted if green-dried) and some cooked sieved spinach.

Chapter 9

SAUCES AND ACCOMPANIMENTS

Herb Sauces

These sauces can bring variety to very many different dishes.

(a) Chervil Sauce

Ingredients:

½ oz. butter *or* oil
1 small onion, finely chopped
½ oz. flour
2 tablesp. fresh chopped or green-dried chervil

· ½ pint vegetable stock
Salt
1 dessertsp. cream, sweet *or* sour

Method:

1. Sauté the onion in the fat until golden.
2. Add the chervil and sauté again.
3. Add the flour and sauté again.
4. Smooth with a little cold water.
5. Add the hot vegetable stock and salt.
6. Cook for 20 minutes.
7. Add the cream before serving.

(b) Fennel Sauce

Adds succulence to boiled or baked fish.

Ingredients:

4 oz. butter
2 tablesp. fresh chopped or green-dried fennel

A little salt

Method:

1. Wash the fresh fennel, or reconstitute the green-dried fennel in water.
2. Melt the butter.
3. Mix the fennel with the hot melted butter, add salt if necessary, and serve.

Note: For any fish dish, add 1 tablesp. fresh chopped or green-dried fennel to a basic white sauce (see Lovage Cream Sauce, page 280).

(c) Lovage Cream Sauce (*makes ½ pint*)

To serve with left-over vegetables, minced meats, or poultry.

Ingredients:

1 oz. butter
1 tablesp. fresh chopped or green-dried lovage
1 oz. flour

½ pint milk
Salt and pepper
¼ cup cream

Method:

1. Melt the butter.
2. Add the lovage and sauté for a few minutes.
3. Stir in the flour and sauté again.
4. Add the milk all at once and the seasoning, stirring until it boils.
5. Simmer for 3–5 minutes.
6. Add the cream, heat again, if necessary, and serve.

Note: The same recipe can be used for Nasturtium Sauce.

(d) Mint Sauce with Lemon (*makes ¼ pint*)

Making the sauce with lemon gives the mint a better chance. Serve with roast lamb and salads.

Ingredients:

2 tablesp. fresh chopped or green-dried mint
1 tablesp. castor sugar

2 tablesp. warm water
¼ pint diluted lemon juice
(3 lemons and 2 oz. water)

Method:

1. Mix together mint and castor sugar.
2. Pour over a little hot water (if green-dried mint is used there should be enough water to be soaked up by the mint).
3. Add lemon juice.
4. Allow to stand for a short time then taste for flavour and add either lemon or sugar according to taste.

Note: ½ pint of white wine vinegar can be used instead of the diluted lemon juice, but taste first how well the mint goes with lemon juice.

(e) Parsley Sauce (*makes ½ pint*)

Ingredients:

2 handfuls fresh chopped parsley
or 3 tablesp. green-dried parsley
1 tablesp. butter
1 tablesp. flour

Pinch of summer savory *or* pepper
(optional)
½ pint stock (fish, chicken, *or* vegetable, according to main dish)

Method:
1. Melt fat and sauté flour, cooking thoroughly.
2. Add the stock and season with pepper.
3. Bring to the boil and simmer for 3–5 minutes.
4. Remove from heat, add parsley and cream.
5. Serve at once; will discolour if left standing.

(f) Sage Sauce (*makes about ½ pint*)

The traditional sauce to serve with boiled or roast mutton.

Ingredients:

3 medium onions, chopped
¼ teasp. salt
1 pint stock *or* water
1 oz. flour

1 oz. butter
¼ pint milk
4 tablesp. cream
2 teasp. fresh chopped or green-dried sage

Method:
1. Cook the onions in the stock with salt for 15–20 minutes.
2. Drain, reserve stock, and pass onions through the mincer.
3. Heat butter in a pan, add flour, and cook for a minute.
4. Remove from heat; beat in milk, reserved stock, and 2 tablesp. cream.
5. Allow to thicken slowly.
6. Add onions and sage to sauce and reheat, adding more salt if necessary.
7. Add rest of cream, and serve spooned round the meat.

(g) Sorrel Sauce (*makes ½ pint*)

Serve with grilled meats, broccoli, or potato dishes.

Ingredients:

2 handfuls of freshly-chopped sorrel
or 2 tablesp. green-dried sorrel
1 tablesp. oil

1 cup stock
2 tablesp. flour
½ cup milk
Pinch of sugar

Method:

1. Wash sorrel and chop finely.
2. Sauté in fat.
3. Add stock and allow to boil until tender.
4. Blend flour with milk.
5. Add to sorrel and allow to boil.
6. Season with salt and sugar.
7. Serve at once.

(*h*) Rosemary Sauce (*makes 1 pint*)

Adds a delicate flavour to fish or lamb, according to kind of stock used.

Ingredients:

1 oz. butter
1 small onion, finely chopped
1 dessertsp. fresh chopped or green-dried rosemary, crushed

1 oz. flour
¾ to 1 pint fish, meat, *or* vegetable stock
2 tablesp. sour cream

Method:

1. Sauté onion in heated butter until transparent.
2. Add rosemary and sauté.
3. Stir in flour; sauté again, and smooth with some cold water or stock
4. Add stock.
5. Add sour cream shortly before serving.

Green Herb Sauce (*makes approx. 1 pint*)

Ingredients:

1 small onion, chopped
1 oz. butter *or* oil
1 oz. wholemeal flour
¾ pint stock
¼ pint milk
1 teasp. lemon juice
2 tablesp. sour cream

2–3 tablesp. of the following mixed fresh chopped or green-dried herbs: parsley, lemon balm, tarragon, lovage, salad burnet, a pinch of marjoram and sage (see GUIDE, page 127, for proportions)

Method:
1. Sauté onion in $\frac{1}{3}$ of the butter or oil until golden.
2. Add half of the chopped herbs and sauté, add flour and sauté.
3. Smooth with a little stock.
4. Add remaining stock and allow to simmer for some time. Add milk and the remaining herbs and lemon juice.
5. Melt the rest of the butter and add this with the cream shortly before serving.

Persillade

Serve with cold lamb and butter beans.

Ingredients:

1 hard-boiled egg
3 tablesp. French Dressing (see Recipe, page 84)

6 tablesp. fresh chopped or green-dried parsley (if green-dried, reconstitute in lemon juice)

Method:
1. Finely chop the hard-boiled egg.
2. Mix together with the French dressing and parsley.
3. Allow to permeate at least 30 minutes before serving.

Sauce Béarnaise

King among French sauces, yet not difficult to make; it is usually served with grilled steak.

Ingredients:

2 tablesp. white wine *or* white wine vinegar
1 teasp. finely chopped onions *or* shallots
3 or 4 peppercorns
1½ teasp. green-dried bay leaves or ¼ fresh bay leaf

1 teasp. each fresh chopped or green-dried tarragon and chervil
2 egg yolks
¼ cup stock *and/or* good gravy*
1½ oz. butter
1 teasp. each fresh chopped or green-dried tarragon and chervil

Method:
1. Boil vinegar with onions, peppercorns, bay leaf, tarragon, and chervil in a small saucepan until reduced to half.
2. Strain and put aside.
3. Mix the egg yolks with 1 tablesp. stock and put in top of double boiler when the water is boiling fast.

* The liquid needed may vary, therefore a little more stock or gravy or both can be added.

4. Stir well.
5. Add the butter when soft in small pieces, stirring constantly.
6. Stir until this mixture thickens, adding stock, and gravy.*
7. Lastly add the boiled onion mixture.
8. Before serving, add tarragon and chervil.

Sauce Hollandaise

Another traditional sauce which can be served with salmon, food fried in batter, cauliflower, scampi, and other fried fish dishes.

Ingredients:

3 tablesp. water
1 tablesp. lemon juice
1 small onion
1 sprig fresh chopped tarragon *or*
   1 teasp. green-dried tarragon

½ bay leaf
1 clove
1 level tablesp. cornflour
½ cup (5 oz.) vegetable stock
2 egg yolks
2 oz. butter

Method:

1. Boil the water, lemon juice, onion, herbs, and clove together until half the liquid has evaporated; strain.
2. Blend cornflour with the vegetable stock; bring to the boil, stirring all the time.
3. Beat egg yolks with the first liquid in a double saucepan over boiling water until creamy.
4. Cook until the sauce thickens; remove from heat.
5. Add small pieces of butter gradually.
6. Add vegetable stock and cornflour very carefully, stirring all the time.
7. Keep hot over boiling water but do not allow to cook any more.

Note: The vegetable stock and cornflour may be omitted, in which case double the quantity of all the other ingredients.

Mousseline Sauce

Method:

1. Make Sauce Hollandaise (see previous recipe).
2. Add ¼ cup (2½ oz.) stiffly beaten double cream just before serving.

* The liquid needed may vary, therefore a little more stock or gravy or both can be added.

Frankfurter Green Sauce (*makes ½ pint*)

A famous traditional spring sauce to be served with boiled beef and new potatoes, with fish, or with boiled potatoes only.

Ingredients:

1 cup mayonnaise (see page 84)
1 hard-boiled egg, chopped
Chopped capers
Gherkins or cucumber, diced
2 tablesp. fresh chopped or green-dried chives

1 tablesp. of the following mixed fresh chopped or green-dried herbs: borage, sorrel, salad burnet (if available); parsley; dill; chervil
or more parsley and
1 tablesp. bouquet for salads

Method:

1. Add to mayonnaise the chopped hard-boiled egg and all other ingredients.
2. Mix lightly but well.

Egg Sauce with Chives

A similar type of sauce for similar types of dishes.

Ingredients:

2 tablesp. fresh chopped or green-dried chives
Juice of half a lemon
3 hard-boiled eggs

4 tablesp. oil
½ teasp. salt
A pinch of sugar

Method:

1. Reconstitute chives with the juice of half a lemon.
2. Pass all the yolks through a sieve.
3. Chop finely whites of eggs.
4. Add oil slowly to yolks (a spoon at a time) and stir well.
5. Add salt and sugar.
6. Add fresh or reconstituted chives.
7. Add chopped whites and mix well.
   Note: Keep in refrigerator and mix again before serving.

Spring Sauce (*makes ¾ cup*)

The traditional 'Seven Herb' sauce to accompany spring dishes, such as new potatoes, lamb, veal; also boiled beef and fish.

Ingredients:

3 hard-boiled eggs (1 egg per person)
1 tablesp. vegetable oil
1 tablesp. lemon juice
½ teasp. salt
⅓ cup double cream
or ⅓ cup sour cream and ⅓ cup yoghourt
2 tablesp. fresh chopped or green-dried chives

1 tablesp. of the following mixed fresh chopped or green-dried herbs:
    Parsley
    Dill
    Borage (optional)
    Chervil
    Sorrel (optional)
    Salad burnet (optional)
or 1 tablesp. bouquet for salads

Method:

1. Peel hard-boiled eggs.
2. Mash yolks with a fork.
3. Chop whites finely.
4. Add oil to the yolks and stir well.
5. Add lemon juice and salt.
6. Add cream, yoghourt, and all the herbs.
7. Mix well – should be of thick consistency.

Tomato Sauces

(*a*) The unobtrusive *vegetable* basis brings out the full flavour of the tomatoes.

Ingredients:

1 tablesp. vegetable fat
1 onion
1 clove of garlic
½ cup mixed of carrots, celery, and leeks
½ lb. tomatoes (approx.)
1 tablesp. flour
½ tablesp. tomato purée

1 pint vegetable stock *or* water
¼ bay leaf
Pinch of fresh chopped or green-dried rosemary
1 teasp. mixed fresh chopped or green-dried basil and thyme
A little hot butter
A pinch of sugar

Method:

1. Cut up vegetables.
2. Melt fat and sauté onions and garlic in it.
3. Add vegetables and sauté in the fat.
4. Cut up tomatoes and add.

5. Cook slowly in a covered pan until the liquid has been absorbed.
6. Sprinkle the flour over the vegetables.
7. Add purée, stock, and herbs and cook for ½ hour.
8. Put through a sieve.
9. Add butter and sugar to improve the flavour.

(b) The *herbs* bring out the full flavour.

Ingredients:

1 tablesp. vegetable fat
1 onion, chopped
1 lb. ripe tomatoes
Salt
¼ bay leaf
A pinch of fresh chopped or green-dried rosemary

½ teasp. fresh chopped or green-dried basil *or* thyme
1 teasp. cornflour
¼ cup (2½ oz.) vegetable stock
2 tablesp. cream
Pinch of sugar, if desired

Method:

1. Melt fat and sauté onion in it.
2. Cut tomatoes in pieces and sauté with the onion.
3. Cover and cook until tender.
4. Put through a sieve.
5. Add herbs.
6. Mix cornflour with stock and cook for a few minutes with the tomato purée.
7. Add cream and sugar if liked.

(c) Simple, *natural*, and delicate in flavour.

Ingredients:

1 lb. tomatoes
Salt

½ teasp. fresh chopped or green-dried basil
2 tablesp. cream or a little butter

Method:

1. Cut tomatoes in pieces, cook until tender with salt and herb.
2. Sieve.
3. Add cream or butter.

Horseradish Sauce

Ingredients:

1 hard-boiled egg
2 teasp. oil
2 teasp. lemon juice
Salt
Drops of onion juice

Drops of garlic juice
1 heaped tablesp. finely grated horseradish
Chopped white of eggs (if used with fish)

Method:

1. Mix the yolk with the oil and the lemon juice to a thick cream.
2. Add salt, a few drops of onion juice and garlic.
3. Add the horseradish (more or less according to taste).
4. Add finely chopped egg-whites.

Apple and Horseradish Sauce

Serve with boiled fish, together with melted butter.

Ingredients:

6 peeled apples, large
2 tablesp. sugar
1 glass white wine

1 glass lemon juice
Grated horseradish (according to taste)

Method:

1. Grate the apples.
2. Add the sugar, the white wine, and the lemon juice.
3. Add grated horseradish.
4. Mix well until the mixture appears frothy.

Burnet-Mint Fish Sauce

This variation of a classic French sauce for grilled fish uses burnet in place of fresh cucumber.

Ingredients:

½ cup burnet leaves
½ cup spearmint leaves
½ lb. butter

Salt
Pepper

Method:

1. Chop burnet and spearmint leaves.
2. Melt butter in a saucepan, add herbs, and simmer for 10 minutes.
3. Season the sauce to taste with salt and pepper.
4. Pour over grilled fillet of sole or plaice.

Pésto Alla Genovese (Genoese Basil Paste)

This delicious Pésto or Paste, originally from Genoa, is traditionally used with all 'Pasta': macaroni, spaghetti, noodles, etc. If a jar of Pésto is prepared and kept, it can be used for this and other dishes such as pizza, canapés, etc., at various times. It is excellent as a spread on toasted French bread (see Herb-Buttered French Loaf, page 313) or a spoonful of the Pésto will give minestrone its authentic flavour. The Pésto Genovese can be made of fresh or green-dried basil if the suggestions for reconstituting are carefully followed.

Ingredients:

1 tablesp. nuts (cashew *or* pine kernels)

¾ cup chopped basil leaves without stems

or 4 tablesp. green-dried basil, reconstituted in 4 tablesp. water (boiled and cooled)

2 cloves of garlic

14 tablesp. Parmesan cheese, finely grated

10 tablesp. oil (sunflower, corn, *or* olive oil)

Salt according to taste

1½ oz. butter

Method:

1. Grind finely, nuts or pine kernels.
2. Chop basil finely without stems or reconstitute green-dried basil in equal quantity of water until all water has disappeared.
3. Chop garlic finely.
4. Add Parmesan cheese.
5. Pound all the above ingredients in a mortar or blend in the blender on half speed.
6. Add oil, drop by drop, while slowly turning.
7. Add salt.
8. Add butter in small pieces slowly and continue stirring or blending until it becomes a firm paste.

Note: The Pésto should be firmly pressed into a jar, and if it is to be kept, a thin layer of melted butter should seal it. The boiled water for reconstituting green-dried basil will keep the paste longer and so will the thin layer of butter on the top. It can be kept in the refrigerator.

Rose Hip Purée and Sauce

Rose hip purée is necessary in order to make Rose hip sauce. The following directions are given for preserving rose hips as purée unless preserved rose hip purée is available in glass jars imported from Switzerland or Scandinavia.

Preparing Fresh Rose Hips for Purée

Ingredients:

2½ lb. rose hips

1 lb. castor sugar for 1 lb. mashed rose hips

Castor sugar for covering jars

1½ pints water

Method:

1. Pick only ripe rose hips, vivid red and slightly soft, after frost has touched them.
2. Select whole, undamaged hips.
3. Top and tail (using scissors if soft).
4. Wash quickly and drain in colander (not aluminium).
5. Put the hips into boiling water in stainless steel or undamaged enamel saucepan and bring again to the boil.
6. Simmer with the lid on until the hips are soft, about 15 minutes (do not over-boil or the colour and flavour will be spoilt, but the hips must be soft enough to sieve).
7. Rub through a fine hair or stainless steel sieve, using a wooden spoon, masher, or pestle.
8. Beat hips and sugar for about 20 minutes, using a wooden spoon or stainless steel mixer.
9. Bring to boil, then cook gently for 10 minutes.
10. Fill well-cleaned, dry and hot earthenware or glass jars.
11. Allow purée to cool.
12. Cover with waxed or greaseproof paper, soaked in alcohol.
13. Cover waxed paper with about half an inch of castor sugar.
14. Cover with cellophane to make jars airtight.

Note: This purée will keep for one year if carefully prepared and stored in a dark, cool, and airy place, but its vitamin content will decrease with keeping.

Rose Hip Sauce

Ingredients:

2½ oz. rose hip purée

1 cup (½ pint) water, clear apple juice, *or* grape juice

2½ oz. sugar

Lemon juice, if liked

1 teasp. each fresh chopped or green-dried lemon balm and sweet cicely

Method:

1. Bring purée, water and sugar to the boil.
2. Add lemon juice and herbs.

Hard Sauce

A pleasant variation of a well known sauce for serving with Christmas pudding and mince pies.

Ingredients:

2 oz. butter

2 oz. castor sugar

1 level teasp. icing sugar

1 tablesp. rum

1 teasp. fresh chopped or green-dried sweet cicely (if green-dried, reconstitute in 1 teasp. rum)

Method:

1. Cream butter.
2. Add castor sugar and icing sugar to butter and blend well.
3. Add the rum and sweet cicely.
   Note: This can equally well be made with brandy.

Elder-berry Sauces

Pick over elder-berries, wash carefully, strip off their stalks, drain well, and express the juice.

(*a*) Uncooked Sauce or Soup

Ingredients:

¾ pint freshly expressed elder-berry juice

1 large eating apple, grated

2 cartons or jars plain yoghourt

1 oz. brown sugar *or* honey

2 teasp. fresh chopped or green-dried sweet cicely

Juice and peel of 1 lemon

Method:
1. Grate the apple.
2. Beat well elder-berry juice with yoghourt, apple, and mix immediately with lemon juice.
3. Sweeten with brown sugar or honey and add sweet cicely.
4. Flavour with some lemon rind.
5. Use it as a sauce with a pudding.

Note: Use it as a breakfast dish with cereal flakes and as a cold sweet with ice-cream for a later summer menu, or as a cold sweet soup.

(*b*) Cooked Elder-berry Sauce

Elder-berry sauce can also be cooked and served hot or cold in the following way.

Ingredients:

½ lb. elder-berries
1 large apple
1½ pints water
¾ oz. cornflour
½ pint apple juice
Peel of a lemon

1 teasp. lemon juice
2 teasp. fresh chopped or green-dried sweet cicely
Brown sugar
2 tablesp. cream *or* top of the milk

Method:
1. Pick over elder-berries, wash carefully, allow to drain well.
2. Cut apple into thin slices.
3. Strip elder-berries of their stalks with a fork.
4. Boil berries and apple in 1 pint of water.
5. Smooth cornflour with ½ pint of water and add to the fruit.
6. Bring to a fast boil.
7. Add apple juice, lemon peel, lemon juice, and sweet cicely.
8. Add sugar according to taste.
9. Before serving, add 2 tablesp. cream and mix well. If too tart, more milk or cream can be added.

Note: Serve hot with a pudding or, if served cold, chill well beforehand and serve with sponge fingers or rusks. Can also be served as a cold sweet soup with ratafia biscuits.

Herb Jellies

(a) Basic Herb Jelly

Herb Jellies make a most refreshing change from the usual main dish accompaniments. Here follows a recipe for a basic jelly which can obtain its flavour from an individual herb or a combination of several.

Ingredients:

2 lb. tart apples *or* crab apples

1 tablesp. red wine vinegar *or* white wine vinegar

¾ cup sugar per ½ pint juice

Per cup of juice (½ pint):

1 sprig of the fresh herb used for flavouring

or 2 teasp. of the green-dried herb, put in a muslin bag

Method:

1. Quarter the apples and just cover with water; boil until soft.
2. Pour into a jelly bag and leave to drain overnight; measure the juice.
3. Add the herb and red wine vinegar for the strong-tasting herbs, or white wine vinegar for the delicate herbs.
4. Boil all the ingredients together for about 10 minutes.
5. Heat the sugar in a warm oven.
6. Add the sugar slowly to the boiling liquid, stirring until it is dissolved.
7. Boil the jelly until setting point is reached or the sugar thermometer registers 219°, then remove the herbs.
8. Pour jelly into warm jars and seal.

Note: If desired, the herbs, chopped finely, can be left in the jelly to provide attractive specks of green.

(b) Herb-flavoured Jellies

Follow Basic Herb Jelly recipe (see previous recipe) for:

BASIL HERB JELLY, served with desserts, fish, game, poultry, and roasts.

MARJORAM HERB JELLY, served with au gratin dishes and fried dishes; with meat, chicken, game, and turkey.

MINT OR PEPPERMINT JELLY, served with lamb, cold poultry, fish; peppermint jelly can also be used for sweets and drinks.

MULTI-FLAVOURED HERB JELLY, a special mint, such as Bowles or Eau de Cologne Mint, can be combined with marjoram and burnet.

ROSE GERANIUM AND BAY JELLY mixed with chopped lemon peel makes an exquisitely flavoured jelly.

SAGE JELLY, served with mutton, lamb, pork, cheese dishes; with all dishes for which sage is usually used.

TARRAGON JELLY, served with fish, meats, salad, poultry, and shellfish.

THYME OR LEMON THYME JELLY, served with cheese dishes, eggs, fish, game, meats, poultry, and shellfish.

Herb Butters

These home-made delicious spreads for so many occasions give the full flavour of uncooked herbs. Use generously on bridge rolls, toast, sandwiches, canapés – which can be garnished with radishes, cucumber, tomatoes – for tea and cocktail parties or picnics. Herb butters kept in the refrigerator will lend the professional touch to steak and fried dishes particularly if the herb butter is shaped into a roll – approximately $1\frac{1}{2}$ in. diameter – packed into foil which is twisted at both ends and placed in the refrigerator. Slices of this can be cut when needed.

(a) Mixed Herb Butter

Ingredients:
   4 oz. butter
   2–4 teasp. fresh herbs
      or 2 teasp. green-dried mixed herbs such as: parsley, tarragon, chervil, chives, mint, lemon balm, sweet cicely, marjoram, basil, summer savory, marigold (for proportions, see GUIDE, page 127)
   Juice of up to half a lemon

Method:
1. Allow butter to soften in room temperature.
2. Cream butter.
3. Reconstitute 2 teasp. green-dried mixed herbs in juice of lemon, but do not use more than the herbs absorb, or use 2–4 teasp. fresh herbs, finely chopped.
4. Blend herbs and salt with the creamed butter and set aside at room temperature for 1–2 hours so that the herbs can permeate the butter.

5. Store in small tightly-covered jars in refrigerator. May be kept until required.

(b) Tarragon Butter

Ingredients:

1 teasp. green-dried tarragon
4 tablesp. butter

1 teasp. lemon to reconstitute tarragon

Method:

1. Reconstitute tarragon in lemon juice.
2. Blend with the butter.
3. Add salt according to taste and allow to permeate.
4. Keep in a cool place. Can be kept in the refrigerator for several days.

Note: Particularly good on grilled steaks. Other herb butters can be made with individual herbs (see GUIDE, page 127, for proportions; and 'Twenty-four Herbs in a Chest', see pages 127–168).

(c) Cucumber and Dill Butter (to serve with fish)

Ingredients:

1 oz. butter
Cucumber
Juice of half a lemon

Salt
1 teasp. fresh chopped or green-dried dill

Method:

1. Peel cucumber and grate it or mash it in blender.
2. Beat butter until soft.
3. Blend all ingredients with the butter, adding salt to taste.
4. Put into a small pot and keep cold until required.

Chapter 10

SWEETS AND DESSERTS, CAKES

Peach Tart (*serves 6*)

An attractive sweet to serve when peaches are cheap.

Ingredients:

Casing:
3 egg whites
⅔ cup sugar
¾ cup flaked coconut
1 tablesp. fresh chopped or green-dried sweet cicely
½ cup cornflake crumbs
⅓ cup chopped toasted almonds

Filling:
2½–3 cups peach slices
1 teasp. fresh chopped or green-dried sweet cicely
Whipped cream
2 teasp. flaked coconut
1 teasp. fresh chopped or green-dried lemon balm

Method:
1. Beat egg whites until stiff.
2. Gradually add sugar, and continue beating until stiff glossy peaks form.
3. Fold in flaked coconut, half of the sweet cicely, cornflake crumbs, and almonds.
4. Spread meringue evenly over bottom and sides of a well-greased 9-in. pie-tin.
5. Bake in a cool oven for 50–60 minutes or until golden. Leave to get cold.
6. Just before serving fill with peach slices.
7. Sprinkle with remaining sweet cicely.
8. Top with whipped cream and sprinkle with coconut mixed with lemon balm.

Orange Chiffon (*serves 4–6*)

A delicate-flavoured dessert to serve after a rich meat dish.

Ingredients:

1 tablesp. gelatine
½ cup sugar
Pinch of salt
1 cup hot water
3 eggs, separated
1 teasp. fresh chopped or green-dried sweet cicely

2 teasp. fresh chopped or green-dried lemon balm
6 oz. orange juice
3 tablesp. lemon juice
½ pint whipped cream
¼ cup halved toasted almonds

Method:
1. Mix together the gelatine, sugar, and salt in a double boiler.
2. Stir in the hot water and cook over boiling water, stirring until the gelatine dissolves.
3. Beat egg yolks slightly and stir into gelatine mixture.
4. Add herbs.
5. Return to double boiler, cook, stirring until mixture coats the spoon.
6. Remove from heat and add orange juice and lemon juice.
7. Chill until it starts to congeal.
8. Beat egg whites until stiff.
9. Fold two mixtures together and chill.
10. Top with the whipped cream and almonds.

Cream Cheese Whip with Berries (*serves 3–4*)

A dish for those who like unusual flavours.

Ingredients:

3 oz. cream cheese
2 tablesp. top of milk *or* cream
1 tablesp. brown sugar
1 tablesp. chopped nuts
1 tablesp. chopped, seedless raisins

Pinch of cinnamon
1 grated eating apple
1 teasp. fresh chopped or green-dried sweet cicely
1 teasp. fresh chopped or green-dried lemon balm

Method:

1. Beat cream cheese with top of the milk or full cream until smooth.
2. Combine with all other ingredients.
3. When all is well mixed, add 5–7 oz. of washed strawberries or any other berries.

   Note: If liked, the mixture can be served in a sponge flan case.

Strawberry Tartlets with Whipped Cream

When strawberries are plentiful, this is a delicious way to serve them.

1. Wash and hull strawberries.
2. Sprinkle with sugar and a little fresh chopped or green-dried sweet cicely.
3. Fill individual pastry cases, top with whipped cream and sprinkle a little sweet cicely on top;

   or Mix whipped cream with sweet cicely before decorating the strawberries;

   or Decorate with whipped cream and hand round small jar of freshly chopped sweet cicely for individual flavouring.

Rhubarb Cream (*serves 3–4*)

All the family will like rhubarb done in this way.

Ingredients:

1 lb. rhubarb
2–3 tablesp. brown sugar
Grated lemon peel
Pinch of cinnamon

2 eggs
2 teasp. fresh chopped or green-dried sweet cicely
1 tablesp. fresh chopped or green-dried elder flowers

Method:
1. Wash and cut the rhubarb into small pieces and cook with a little water or apple juice; sieve.
2. Add 2 tablesp. brown sugar, grated lemon peel and cinnamon. Allow to cool.
3. Beat yolks with 1 tablesp. brown sugar, sweet cicely, and elder flowers and add to cooled rhubarb.
4. Beat the two whites of egg until stiff and add to the mixture.
   Note: If liked, 8 tablesp. double cream, whipped stiffly and folded into the mixture, will improve the flavour.

Fresh Lemon Ice-cream (*serves 6–8*)

An ideal dish to serve as dessert at a party or barbecue.

Ingredients:

1 cup double cream	2 teasp. grated lemon peel
1 egg	1 teasp. fresh chopped or green-dried lemon balm
¾–1 cup sugar	
⅓ cup lemon juice	Pinch of salt
	1½ cups milk

Method:
1. Beat, in an electric mixer, the cream and egg, until blended and thickened.
2. Add sugar gradually while beating until mixture is stiff.
3. Beat in the lemon juice, lemon peel, lemon balm, and salt.
4. Add the milk and beat again.
5. Immediately turn into a large refrigerator tray.
6. Leave in the freezer until firm, about 4 hours.
   Note: This quantity can be halved for a smaller family.

Herbed Fruit Salad (*serves 6 or more*)

A fresh fruit dish for a hot summer's day, to which the herbs give sweetness, reducing the sugar; the extra tang from the lemon thyme replaces Kirsch.

Ingredients:

Juice of 2 oranges *or* the equivalent of apple juice	1 banana, sliced
3 oranges *or*	1 teasp. fresh chopped or green-dried sweet cicely
2 oranges and 1 grapefruit	Pinch of fresh chopped or green-dried lemon thyme
1 apple, finely sliced	
1 pear, finely sliced	½–1 oz. sugar *or* sweetening tablets

Method:

1. Peel oranges and remove all pith; halve the peeled orange across the middle and then cut each half into 8 pieces – 16 pieces in all. Cover well.
2. Place all other sliced fruit into a bowl.
3. Add oranges and grapefruit.
4. Add sugar or dissolved tablets.
5. Add herbs and juice.
6. Mix gently but thoroughly.
7. Press gently with a plate and keep covered.
8. Allow to permeate for 1 hour and chill before serving.

Note: Can be served with liquid or whipped cream.

Plum Salad (*serves 4*)

Use dessert plums for this salad and no extra sugar is needed.

Ingredients:

1 lb. plums
1 tablesp. fresh chopped or green-dried sweet cicely
1 teasp. fresh chopped or green-dried lemon balm

¼ cup cream
¼ cup yoghourt *or* sour cream
Lemon juice

Method:

1. Stone plums and dice.
2. Sprinkle herbs over plums.
3. Make a dressing of cream and yoghourt or sour cream with lemon juice; mix well.
4. Add to plums.
5. Allow to permeate and then taste; add sugar if necessary.
6. Serve chilled.

Banana Sweet (*serves 3–4*)

A hot party sweet for a cold winter's night.

Ingredients:

4 bananas

2 oranges

1 teasp. rum or curaçao

1 teasp. fresh chopped or green-
dried sweet cicely

or 1 teasp. mixed fresh chopped
or green-dried sweet cicely and
lemon balm

Pinch of peppermint (optional)

Piece of butter, size of walnut

1 teasp. honey

or 1 teasp. brown sugar

Method:

1. Squeeze juice of 2 oranges and add the liqueur – if the oranges are very sweet, add a little lemon juice.
2. Add the herbs to this liquid and allow to stand for 10 minutes.
3. Melt the butter in small frying-pan or skillet.
4. Add the orange juice mixture and the honey or sugar. Bring to the boil.
5. Add the peeled whole bananas and baste with the mixture; cook for 5–7 minutes.
6. Serve the bananas straight from the skillet *or* remove carefully on to a hot flat dish and cover with mixture which should have been left cooking for a little longer after removing the bananas.

Almond Peaches (*serves 6*)

Peaches and almonds combine to make this a good party sweet.

Ingredients:

6 fresh peaches

½ cup finely ground almonds

½ cup icing sugar

2 tablesp. butter

½ teasp. grated lemon peel

1 teasp. fresh chopped or green-
dried sweet cicely

1 teasp. fresh chopped or green-
dried lemon balm

½ cup orange juice

⅓ cup granulated sugar

Double cream

Method:

1. Mix with a spoon the ground almonds, icing sugar, butter, lemon peel, and herbs; blend well.
2. Stir in about 1 tablespoon orange juice to make a good consistency for shaping.
3. Peel, halve, and pit peaches.

4. Stuff centre of each peach with the almond mixture.
5. Put halves together again and arrange in greased baking-dish.
6. Pour remaining orange juice over peaches; sprinkle with granulated sugar.
7. Bake in a moderate oven (375°) for 20–30 minutes, or until tender, basting several times.
8. Serve warm with cream.

Flavoured Salzburger Nockerls (*serves* 6)

This famous sweet was invented in Salzburg and is served in coffee houses with variations in flavour. It is a very unusual dessert, but is not a difficult one to make; it should be prepared and served quickly.

Ingredients:

6 egg whites	Milk
¼ teasp. salt	2 tablesp. grated orange peel
3 tablesp. castor sugar	2 tablesp. fresh chopped or green-dried lemon balm
2 level tablesp. flour	
3 egg yolks	A pinch of fresh chopped or green-dried lemon thyme
Butter	

Method:

1. In a large bowl beat egg whites with salt until frothy.
2. Gradually beat in sugar, adding 1 tablesp. at a time, beating after each addition, until the whites form stiff peaks.
3. Beat egg yolks with flour until thick and light.
4. Grate fresh orange peel into egg mixture and add herbs.
5. Carefully fold egg yolk mixture into the whites.
6. Melt butter over low heat in large frying-pan at least 10 in. in diameter, until butter bubbles.
7. Spoon egg mixture into pan, piling it into mounds.
8. Cook egg mounds over low heat, until undersides are golden (about 2 minutes).
9. Turn the nockerls over carefully, cook for further 2 minutes.
10. Then place them in a fireproof shallow dish in which there is already a ¼ in. boiling milk and a knob of melted butter.
11. Put this dish into the oven (325°).
12. Allow the nockerls to rise, but they should not get too dark.
13. Serve as quickly as possible with a sprinkling of icing sugar; they are very delicate and may fall.

Carthusian Dumplings (*serves 4–6*) **(B)**

A satisfying sweet for all the family.

Ingredients:

½ small wholemeal loaf *or* French loaf
¼ pint milk
1 egg
1 tablesp. fresh chopped or green-dried lemon balm
1 tablesp. fresh chopped or green-dried sweet cicely

Pinch of lemon thyme
Butter for frying
Sugar and ground cinnamon mixed (proportion: 1 teasp. cinnamon to 4 tablesp. sugar)

Method:

1. Grate off rind of loaf and keep the grated crumbs.
2. Cut bread into thick slices and then across again (should give squares of 2 in.).
3. Beat well together the milk with sugar, whole egg, and half the mixed herbs.
4. Allow bread cubes to soak in this mixture.
5. Before frying, take out cubes and place on a plate.
6. Mix well grated breadcrumbs and remaining herbs.
7. Cover bread cubes with the breadcrumb mixture, on all 4 sides.
8. Fry in hot butter, turning frequently.
9. Serve with sugar and cinnamon (mixed).
    or
   Serve with wine sauce:

Sauce

Ingredients:

1 cup white wine *or* apple juice
1 egg
1 teasp. lemon juice
A little grated lemon peel

1–2 tablesp. sugar
2 teasp. flour *or* cornflour (smoothed with a little water)

Method:

1. Mix all ingredients, except the flour, in a saucepan and bring almost to the boil, beating with an egg-beater all the time.
2. When it bubbles, take off heat, let it settle down, and add smoothed flour.
3. Bring to the boil again.

Elder Flower Fritters (*allow 2–3 fritters per person*)

A delicately-flavoured sweet to be made when elder flowers are in full bloom.

Ingredients:

Prepare batter as Recipe, page 312
Freshly picked elder flower heads
Oil
½ teasp. marigold petals

Sugar
or sugar and cinnamon mixed (proportion: 1 teasp. cinnamon to 4 tablesp. sugar)
1 teasp. fresh chopped sweet cicely

Method:

1. Dip the whole heads of elder flowers into the batter, holding them by the short stalks.
2. Immediately deep-fry in hot oil until golden brown; drain.
3. Serve quickly with either sugar, or sugar mixed with cinnamon, or less sugar mixed with fresh chopped sweet cicely.

Note: Marigold petals should be mixed with the batter. Sweet cicely, if fresh, can be used with sugar to be sprinkled on the fritters or, if used green-dried, can also be added to the batter.

Elder-berry Dumplings (*serves 6*)

Wild elder-berries have not only been used on the Continent but also in the early days of the American pioneers; they have been a healthy addition to their food. Blackcurrants or blackberries can be used instead, if liked.

Ingredients

Sauce:

2 cups washed elder-berries, without stems
¾ cup sugar
1 tablesp. flour
2 tablesp. lemon juice
¾ cup water

Dumplings:

American recipe uses baking powder, but the equivalent continental recipe uses yeast (see Yeast Dough, page 311)
¾ cup flour
1½ teasp. baking powder
¼ teasp. cinnamon
Salt
¼ cup sugar
¼ teasp. lemon peel
1 teasp. fresh chopped or dried marigold petals (if available)
¼ cup milk
1 egg slightly beaten

Method:
Sauce
1. Put elder-berries in a saucepan.
2. Mix sugar and flour, and smooth with lemon juice and water.
3. Pour over the berries.
4. Bring to the boil.
5. Reduce heat just enough to keep berries hot.

Meanwhile, make **Dumplings**

1. Sift flour and mix with baking powder.
2. Add cinnamon and salt.
3. Add sugar and lemon peel.
4. Combine milk and egg.
5. Stir into dry ingredients until blended.
6. Pour elder-berry mixture into an 8-in. square baking-tin or fireproof dish.
7. Drop the dumpling mixture into the elder-berry sauce by the tablespoonful (there should be exactly 6 dumplings). If yeast dough is used, shape into walnut-size pieces.
8. Bake in a hot oven (400°) 25–30 minutes or until the tops of the dumplings are golden.
   Note: Can be served warm with thick cream.

Sorrel Turnover (*serves 4–6*)

A most unusual sweet.

Ingredients:

1 cup dry pastry mix using Pastry Recipe, page 310
3 teasp. fresh chopped or green-dried sorrel
2 teasp. fresh chopped or green-dried sweet cicely
1 tablesp. lemon juice to reconstitute
2 tablesp. brown sugar

Method:
1. Add enough water to pastry-mix to make a firm dough.
2. Roll out and cut into two rounds.
3. If dried herbs are used, reconstitute herbs in lemon juice, otherwise add less lemon juice.
4. Mix herbs and brown sugar and spread on round of pastry.
5. Wet edges of pastry and put second round on top, pressing down lightly.

6. Place in shallow dish or on a baking-tin and bake in moderate oven (350°) for about 15 minutes or until golden.

Note: If preferred, make individual turnovers.

The following three recipes make unusual tea-time treats:

Rosemary Biscuits (*makes approx. 4 dozen small biscuits*)

Ingredients:

4 oz. butter
2 oz. sugar
6 oz. flour

2 tablesp. fresh chopped or green-dried crushed rosemary

Method:
1. Cream butter and sugar together until light.
2. Add flour and rosemary to butter mixture.
3. Knead well with hands until it forms a dough.
4. Gently roll out on lightly floured board.
5. Cut into small rounds with biscuit-cutter.
6. Place biscuits on greased baking sheet.
7. Bake in hot oven 450° for 10–12 minutes until golden and firm.
8. Remove at once to cool on wire tray.

Marigold Sweet Buns (*makes 20*)

Ingredients:

2 eggs
Their weight in:
  Plain flour
  Castor sugar

2 tablesp. fresh chopped or dried marigold petals

Method:
1. Separate the eggs.
2. Add the sugar to the egg yolks and beat well.
3. Fold in flour and marigold petals.
4. Beat egg whites until stiff.
5. Add to yolk mixture, mixing well together.
6. Divide in greased bun-tins topped with more marigold petals and a sprinkling of sugar.
7. Bake in a moderate oven for about 10 minutes.

Marigold Yeast Buns

1. Use Yeast Dough (Recipe, page 311) omitting butter and adding 1 tablesp. marigold petals to the milk; otherwise follow recipe.
2. Form into 12 small buns, brush with beaten egg and top with marigold petals.
3. Bake on a greased baking-tin for approximately 30 minutes in a moderate oven until golden.

Cream Cheese Cake

Ingredients:

5 oz. butter
5 oz. sugar
6 egg yolks
¾ lb. soft cream cheese
Grated rind of half a lemon

5 oz. almonds, skinned and ground
2 teasp. fresh chopped or green-dried lemon balm
6 egg whites

Method:

1. Cream butter, sugar, yolks, and cream cheese together.
2. Add lemon rind, herbs, and ground almonds.
3. Fold in beaten egg whites.
4. Place in greased sponge tin.
5. Bake for ¾ hour at 300–350°.

Savoury Sandwiches

These sandwiches can be made equally well with either white or wholemeal bread, but the slices need to be thinly cut. For figure-watchers, Pumpernickel or rye bread make low-calorie sandwiches.

(a) Nasturtium Sandwiches

Chop nasturtium leaves finely, butter slices of wholemeal bread and arrange nasturtium leaves between the buttered bread. Cut neat, small triangular sandwiches. Prepare shortly before required.

(b) Tarragon and Chives Sandwiches

Blend well together, ½ lb. cream cheese, 2 teasp. (each) fresh chopped or green-dried tarragon and chives, and leave to permeate for 5–10 minutes before putting in between the sandwiches.

(c) Herb Egg Spread Sandwiches

2 eggs, hard-boiled	2 teasp. bouquet for omelettes
2 tablesp. butter	*or* 2 teasp. mixed of fresh chopped
1 teasp. yoghourt	or green-dried chives, parsley,
Pinch of salt	chervil
	A pinch of fresh chopped or green-dried marjoram or thyme

Mix the finely chopped hard-boiled eggs with the softened butter. Add all the herbs, salt, lemon juice, and yoghourt and mix well until smooth. Spread fairly thick on either wholemeal or white sandwiches.

(d) Cucumber and Dill Sandwiches

Cut fine slices of cucumber, arrange on buttered bread and sprinkle generously with dill before adding the second slice of bread.

(e) Chicken and Marjoram Sandwiches

3–4 oz. minced cooked chicken
¼ cup sour cream
1 teasp. fresh chopped or green-dried onion green

½ teasp. fresh chopped or green-dried marjoram
¾ teasp. salt
¾ teasp. paprika

Blend together well before using as a spread.

(f) Tomato and Basil Sandwiches

Cut slices of tomato, place on buttered bread, and sprinkle generously with basil, before adding the second slice of bread.

Note: The basil is used instead of pepper and often replaces the salt, but if a little salt is required, this can be added.

Pastry for Herb Recipes

(a) Short Pastry

Ingredients:
¼ lb. butter
½ lb. flour
Salt
Water
} This makes 2½ cups of dry pastry mix

Method:
1. Sift flour and salt into a bowl.
2. Rub butter into flour until it resembles breadcrumbs.
3. Add sufficient water to make a firm dough.

(b) Yeast Dough for Pastry (savoury – for Pizza, Rolls, etc.)

Ingredients:
8 oz. flour, 2 oz. of which can be wholemeal
2 oz. butter

Salt
1 oz. yeast or more
4–6 tablesp. milk

Method:
1. Sift flour and salt into a bowl, make a well in centre and put in a warm place.
2. Cut the butter into small pieces and dot on the flour.
3. Mix the yeast with 2 tablesp. milk, pour into well, and mix with a little flour to make a thick paste.
4. Cover bowl with a cloth and put in a warm place till the dough in the well doubles its size.
5. Add the rest of the milk and knead the flour into the dough.
6. Beat dough until smooth and allow to rise in a warm place, covered by a cloth until approximately double the size.
7. Roll out and line baking-tin, or use according to recipe.

(c) Yeast Dough for Dumplings, Buns, etc.

Ingredients:

6 oz. flour

$\frac{1}{3}$–1 oz. yeast

1$\frac{1}{2}$ oz. butter

Approx. 4–5 tablesp. milk *or* more

1$\frac{1}{2}$ oz. sugar

1 egg

Salt

Method:
1. Working in a warm place, sift flour into a bowl and make a well in the centre.
2. Put dabs of butter, sugar, and salt round the edge.
3. Mix yeast with a little of the milk; pour into the well.
4. Mix to a thick paste with a little flour.
5. Sprinkle with a little sugar, cover with a cloth, and leave to rise in a warm place.
6. When the dough in the well has doubled its size, work in the remaining flour, add the egg and the rest of the milk.
7. Knead to a dough and beat well until smooth.

For Elder-berry Dumplings

Omit butter

Add: 1 teasp. grated peel; $\frac{1}{2}$ teasp. ground cinnamon; 1 teasp. marigold petals (if available)

Add these with the milk.

(d) Choux Pastry (*makes 14 savoury or sweet puffs*)

Ingredients:

2 oz. butter	3 oz. plain flour
¼ pint cold water	2 large eggs
Pinch of salt	

Method:

1. Place the water, butter, and salt into a saucepan, and bring to boil.
2. Immediately add all the flour.
3. Remove from the heat and beat until the mixture leaves the sides of the pan.
4. When cool, beat in the eggs a little at a time.
5. Place dessertspoons of the mixture, spaced well apart, on to a greased baking-sheet, or it can be pressed through a forcing bag into any shape desired.
6. Bake in oven (400°) for about 40 minutes.
7. Split and allow to cool.

Note: Add 1 tablesp. sugar for sweet puffs, grated nutmeg for savoury puffs.

(e) Batter for Vegetable and Fruit Fritters

Ingredients:

4 tablesp. flour	6 tablesp. water
Salt	1 egg, separated

1. Sift flour and salt in a bowl.
2. Mix to a smooth paste with the water and yolk of egg, and leave to rest for at least half an hour.
3. Then fold in gently, the stiffly beaten white of egg until well mixed, shortly before using the batter.

(f) Easy Pastry made with Oil (*sufficient for 1 pie-cover or 1 flan*)

Ingredients:

¼ cup sunflower *or* corn oil	1 cup sifted flour
2–3 tablesp. cold creamy milk	¾ teasp. salt

Method:
1. Put the oil and the milk together in a cup; do not stir.
2. Mix the flour and salt in a bowl.
3. Pour in oil and milk, mixing with flour.
4. Press into a ball.
5. Place between 2 sheets of waxed paper (12 in. square).
6. Dampen table-top to prevent slipping.
7. Roll out until circle reaches edges of paper and peel off top paper.
8. Place pastry, paperside up, in 8- or 9-in. flan-tin, remove paper, and fit to pan.
9. Prick pastry in several places with a fork.
10. Bake in hot oven (425°) for about 10 minutes.
10A. If used as a pie-cover, place over filling and bake in hot oven for about 40 minutes.

Note: This pastry may be kept unbaked in refrigerator or deep freeze for use at any time. Wrap in aluminium foil to retain moisture.

Hot Herb-buttered French Loaf

Easy to prepare, excellent on its own and one of the best accompaniments to any savoury dish. A great stand-by to eke out the meal, when unexpected guests arrive.

Ingredients:

1 long French stick	Herb butter (see Recipe, Chapter 9, page 294)

Method:
1. Prepare herb butter.
2. Cut a long French stick across into small slices.
3. Spread herb butter generously all over one side of each slice.
4. Press closely together again.
5. Wrap foil round loaf and seal well.
6. Place in medium oven (350°) for 20–30 minutes or until crisp.
7. Unwrap and serve at once.

Cheese Herb Bread (*makes one 2-lb. loaf*)

Ingredients:

3¾ cups flour
2 tablesp. melted butter
1 tablesp. sugar
1 teasp. salt
½ teasp. fresh chopped or green-dried marjoram

1 teasp. fresh chopped or green-dried thyme
1 cup milk
1 cup grated Cheddar cheese
1 packet dried yeast
2 tablesp. warm water

Method:

1. Blend 3 tablesp. flour with butter, sugar, salt, marjoram, and thyme in saucepan over medium heat.
2. Stir in milk.
3. Cook, stirring until thick and smooth; remove from heat.
4. Add cheese and stir until cheese melts; keep just warm.
5. Soften yeast in the warm water; add to cheese mixture.
6. Gradually add flour, beating until smooth after each addition, mixing to a stiff dough.
7. Turn dough on to a lightly floured board.
8. Knead gently until dough is a smooth ball.
9. Return to pan, grease top of dough, cover with damp cloth.
10. Stand pan in a warm place and allow dough to rise – about 50–60 minutes.
11. Return dough to floured board, punch it down and shape into a loaf.
12. Place in greased loaf-tin (2 lb. size); cover with damp cloth and allow to rise until almost double the size.
13. Brush with melted butter.
14. Bake in moderately hot oven (375°) for 35 minutes.
15. Turn out on wire tray and cool before storing.

Cream Cheese Puffs

Ingredients:

Savoury Choux Pastry (see Recipe, page 312)
7 oz. cream cheese
2 tablesp. each milk and cream
3 tablesp. grated cheese
1 tablesp. chopped or green-dried chives

½ teasp. each fresh chopped or green-dried summer savory and thyme
Salt
Marmite *or* other yeast extract, thickly diluted with a few drops of water

Method:

1. Prepare Choux pastry.
2. Shape into small but longish rolls; place on baking-sheet.
3. Bake in moderate oven (350°) for about 15 minutes.
4. Beat cream cheese until it is of a soft creamy consistency.
5. Add other ingredients and beat well together.
6. Cut rolls in half, lengthways; pipe or fill with stuffing.

Note: A suggestion for a sweet cream cheese filling is Banana Cheese Cream (page 111).

Savoury Turnovers (*makes approx. 20*)

A savoury accompaniment to vegetables and thick soups.

Ingredients:

Full quantity of Short Pastry (see page 310)
5 oz. cream cheese
1 egg
1 tablesp. cream *or* top of milk
1 tablesp. flour
Salt
1 tablesp. fresh chopped or green-dried chives

½ teasp. each fresh chopped or green-dried summer savory, basil tarragon, and lovage
Nutmeg ⎫
Paprika ⎬ According to taste
Caraway *or* poppy seeds ⎭

Method:

1. Prepare pastry and roll out ¼-in. thick.
2. Cut into 4-in. squares.
3. Mix other ingredients together and put 1 teasp. of this filling on each square.
4. Brush edges with water, turn over to make triangle, and press edges well together.
5. Brush top with egg yolk.
6. Sprinkle with caraway or poppy seeds.
7. Bake in moderate oven (350°) until golden brown.

Note: The fillings can be made in a number of different ways – with minced meat, poultry, fish, mushrooms, or cabbage in place of the cream cheese. Originally a Russian recipe, the turnovers can be eaten with any meal instead of bread.

For cocktail or party purposes, they are delightful if made smaller (3-in. squares).

Pizza Napolitana with Basil (*makes approx. 10*)

An easy and excellent way to make this traditional Italian dish for which herbs are of such importance.

Ingredients:

Yeast Pastry (see page 310)
6 ripe tomatoes, skinned
3–4 oz. Gruyère *or* Cheddar cheese, in slices
1 tablesp. mixed fresh chopped or green-dried rosemary and parsley
Oil for brushing

Pésto:

2 tablesp. grated Parmesan cheese
1 clove garlic
1 level teasp. fresh chopped or green-dried basil
1 tablesp. sunflower oil
1 tablesp. butter
or Genoese Pésto (Recipe, page 289)

Method:

1. Prepare yeast pastry.
2. Roll out to about ¼-in. thick and cut into rounds 4–5-in. in diameter.
3. Put on baking-sheet.
4. Brush edges of each round with oil.
5. Mix Parmesan cheese, garlic, basil, oil, and butter into a thick paste or use Genoese Pésto.
6. Spread some of the paste thinly on the centre of each round where not touched by oil.
7. Put some slices of tomato on top.
8. Sprinkle a little of the other mixed herbs on the tomato slices.
9. Top with slices of cheese.
10. Allow to rise again.
11. Bake in oven (400°) for 10–20 minutes.

Savoury Herb Pastry to Serve with Soup

(a) Parsley Biscuits (*makes 2 dozen*)

These can be made with either lovage or marjoram in place of parsley.

Ingredients:

1½ cups Short Pastry Mix (see page 310)
¼ cup finely minced parsley
or 2 tablesp. green-dried parsley

1 tablesp. onion, finely chopped
¼ cup milk

Method:
1. Mix parsley and onion with pastry mix.
2. Add milk to make a stiff dough.
3. Turn on to a floured board and knead well.
4. Roll out to $\frac{1}{2}$-in. thickness.
5. Cut into 1-in. squares or diamonds.
6. Place on baking-sheet and bake in moderate oven (375°) for 15–20 minutes. Serve hot.

(b) Cheese and Ham Twists (*makes approx. 30*)

Ingredients:

1 cup pastry mix (see Recipe, page 310)
1 teasp. fresh chopped or green-dried chives
$\frac{1}{2}$ teasp. fresh chopped or green-dried summer savory
2 oz. grated Cheddar cheese

$\frac{1}{4}$ cup milk
1 tablesp. melted butter
2–3 oz. chopped ham
1 teasp. fresh chopped or green-dried tarragon

Method:
1. Mix pastry, cheese, and herbs (except tarragon) together.
2. Add milk and knead lightly.
3. Turn on to a floured board and roll out $\frac{1}{4}$ in. thick to a rectangle.
4. Brush this pastry with the butter.
5. Mix ham and tarragon well; spread this mixture over the pastry to within 1 in. of the edge.
6. Fold lengthwise and pinch-seal the edges.
7. Cut into $\frac{1}{2}$-in. strips and twist each.
8. Place on greased baking-tin and bake in moderate oven (375°) for 20–25 minutes. Serve hot.

(c) Cheese Logs (*makes 16*)

Ingredients:

2 oz. soft butter
1 teasp. hot water
4 oz. flour

2 oz. grated Cheddar cheese
1 teasp. fresh chopped or green-dried thyme
Poppy seeds (optional)

Method:

1. In an electric mixer, whip butter with hot water for 2 minutes at medium speed.
2. Add flour, making a soft dough.
3. Add cheese and thyme, mixing well.
4. Chill in refrigerator until stiff enough to handle.
5. Turn on to a floured board, roll into logs ½ in. round and 2 in. long.
6. Brush with beaten egg, roll in poppy seed and place on greased baking-tin.
7. Bake in a moderate oven (375°) for about 20–25 minutes.

Rosemary Ring

A savoury pastry to accompany vegetables, excellent as a snack, hot or cold, with soup or coffee.

Ingredients:

½ lb. yeast dough (see Recipe, page 310

2 tablesp. butter

1 tablesp. fresh chopped or green-dried rosemary

2½ oz. Cheddar cheese, grated

Method:

1. Roll out dough to ½ in. thick, cut into biscuit rounds.
2. Melt the butter and add the rosemary.
3. Brush tops of biscuits with this mixture.
4. Arrange the biscuits in a round cake-tin to overlap each other.
5. Brush the tops again with the remaining butter.
6. Sprinkle with the grated cheese.
7. Bake in a hot oven (425°) for about 10 minutes until golden brown.

Meat and Vegetable Pasties

For the lunch-box and the picnic basket.

A perfect alternative to sandwiches, these pasties provide a complete meal, containing such important proteins as meat, eggs, cheese, and nuts, wrapped in a yeast crust. This means less calories and a better proportion of starch to protein than sandwiches.

They can be eaten with the fingers and require no plates or cutlery. Heated up, and wrapped well in 2–3 layers of foil, they will stay hot for several hours.

Pasties can also be frozen and thawed pasties can be heated in a 300° oven for about 15 minutes. They can be served plain or with a sauce or as accompaniment to a salad when they supply a whole meal.

Make Yeast Pastry (see page 310) from 1 lb. flour to provide 18 pasties – 6 for each of the 3 following fillings,
or
Buy 1 packet bread mix (white or brown) and follow the directions on the package.

Ingredients:

Yeast pastry *or* 1 packet bread mix

Caraway and poppy seeds (optional)

Method for Pasties:
1. When the dough has risen sufficiently, turn on to a floured board.
2. Roll out to about ½ in. thickness, making a rectangle of about 16 in. by 24 in.
3. Cut the dough with a sharp knife into 8 in. squares.
4. Have ready a choice of 3 fillings and place 2 tablesp. cold filling in the centre of each square.
5. Brush all 4 edges with water.
6. Bring corners together at the centre of the square and pinch edges together to seal, making 4 diagonal seals.
7. Brush with beaten egg yolk and sprinkle with caraway or poppy seeds.
8. Place on well-greased flat tin.
9. Bake in moderate oven (350°) for 30 minutes or until golden brown.

(a) Beef and Cabbage Filling (6 pasties)

Ingredients:

½ medium-sized onion, chopped
1 tablesp. butter *or* margarine
½ lb. minced beef
¼ teasp. salt

1 teasp. each fresh chopped or green-dried lovage and summer savory
1 small cabbage head, chopped

Method:

1. Brown onions in butter and add the meat, stirring until red-ness disappears.
2. Add salt, herbs, and cabbage, and simmer for 45 minutes, covered, stirring occasionally.
3. Set aside to cool.

(b) Egg and Carrot Filling (6 pasties)

Ingredients:

½ lb. carrots, cooked and finely chopped
1 tablesp. butter *or* margarine
¼ teasp. salt
1 teasp. each fresh chopped or green-dried tarragon, summer savory, and basil
½ teasp. fresh chopped or green-dried marjoram
or 1 teasp. bouquet for omelettes

3 hard-boiled eggs, chopped
2 tablesp. fresh chopped or green-dried parsley
Nutmeg and paprika
1 tablesp. thin cream

Method:

1. Sauté the carrots in the butter for 5 minutes.
2. Remove from heat.
3. Stir in salt, herbs, eggs, parsley, nutmeg, paprika, and cream.
4. Cool and then use for filling.

(c) Cheese, Nuts, and Aubergine Filling (6 pasties)

Ingredients:

1 medium-sized onion, chopped
2 tablesp. butter *or* margarine
¾ lb. grated cheese
Salt
1 tablesp. fresh chopped or green-dried onion green

1 teasp. each fresh chopped or green-dried lovage, summer savory, and tarragon
1 medium-sized aubergine, peeled and chopped
¼ cup nuts or slivered almonds
Nutmeg

Method:

1. Sauté the onion in butter for 5 minutes.
2. Add onion green and sauté, add the aubergine, salt, and all herbs.

3. Cover and allow to simmer on low heat for 10 minutes.
4. Stir in the cheese and the nuts and nutmeg then allow to melt.
5. Remove from heat, drain excess fat, and cool.

Savoury Bread Mixture (B)

Tastier than sausage mixture or minced meat; to be used for stuffings, dumplings, roasts.

Ingredients:

4 oz. bread	Salt
8 tablesp. chopped onion	Grated nutmeg
3 tablesp. fresh chopped or green-dried parsley	Ground ginger
	1–2 eggs
4–5 tablesp. fresh chopped or green-dried onion green	

Method:

1. Soak bread (preferably wholemeal) in cold water until the crust is soft.
2. Take it out and squeeze well so that it is mashed and fairly dry.
3. Sauté chopped onion in oil until golden.
4. Add parsley and sauté again.
5. Then add onion green and sauté again (a few more herbs such as celery leaves, lovage, and a small quantity of marjoram can be added according to taste).
6. Add to this the squeezed bread.
7. Mix well and sauté, turning over all the time, until all the moisture has disappeared and the mixture is fairly dry.
8. Allow to cool.
9. Season with salt, grated nutmeg, and ground ginger, according to taste.
10. Add eggs and mix all well.

Note: This stuffing can be used for stuffed cabbage leaves, spinach leaves, vine leaves, stuffed tomatoes, marrow, potatoes, in fact all kinds of stuffing.

Bread Dumplings

1. Roll the same mixture between wet hands without pressure, to form small balls.

2. The dumplings should be cooked in salted water or stock.
3. Cook one dumpling and, if it does not hold well together, add another egg and more breadcrumbs to the mixture.
4. Place dumplings into the boiling liquid, allow to simmer and when they come up to the surface, they are ready.

Note: Dumplings the size of a walnut can be served in clear broth; larger dumplings – the size of a plum – should be drained well and can be served with melted butter and fried onions on a heated shallow dish.

Roasted Loaf

The bread mixture can also be shaped into a loaf and roasted like a joint in a heavy saucepan or in the oven. To make a full meal, 1 or 2 hard-boiled eggs can be placed into the centre of the loaf.

Savoury Marjoram Rolls (*makes approx. 15*)

A savoury pastry similar to scones for tea or as a snack.

Ingredients:

Yeast pastry (see page 310)   3 teasp. fresh chopped or green-dried marjoram

Method:
1. Make yeast pastry according to recipe, and add the marjoram to the dry ingredients.
2. Finish pastry according to recipe, and roll out ½ in. thick.
3. Cut rounds with biscuit-cutter.
4. Allow to rise until double the size.
5. Brush top with water.
6. Bake in a moderate oven (350–375°) approximately 30 minutes.
   Note: Eat when fresh, cut across and spread with butter.

Chapter 12

HERBED DRINKS – ALCOHOLIC AND NON-ALCOHOLIC

Herb-Fruited Wine Cup (*makes 20 glasses*)

Ingredients:

2 bottles sweet white wine, such as Sauterne or Yugoslav Riesling

1 bottle champagne *or* soda water

2 sprigs each fresh *or* 1 teasp. each of green-dried lemon verbena, sage and mint

1 small sprig rosemary *or* ½ teasp. green-dried rosemary

4 fresh *or* green-dried whole scented rose geranium leaves

1 lb. strawberries, fresh *or* frozen

2 tablesp. honey (preferably flower or herb honey)

Additional scented rose geranium leaves for garnish

Method:

1. Lightly crush fresh sprigs and 4 rose geranium leaves in bottom of a large jar.
2. Cool wine and pour over herbs.
3. Steep for 3 hours at room temperature (covered).
4. Clean and crush strawberries; if fresh, sweeten with honey.
5. Chill for 30 minutes in refrigerator.
6. Add sweetened berries to wine.
7. Chill well and keep chilled by placing jug of crushed ice in centre of punch-bowl.
8. Just before serving, pour in champagne or soda-water.
9. Serve in chilled punch-cups with one small rose geranium leaf floating on top.

Note: If green-dried herbs are used, strain before adding fruit.

Woodruff Cup

If woodruff is available, this makes the best May wine cup or herb cup, but the fresh woodruff must be dried in a well-covered china or earthenware bowl for 2 days before using. If woodruff is carefully green-dried, and thus becomes available the whole year, approximately ⅛ oz. green-dried woodruff (whole leaves) should be used.

Method:

1. Add ¼ of the quantity of white wine being used to the woodruff (or clear apple juice if wanted for a non-alcoholic cup).
2. Allow to steep for half an hour.
3. Filter and add more wine (or juice).

4. Flavour with lemon juice and rind, and add strawberries or peaches, sugar, and champagne or soda water, according to taste.

Note: An excellent, even exhilarating drink can be made when woodruff is allowed to steep in clear, undiluted apple juice.

Burnet Cocktail

Ingredients:

Sprigs of burnet leaves
A tot of whisky
½ teasp. icing sugar

Juice of ½ lemon
Crushed ice

Method:

1. Bruise a sprig of burnet leaves in a well-chilled cocktail glass.
2. Combine the whisky, icing sugar, and lemon juice.
3. Add another whole sprig of burnet to the mixture.
4. Pour into an electric blender with crushed ice and whirl until the ice is powdered. Strain the snow through a fine mesh strainer over a cone-shaped mound of crushed ice in each cocktail glass.
5. Decorate with a sprig of burnet and serve with a straw.

Melissa Liqueur

Method:

1. Place a handful of fresh or dried whole melissa leaves (lemon balm) *or* 2 tablesp. green-dried lemon balm in 1 pint of brandy or kirsch and leave in a warm place for 24 hours.
2. Remove leaves from liquid and sweeten with ½ lb. sugar.
3. Pour into bottles; seal well.

Miner's Arms Long Herb Drink

A long drink can be made by using a herb decoction which is made up beforehand. This herb mixture should be allowed to steep for at least two days before use and can be kept indefinitely in a screw-top bottle for use as required. The decoction may ferment so the bottle should be opened from time to time to release the pressure, but otherwise fermentation enhances the result.

This is an invention of the host at the Miner's Arms in Priddy,

Somerset, and produces an excitingly pleasant long drink which seems to be preferred to Pimm's and other similar drinks. He reports that it has an enlivening and exhilarating effect beyond that normally contributable to the brandy.

Herb Mixture:

Equal portions of freshly chopped or green-dried mint and borage with 2 fl. oz. lemon juice, together with the yellow rind of 1 lemon and 1 good teasp. each of borage and lemon balm.

This drink is made as follows:

1. Put into a large glass (about 8 oz.) a piece of ice.
2. Add about 6 drops of Angostura bitters and the same quantity of the decoction of herbs in lemon juice (see above).
3. Add an even slice of lemon, a large measure of cognac, and top up with a baby bottle of Schweppes' tonic water.

Mint Julep

Ingredients (per glass):

3–4 fresh mint leaves
or 1 tablesp. green-dried mint
1–4 teasp. sugar syrup (according to taste) made with equal parts sugar and water

1 fl. oz. whisky
Crushed ice
Whisky to fill up the glass
2 sprigs of mint for decorating

Method:

1. Place a little of the crushed ice in the bottom of a glass.
2. Add the sugar syrup according to taste.
3. Add whisky and mint.
4. Stir well, crushing the mint.
5. Fill the glass with crushed ice and pack tightly to the top.
6. Slowly fill with whisky.
7. Stick in 2 sprigs of mint to decorate the top; let it stand for a minute or two.
8. When the glass starts to frost, the Julep should be served.

Note: Crush the ice – which is important – either (*a*) by a blender; *or* (*b*) by packing ice cubes in a tea towel or canvas bag and hammering it until flat. This is to keep the ice dry.

Cider Cup with Borage (*makes approx. 3 pints*)

Ingredients:

1 quart cider	½ cup sherry
1 lemon	½ gill brandy
1 pint orange juice	Sugar ⎫ According
1 handful fresh or green-dried whole borage leaves	Soda-water ⎭ to taste

Method:

1. Finely peel lemon so that the skin remains in one piece and attached at one end.
2. Prick the lemon with a fork and immerse in the cider.
3. Add borage to the cider.
4. Cover and leave to stand for about 2 hours.
5. Add orange juice, the sherry, brandy, and sugar.
6. Chill.
7. Add soda-water, shortly before serving.
   Note: Remove lemon (optional).

Fresh Mint Punch (*makes about 2 pints*)

Ingredients:

6 good sprigs of fresh mint	¾ pint apple juice
Juice of 3 oranges	6 tablesp. sugar
Juice of 2 small lemons	½ pint cider

Method:

1. Wash and bruise the mint and place it in the bottom of a large jug.
2. Pour over the orange, lemon, and apple juice.
3. Add the sugar and stir well.
4. Allow to stand at room temperature for 1 hour, then chill in the refrigerator.
5. Just before serving, fill up with cider (up to 2 pints can be added).
6. Put layers of crushed ice into bowl and pour mixture over, or serve in individual glasses containing some crushed ice.

Mint Syrup (*makes 1 cup*)

Ingredients:

6 sprigs fresh *or* 6 tablesp. green-   3 cups sugar
   dried mint *or* peppermint   1 cup water

Method:
1. Select fresh, crisp mint. Wash and dry thoroughly.
2. Crush or bruise leaves and stems in small bowl.
3. Pour water into heavy saucepan; dissolve sugar in water.
4. Add mint.
5. Bring to the boil over medium heat.
6. Boil 5 minutes, stirring occasionally.
7. Remove from heat and allow to stand for 15 minutes.
8. Remove mint sprigs, or strain if green-dried mint is used.
9. When syrup is cool, pour into bottle; cork tightly.

   Note: Use as a flavouring for drinks; also with fresh fruit cups and desserts.

Mint Lemonade (*makes ½ pint*)

Ingredients:

Juice of large lemon   ¼ pint apple juice
Juice of 1 orange   Sprigs of fresh mint for garnish
5 tablesp. mint syrup (see above)

Method:
1. Mix together lemon and orange juice.
2. Add mint syrup and shake well.
3. Stir in apple juice.
4. Serve chilled and garnished with fresh mint.

Hibiscus Punch – Hot or Cold

Ingredients (per pint of boiling water):

2 heaped teasp. hibiscus flowers   ½ stick cinnamon
⅔ vanilla pod   Honey to sweeten
2 or 3 cloves

Method:

1. Place flowers, vanilla, cloves, and cinnamon in a warmed pot.
2. Cover with the boiling water and allow to draw 5–10 minutes; strain.
3. Sweeten with honey.
4. Serve hot in winter or chilled in summer.

Note: Add half of the quantity red wine if desired.

Fragrant milk drinks for those with a delicate palate:

Elder Flower Milk

Ingredients:

1 head of elder flowers
or 1 tablesp. dried elder flowers
1 teasp. fresh chopped or green-dried lemon balm
¼ pint milk
1 teasp. honey

Method:

1. Pour hot milk (not boiling) over elder flowers and lemon balm.
2. Allow to draw 5–10 minutes in a warm place.
3. Strain, add honey, and mix well.
4. Allow to cool. Serve cold.

Orange-Apple Milk Drink

Ingredients:

¼ pint milk
2 oz. orange juice
2 oz. apple juice
1 teasp. honey
1 teasp. fresh chopped or green-dried sweet cicely
Few drops of lemon juice

Method:

1. Mix all ingredients together, whisking well, or whirl in a blender.
2. Leave to stand at room temperature for about half an hour.
3. Strain and serve chilled.

Raspberry Milk

Ingredients:

¼ pint milk
1 oz. blackberry juice ⎫ or 1 tablesp.
1 oz. raspberry juice ⎭ raspberry syrup
1 teasp. honey
1 teasp. mixed fresh chopped or green-dried sweet cicely and
lemon balm

Method:

1. Mix all ingredients together, whisking well, or whirl in a blender.
2. Allow to stand at room temperature for half an hour, then strain.
3. Serve chilled.

Note: When fresh berries are available, they can be used freshly expressed with added honey; they are of most value to health.

INDEX

*Bold page numbers are given where each of the main
Twenty-four Herbs are discussed in detail.*

ALL RECIPES are listed at the beginning of the following chapters:
Part One Chapter 4 – Salads and Health Dishes, pages 80, 88, 106
Chapter 5 – Herbs in Invalid Cooking, pages 113, 114
Part Three Chapters 1 – 12 – General Cookery Recipes, see page 6

Recipes are also mentioned in the Index under the name of the herb
if this name appears in the recipe heading.